IMAGES
of America

WILMERDING AND THE WESTINGHOUSE AIR BRAKE COMPANY

IMAGES
of America

WILMERDING AND THE WESTINGHOUSE AIR BRAKE COMPANY

Wilmerding World Wide

ARCADIA
PUBLISHING

ISBN 978-0-7385-1078-1

Published by Arcadia Publishing
Charleston, South Carolina

Printed in the United States of America

Library of Congress Catalog Card Number: 2002107336

For all general information contact Arcadia Publishing at:
Telephone 843-853-2070
Fax 843-853-0044
E-mail sales@arcadiapublishing.com
For customer service and orders:
Toll-Free 1-888-313-2665

Visit us on the Internet at www.arcadiapublishing.com

Contents

ACKNOWLEDGMENTS

We would like to acknowledge Cyrus Hosmer III, Val Travisano, David T. Kerr, Barbara R. Hiquet, George J. Belchick, Margaret M. Hudak, Richard Shumaker, and Lillian Shumaker.

The majority of the images contained in this book are from original photographs taken by Westinghouse Air Brake Company photographers.

INTRODUCTION

Wilmerding and the Westinghouse Air Brake Company tells the story of a community indivisible from a man of vision: George Westinghouse Jr. and his first company, the Westinghouse Air Brake Company. Westinghouse's air brake was a boon to the railroad, making it a giant industry, as well as safer and more traveled. As the Westinghouse Air Brake Company revolutionized railroad travel in the early days of an expansive America, the small borough Westinghouse founded in 1890 was a model for society—unsullied and principled, nestled in a quiet valley, safeguarded by wooded hills.

At a time in history when industrial towns and cities sprung up and haphazardly mushroomed, George Westinghouse and his associates planned Wilmerding, specifically in conjunction with his factory, to manufacture the revolutionary air brake and related equipment for the railroad industry. Westinghouse turned 500 acres of farmland into a centerpiece for industrial development in southwestern Pennsylvania.

Not the typical historical town associated with the Revolutionary War's Williamsburg, Virginia, or the Civil War's Gettysburg, Pennsylvania, Wilmerding was a simple middle-class culture, replete with both skilled and unskilled laborers from numerous western and eastern European countries, as well as black Americans from the South, all working and living together harmoniously.

Westinghouse made sure that Wilmerding residents had affordable, comfortable living conditions. Home designs varied, but upscale styles such as Tudor and Victorian were common. Streets and sidewalks were paved. Schools were built on both sides of Turtle Creek, a creek that flowed through the middle of the borough. Churches of all denominations flourished, along with independent stores. A police department, fire department, and post office were created. Since the area was situated along the main line of the Pennsylvania Railroad, a depot for passengers and freight was constructed. Recreational facilities were not forgotten either; an ornate castle housed a bowling alley and pool, and a lush green park sprouted in the center of the community. Public transportation services were available to nearby communities. The company launched a band to provide musical entertainment. Everyone attended the municipal celebrations that were organized.

The company's air brakes, related railroad equipment, and industrial pneumatic devices have been exported throughout the world, bringing safety and comfort to millions of people and recognition to the borough of Wilmerding—all thanks to the vision and humanitarian efforts of a most unique and distinguished industrialist and prolific inventor. George Westinghouse Jr. turned farmland into an incredible thriving community with just a pen and a plan.

This book focuses on the formation of Wilmerding in 1889 through the mid-1960s.

One

THE EARLY YEARS

On what appeared to be an uneventful train ride from Schenectady to Troy, New York, in 1869, a sudden collision between two engines gave passenger George Westinghouse Jr. food for thought. He heard the brakeman say these words, which he never forgot: "You can't stop a train in a moment." Thereafter, he worked to resolve the problem of railroad safety.

Not long after, Westinghouse sat leafing through a magazine in his father's machine shop. He was struck by one particular article detailing how compressed air had powered a drill to tunnel through a mountain. Young George began to think how he could use compressed air to power a braking system. After all, if compressed air could power an apparatus to tunnel through a mountain, why not use it to force a brake against a wheel?

In short order, George Westinghouse found himself in Pittsburgh in search of a local steel manufacturer. Lost in a strange city, Westinghouse chanced to ask a stranger, Ralph Bagaley, for directions. From that moment, the two formed a lifelong friendship.

A man of means, Ralph Bagaley backed the young inventor, providing personal funds to develop equipment for test purposes. One day, W.W. Card, superintendent of the Steubenville division of the Panhandle Railroad, contacted Westinghouse, liked his invention, and appealed to his superiors to test the novel braking system.

On the day of the trial, engineer Dan Tate throttled the test train through the Grant Hill Tunnel in Pittsburgh when he suddenly came upon a huckster's wagon stuck on the track. In a flash, engineer Tate grabbed the air brake handle and twisted it. The train dramatically stopped a mere four feet from the huckster. This successful test laid the foundation for the Westinghouse Air Brake Company.

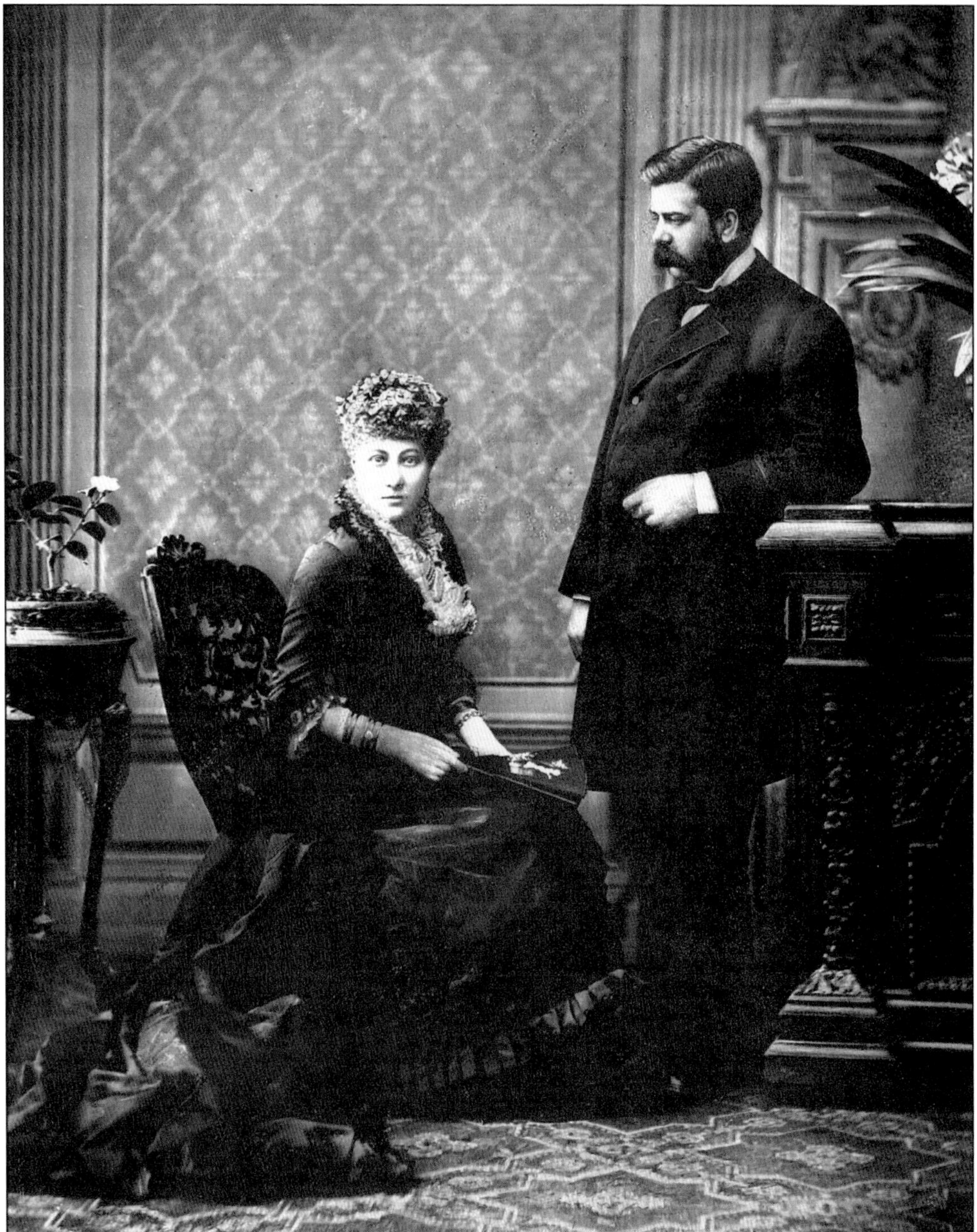

George Westinghouse Jr. poses with his lovely wife, Marguerite, *c.* the 1870s. Since his life revolved around railroads and the railroad industry, it was only natural for young George to meet the love of his life on a train, the New York Central & Hudson River Railroad. After their initial meeting in June 1867, he proudly told his parents he had met his future wife. As was that day's custom, Westinghouse procured letters attesting to his good character and pursued the hand of the beautiful Marguerite Erskine Walker. The wedding took place on August 8, 1867. From the very beginning, George shared all of his dreams with Marguerite and kept in daily communication with her. He said that he owed everything he accomplished in life to his wife. Marguerite bore only one son to George.

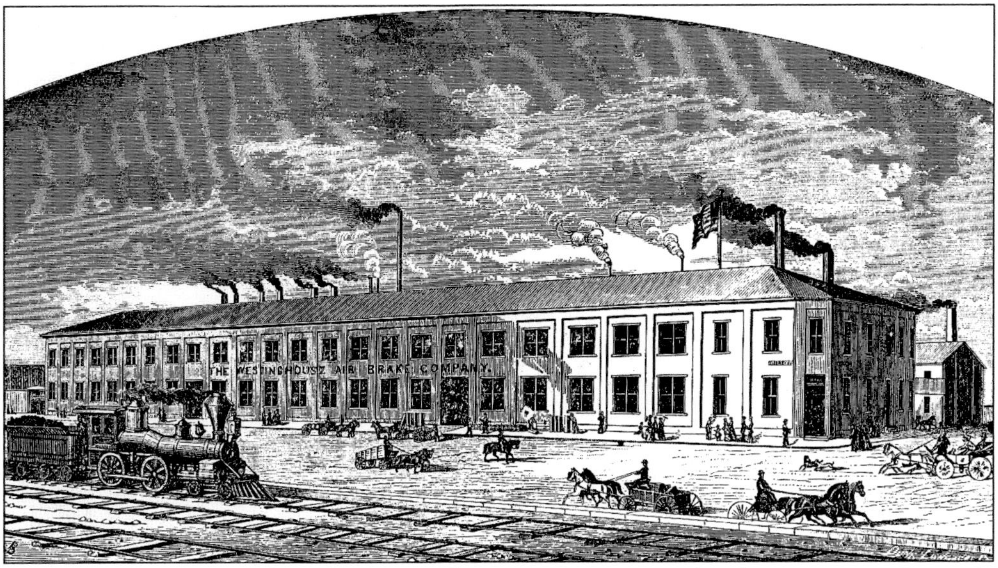

George Westinghouse's first plant, on Liberty Avenue in Pittsburgh, is seen in this early engraving. The Westinghouse Air Brake plant opened in 1870 with 105 employees and an initial capitalization of $500,000. The first officers were George Westinghouse Jr., president; Ralph Bagaley, vice president and secretary; and Robert Pitcairn, treasurer. The company remained at this location until increased production demands necessitated a move to larger quarters in Allegheny (Pittsburgh's present-day North Side).

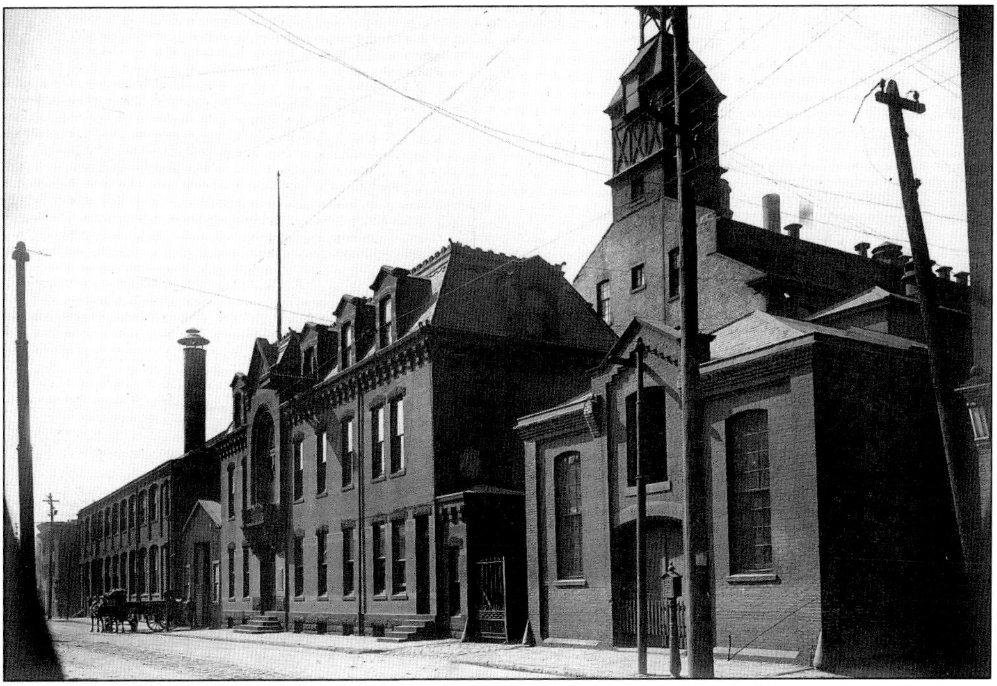

Between 1880 and 1889, the Westinghouse Air Brake Company plant stood here in Old Allegheny, Pennsylvania. The new plant was located on Lacock and General Robinson Streets. Demand by railroads throughout the world for what was rapidly recognized as the standard of railroad braking grew to where it had become necessary to move the operation to a bigger facility.

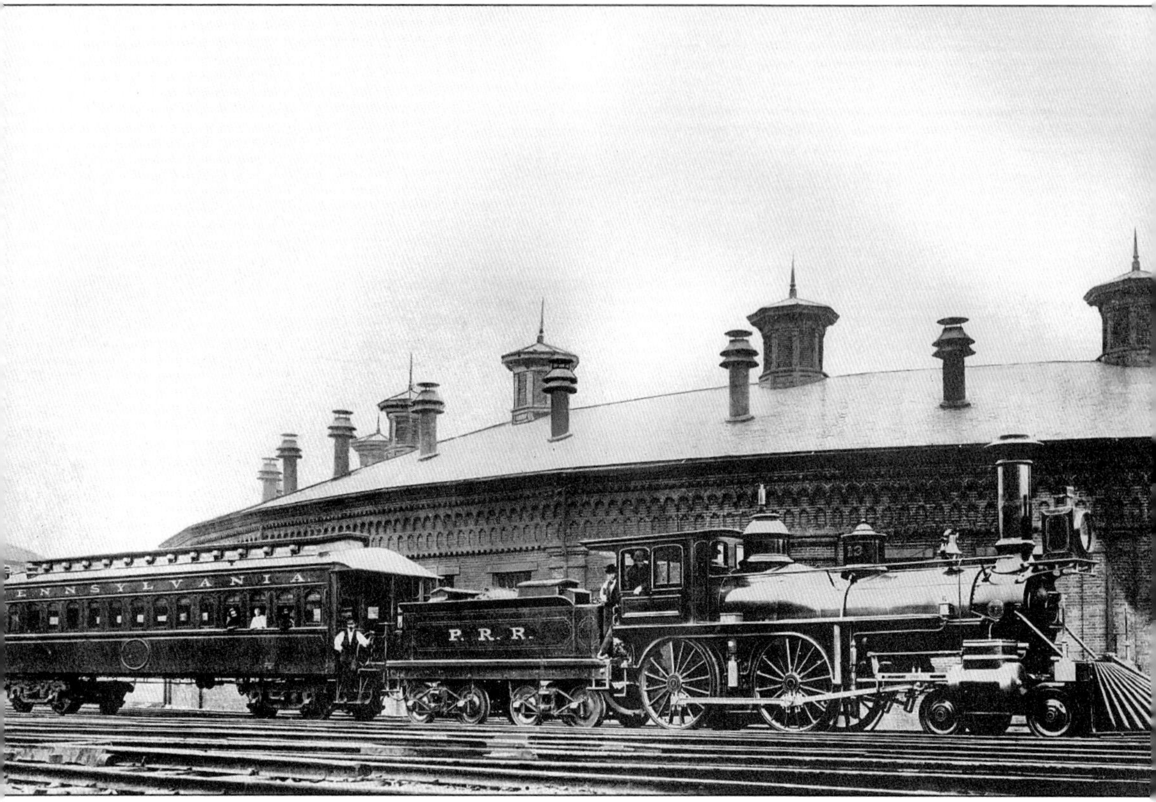

The first locomotive equipped by George Westinghouse with Westinghouse Atmospheric Brakes is shown in this photograph. Installation was on a Pennsylvania Railroad locomotive, which is shown parked in front of the 28th roundhouse in Pittsburgh, Pennsylvania, *c.* 1869. Although the Panhandle Railroad was the first to recognize the merits of the Westinghouse air brake and give him the all-important first test of his new equipment, the Pennsylvania Railroad was the first to actually install air brakes on their locomotives. The advent of the air brake revolutionized the railroad industry. Air brakes stopped trains more quickly, safely, and efficiently than any other braking system known. Longer freight trains were possible. Passenger service increased. On March 2, 1893, Congress passed the Federal Safety Appliance Act, which forced the railroads to equip trains with air brakes and employ other safety measures.

Two

A Town Is Born

At the tender age of 22, George Westinghouse Jr. became president of the Westinghouse Air Brake Company, by unanimous vote. Ralph Bagaley was elected vice president and secretary, and Robert Pitcairn was elected treasurer.

Production began in 1870 at the new plant on Liberty Avenue, between 24th and 25th Streets in Pittsburgh. By the end of the 1870s, the demand for the air brakes and all related railroad equipment soared so that it became necessary to move to a larger plant on Lacock and General Robinson Streets in Allegheny. Thus, the Westinghouse Air Brake Company joined the other giants of the 19th century on the North Side of Pittsburgh. This included the growing coal, iron, and steel industry, men like Frick and Carnegie, as well as others. Pittsburgh was, indeed, the hub for industry.

At first, the Westinghouse air brake was only used on passenger trains, but continued experimentation and testing developed a brake for freight trains. Thus, freight service expanded rapidly. Use of Westinghouse Air Brake equipment was not restricted to America but was manufactured and sold throughout the world. In time, the Westinghouse Air Brake Company led the industry when it came to innovation and production of brake equipment systems for passenger and freight trains. The company became known for quality and workmanship, traits still admired today.

Increased demand and production necessitated one final move. In 1887, George Westinghouse purchased 500 acres of farmland in the Turtle Creek Valley, where he began construction of a modern plant, foundry, and the borough of Wilmerding.

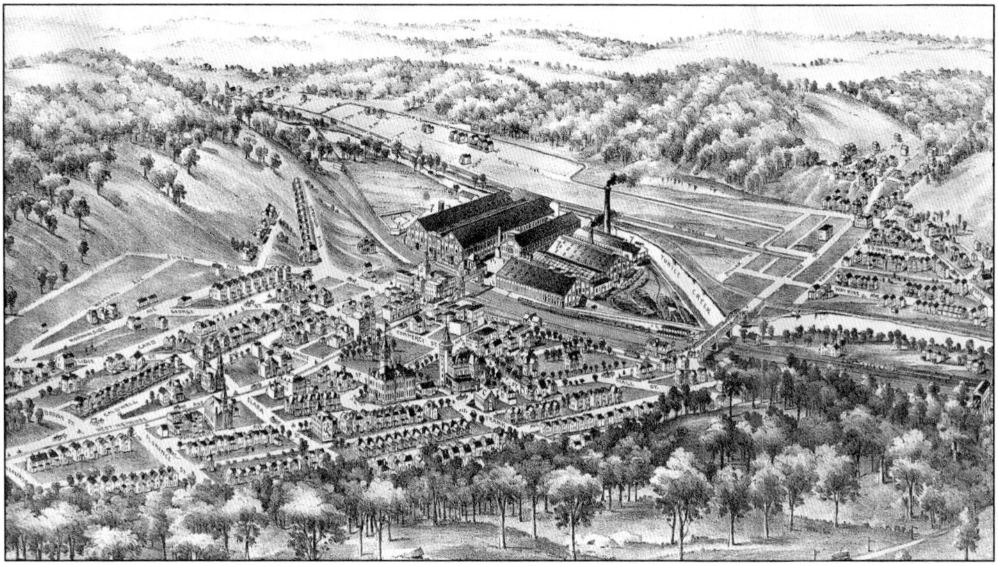

Here is an early drawing of the borough of Wilmerding, as it appeared in 1897. Wilmerding was divided into two parts by Turtle Creek, which ran parallel to the Pennsylvania Railroad tracks. Residents could access either side by crossing the Bridge Street Bridge. To the north of Wilmerding lay Patton Township-Monroeville; to the east, Wall and Pitcairn; to the south, East McKeesport and North Versailles; and to the west, Turtle Creek.

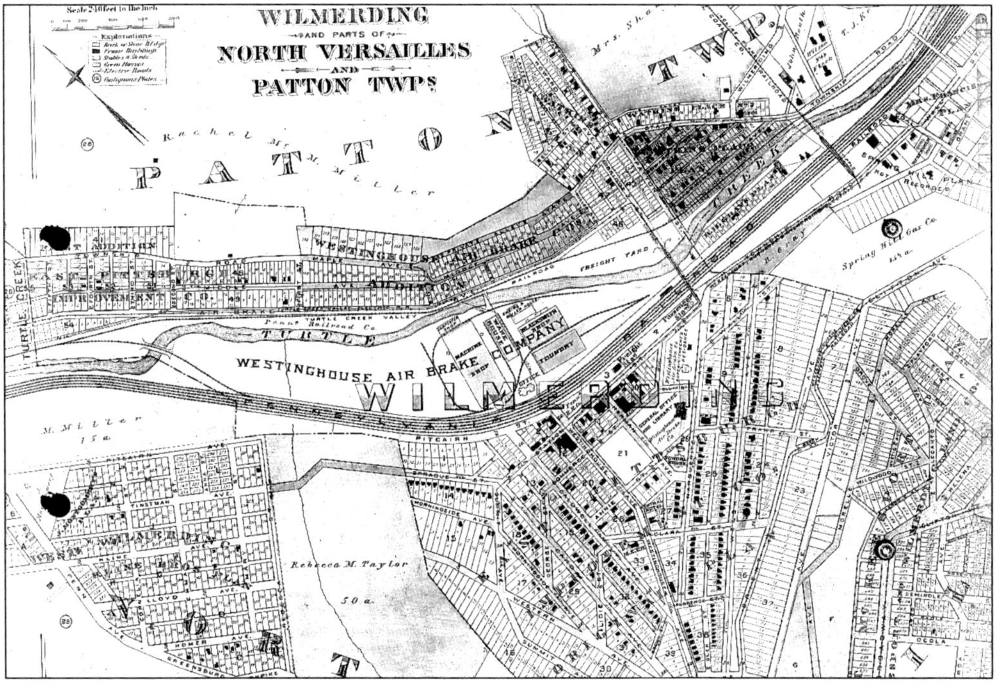

A c. 1903 plan of the borough of Wilmerding is shown here. As the Westinghouse Air Brake Company captured an ever-increasing share of the market for passenger and freight air brake systems, a much larger manufacturing facility was needed. In 1890, George Westinghouse moved 13 miles east of Pittsburgh into the Turtle Creek Valley and constructed a new plant in the borough he founded, Wilmerding.

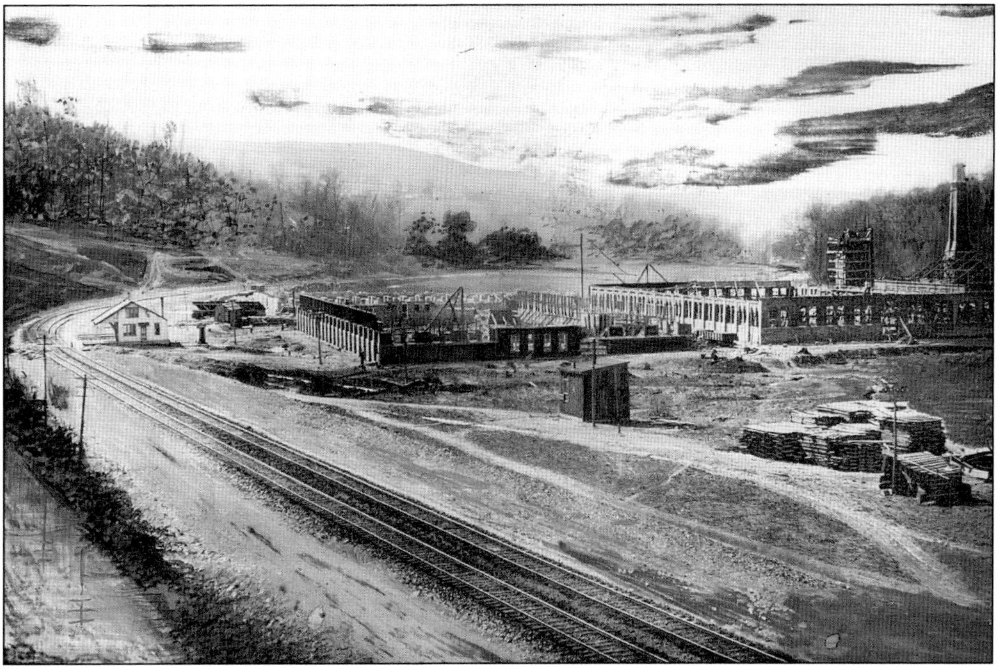

Workers erect the Westinghouse Air Brake Company foundry in the summer of 1889. The company became known for its foundry, and in later years, continued renovations helped to maintain its reputation. The Pennsylvania Railroad's flag stop railroad station is shown at the left on its main line at the end of Herman Avenue.

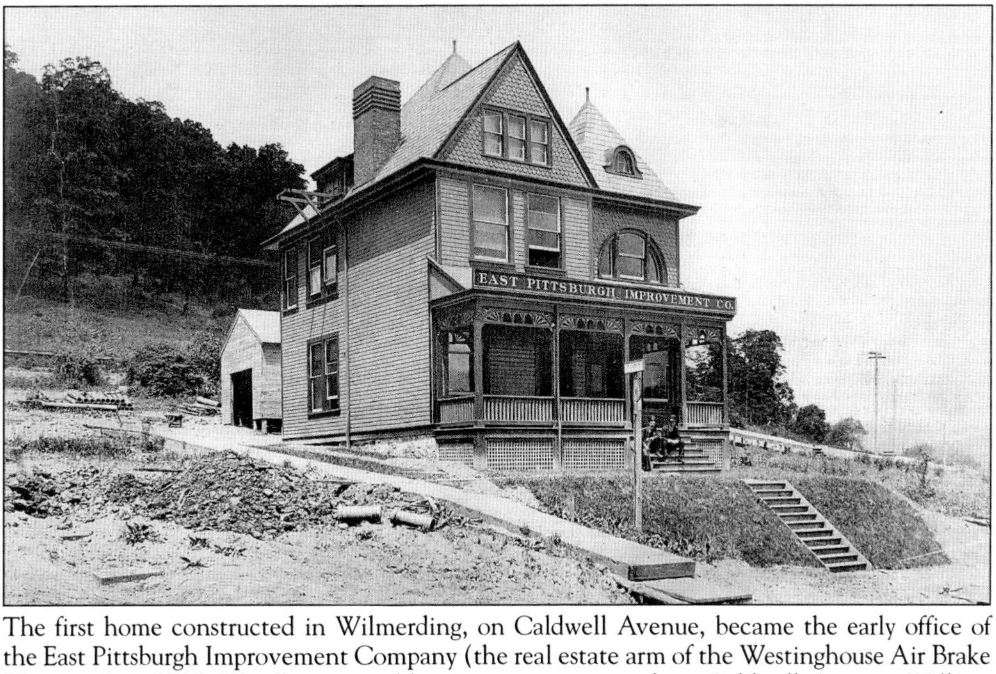

The first home constructed in Wilmerding, on Caldwell Avenue, became the early office of the East Pittsburgh Improvement Company (the real estate arm of the Westinghouse Air Brake Company) *c.* 1889. The first row of homes was constructed on Caldwell Avenue. William Moles was the first occupant. He was a machinist with the Westinghouse Air Brake Company from 1884 (starting at the North Side Pittsburgh plant) until his retirement in 1929.

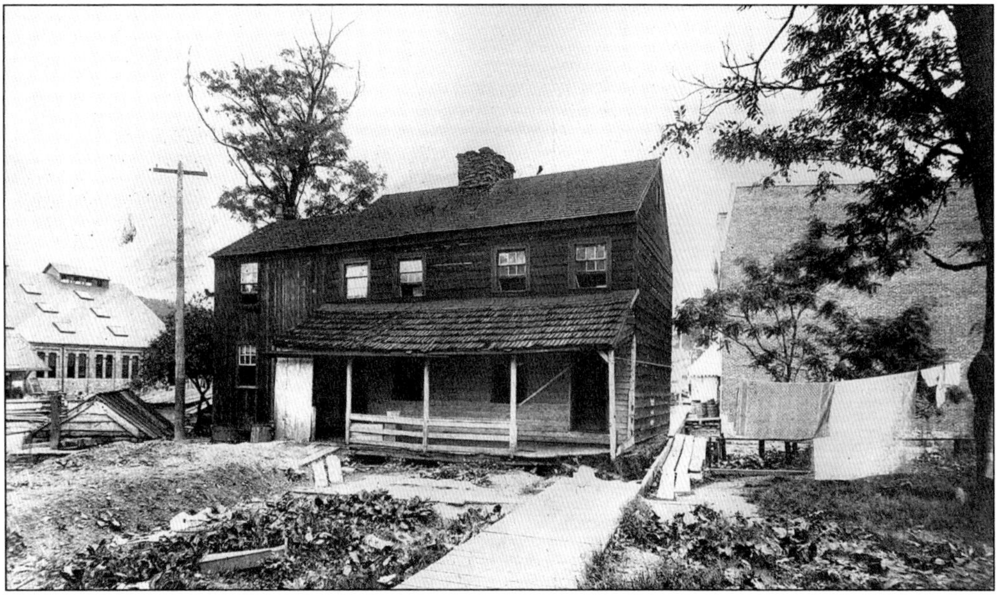

The Osborne residence, located on the Osborne Farm, was one of the tracts of land purchased by George Westinghouse in 1887. The new company foundry can be seen at the far left, along with the first flag stop railroad station. This photograph was taken on August 23, 1889. The Osborne residence was razed in 1890.

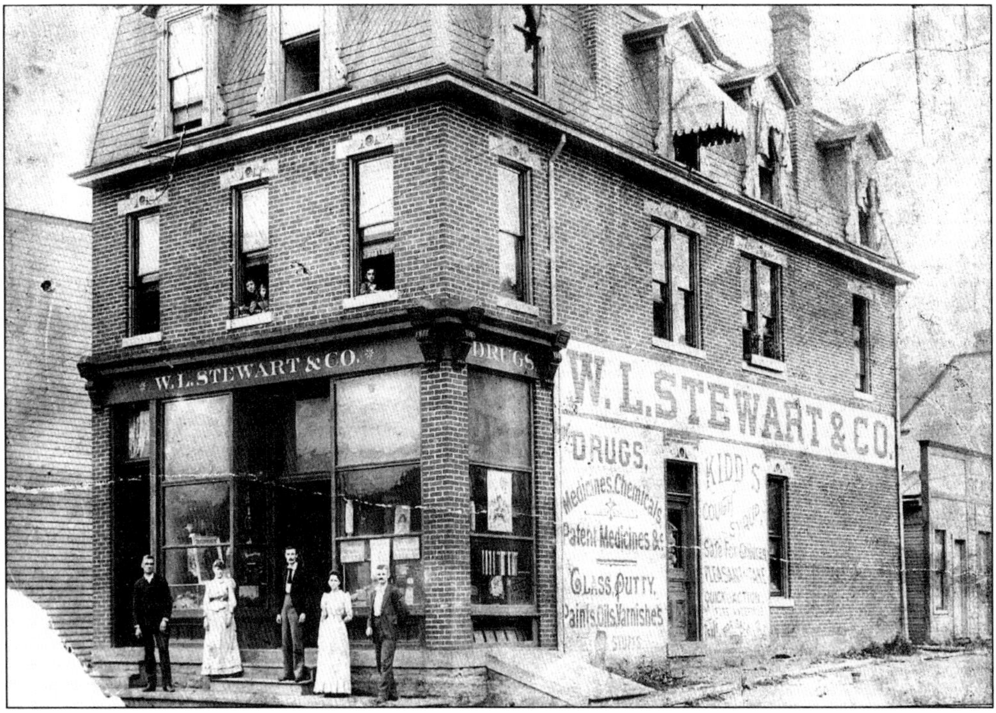

The first drugstore, owned by W.L. Stewart & Company, was located at the corner of Westinghouse Avenue and Station Street. The name was later changed to Stewart & Hankey. Wilmerding's first post office was located in the front part of the drugstore. William L. Stewart was the first postmaster. This photograph was taken c. 1890.

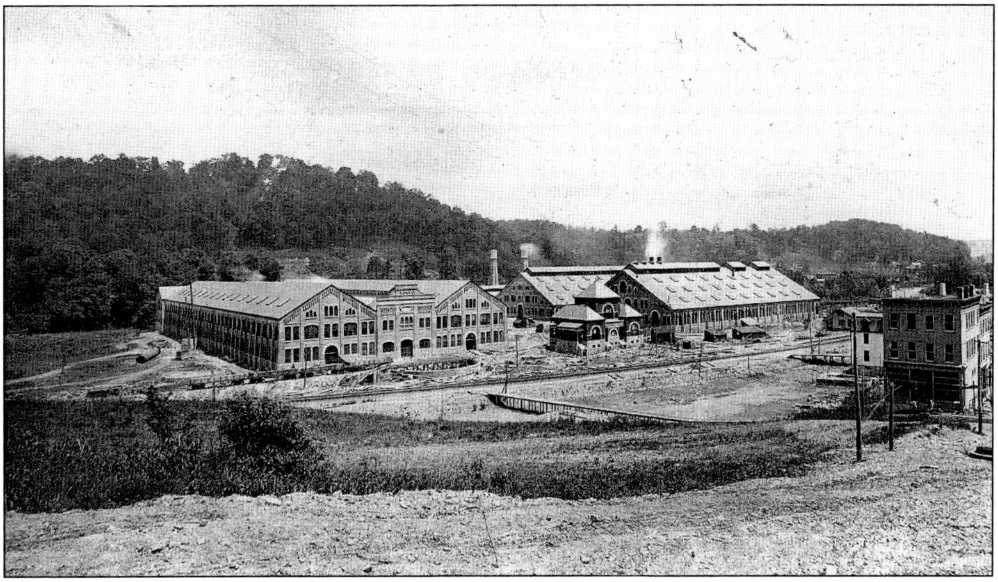

The Westinghouse Air Brake Company begins construction of its new plant along the Pennsylvania Railroad in the Turtle Creek Valley. George Westinghouse purchased four tracts of land (about 500 acres) in the Turtle Creek Valley during 1887 and 1888. The view shows, from left to right, the machine shop, blacksmith shop, superintendent's building, and foundry. Construction began in the summer of 1889, and by fall, 200 employees worked in the foundry. By completion, 1,400 were employed.

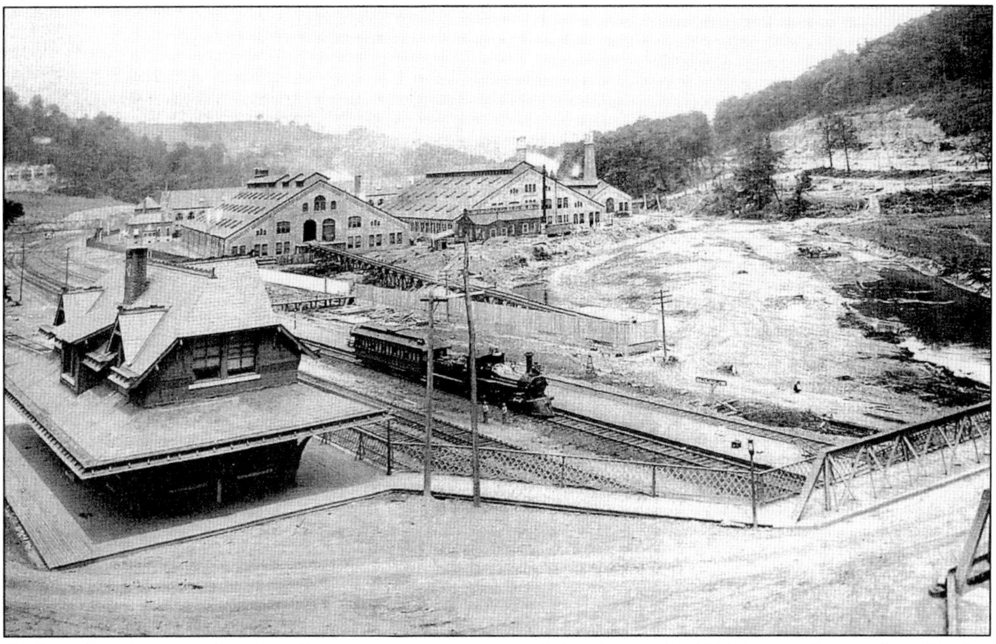

Wilmerding's second railroad station, as it appeared in the early 1890s, was located at Bridge and Station Streets. The new Westinghouse Air Brake plant can be seen toward the rear. Note that Turtle Creek has been relocated to the right. Turtle Creek had originally curved as it entered Wilmerding from the east. Its course was changed to conform more directly to the Westinghouse Air Brake Company's property line.

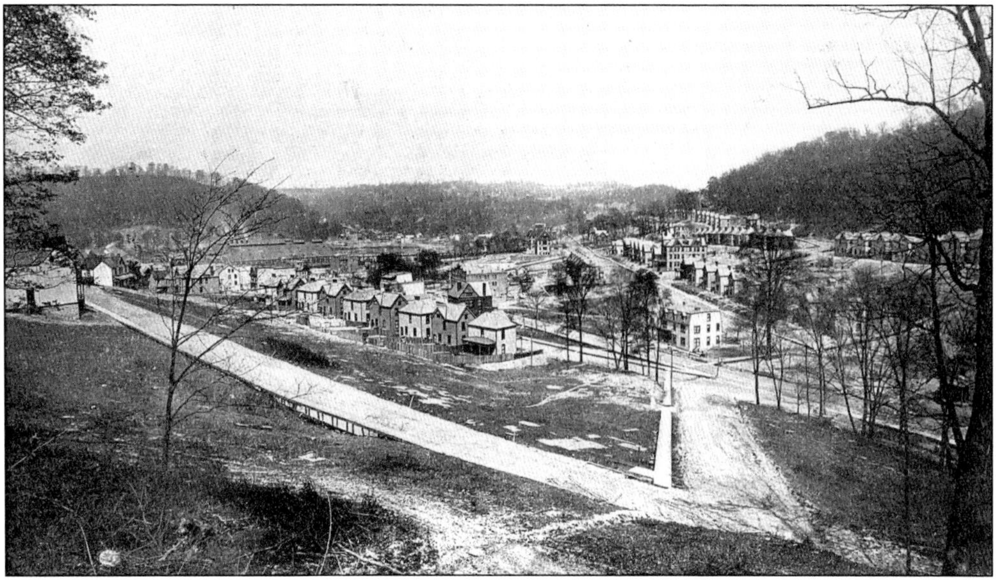

This photograph was taken at the south end of Wilmerding, looking northeast toward the Westinghouse Air Brake Company plant. The dirt roads in the foreground became Card Avenue and Brown Street. At the foot of Brown Street is where Caldwell and Westinghouse Avenues intersect. The other major road shown is Marguerite Avenue. The large building on the right side of Marguerite Avenue is the Glen Hotel.

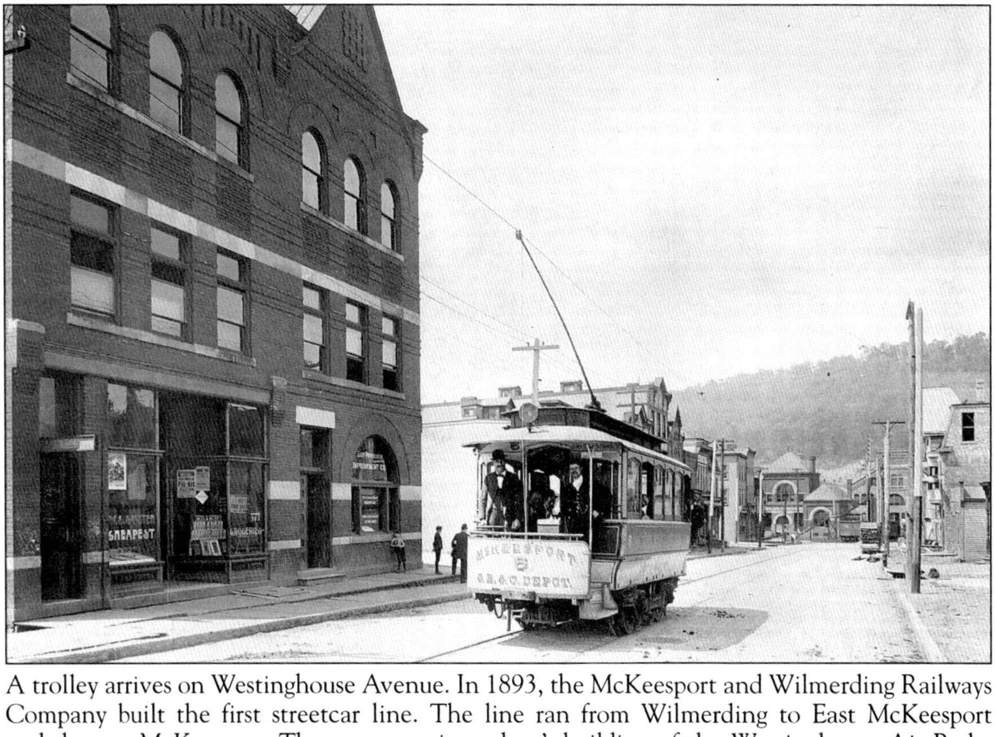

A trolley arrives on Westinghouse Avenue. In 1893, the McKeesport and Wilmerding Railways Company built the first streetcar line. The line ran from Wilmerding to East McKeesport and then to McKeesport. The new superintendent's building of the Westinghouse Air Brake Company can be seen at the end of the street. The building on the left housed the offices of the East Pittsburgh Improvement Company.

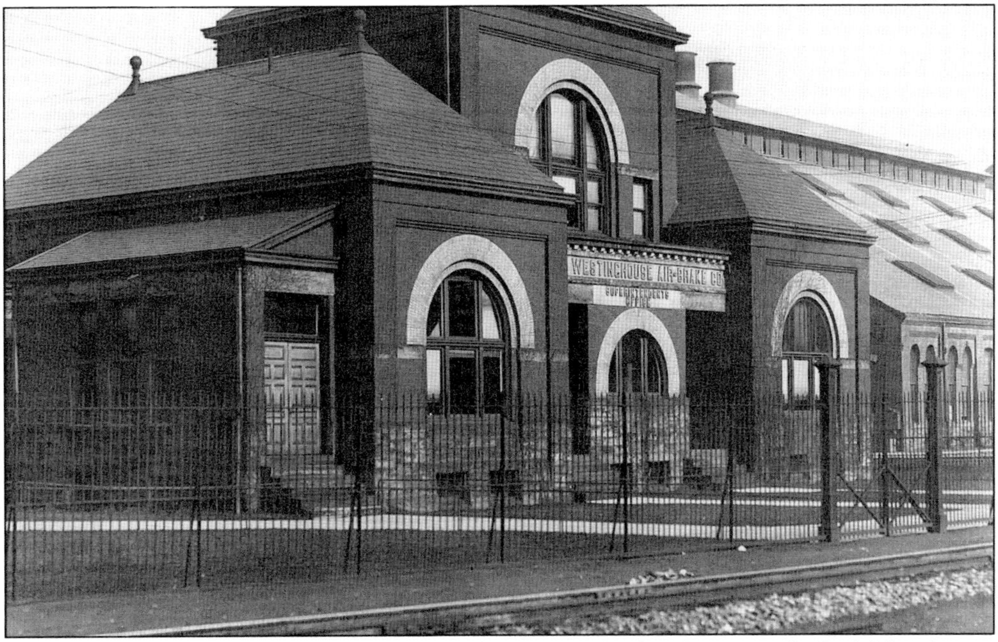

The superintendent's office of the Westinghouse Air Brake Company looked like this in the 1890s. T.W. Welsh was the first superintendent at the Wilmerding plant. The foundry appears to the right, and the Pennsylvania Railroad tracks are shown in the foreground. Note that the early buildings have letters to identify them. The letters were placed on the buildings during construction.

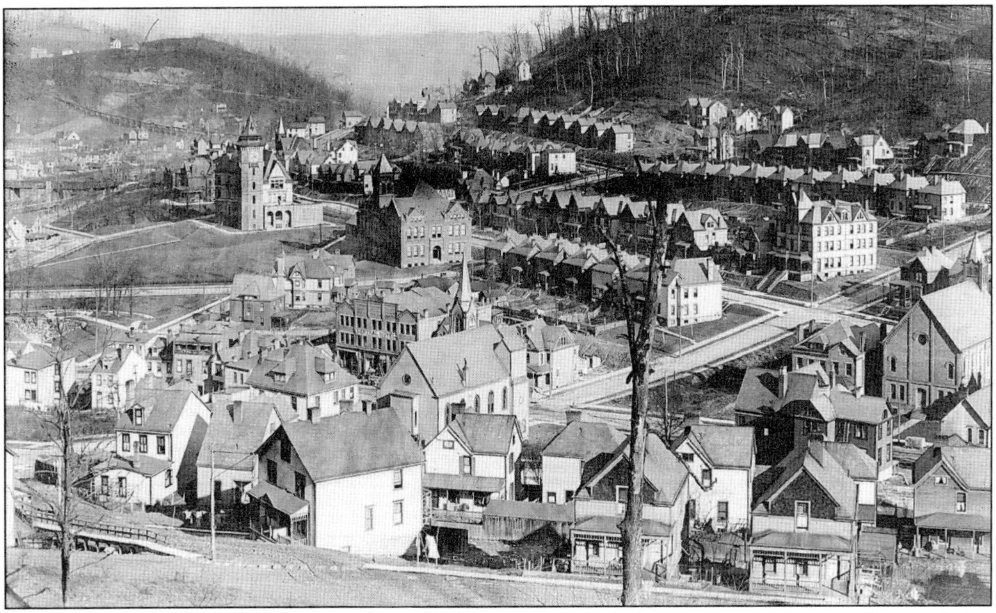

An 1896 photograph of Wilmerding looks east toward the new executive offices of the Westinghouse Air Brake Company. The castlelike building was destroyed by fire on April 8, 1896, but was immediately reconstructed on the same foundation. This time, a turret with four synchronized clock faces was added. The Club House, as it was called, no longer maintained recreational activities, only offices. The building became known as the G.O.

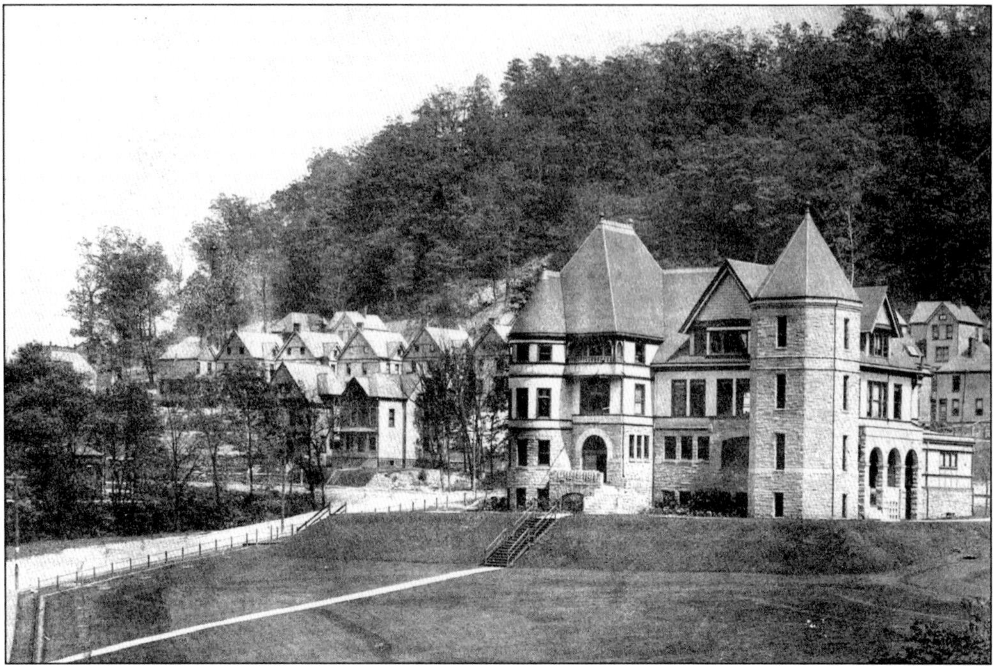

The Westinghouse Air Brake Company general office was built *c.* 1890 on Marguerite Avenue. Known as the Club House, the building contained a swimming pool, two bowling alleys (both on the first floor), a restaurant (second floor), and a library (second floor). George Westinghouse Jr.'s office was on the third floor, along with his staff and accountants.

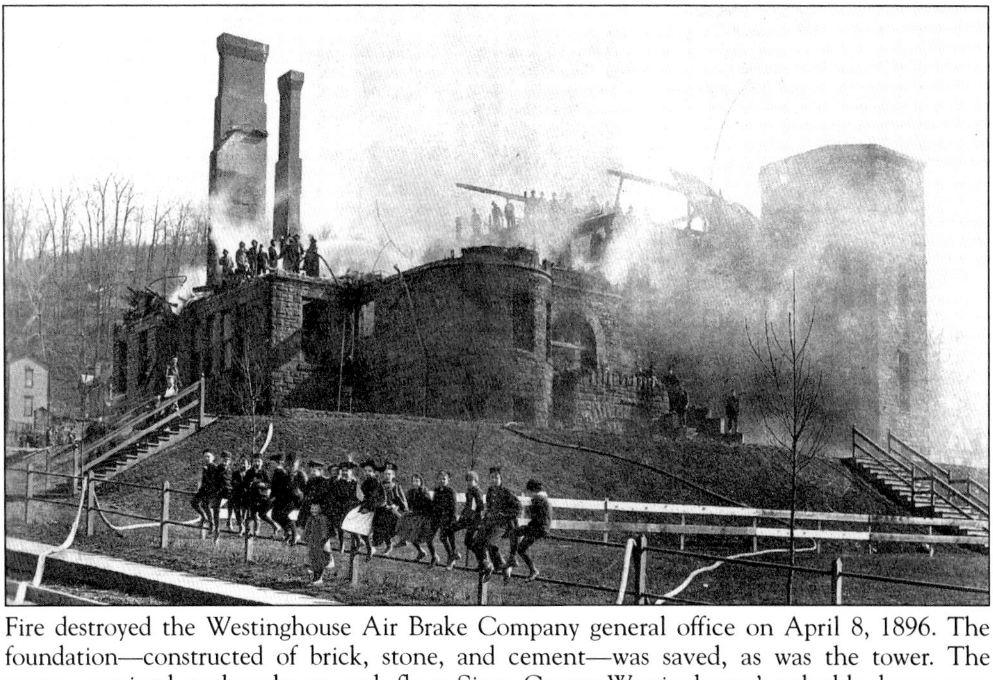

Fire destroyed the Westinghouse Air Brake Company general office on April 8, 1896. The foundation—constructed of brick, stone, and cement—was saved, as was the tower. The tower contained steel vaults on each floor. Since George Westinghouse's valuable documents, inventions, and drawings were stored in the vaults, they remained intact during the fire. Reconstruction of the building began immediately.

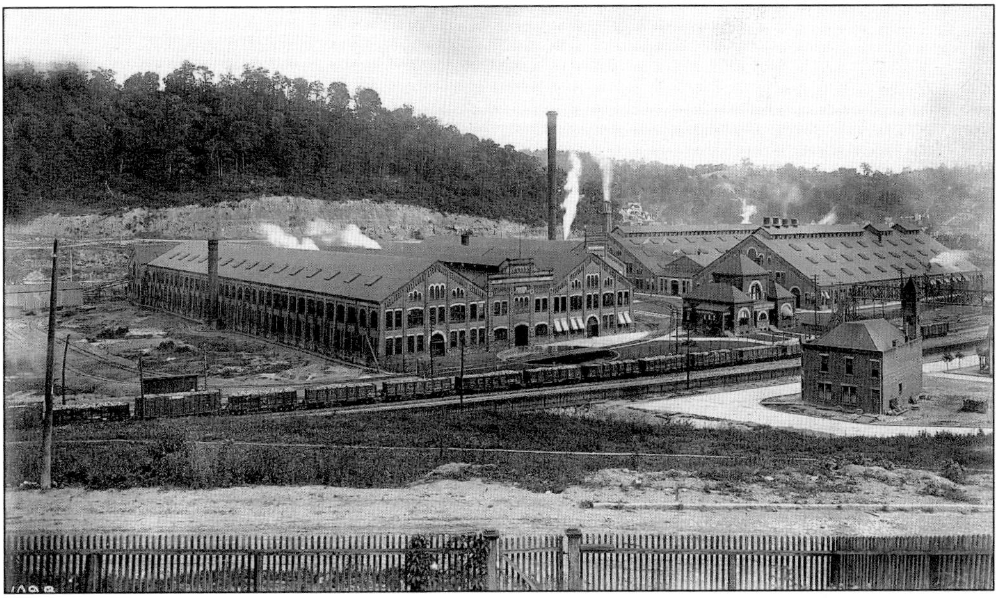

Here is a photograph of the Westinghouse Air Brake plant as it appeared in the late 1890s. The building in the foreground and to the right is Wilmerding's first borough building. In only 10 years, Wilmerding was already considered an example of a successful industrial town with conveniences and services found only in larger cities.

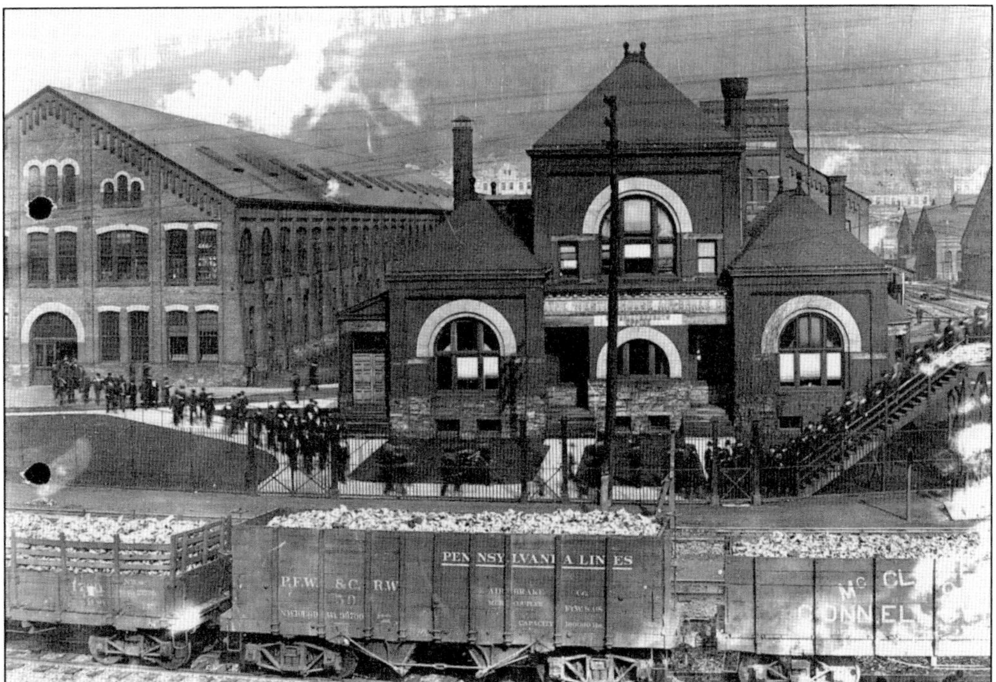

Westinghouse Air Brake Company workers go home for lunch, leaving the plant and walking over Wilmerding's first bridge. An obvious advantage to working for the Westinghouse Air Brake Company was returning home to eat lunch with family. Freight cars sitting in the foreground are loaded with coke. This photograph was taken in the late 1890s.

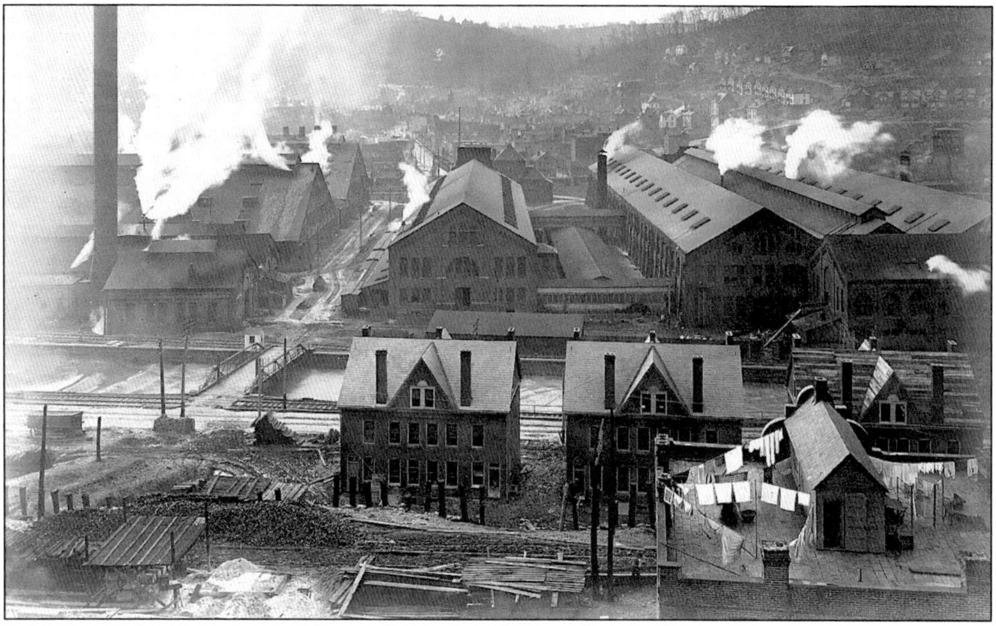

Looking south, this rear view shows the Westinghouse plant with the borough of Wilmerding in the background and Airbrake and Middle Avenue houses under construction in the foreground. The buildings on the left are the boiler house, light station, blacksmith shop, and foundry. The building in the center is the warehouse, and to the right is the machine shop. The carpenters shop is on the far right.

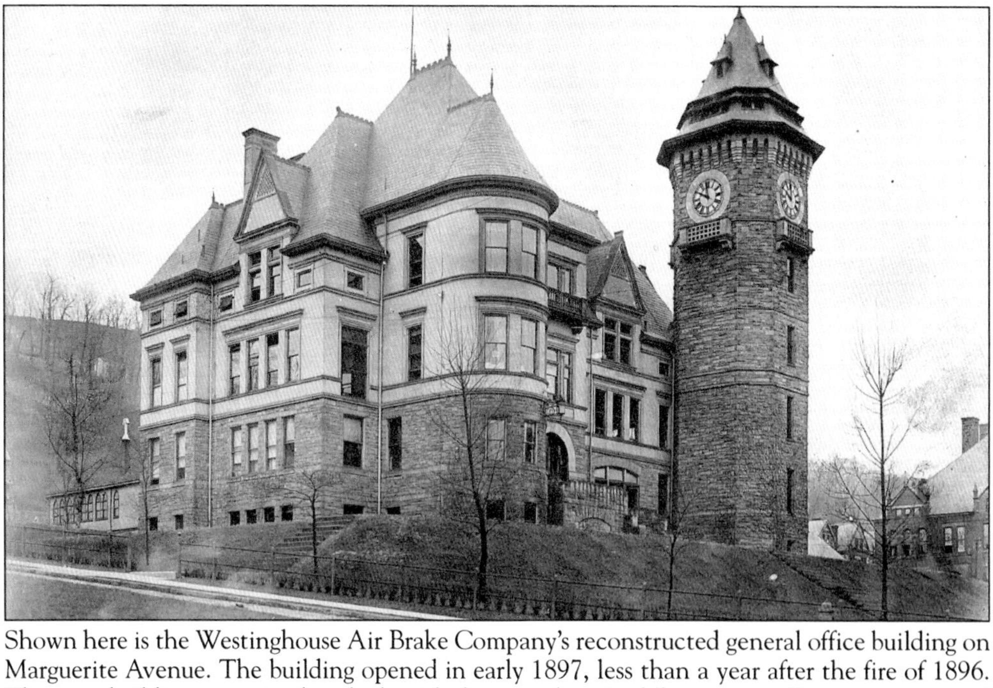

Shown here is the Westinghouse Air Brake Company's reconstructed general office building on Marguerite Avenue. The building opened in early 1897, less than a year after the fire of 1896. The new building contained a clock with four synchronized faces in a taller tower operated by a system of chains and pulleys. The tower clock, built by the E. Howard Watch & Clock Company in Boston, still operates today.

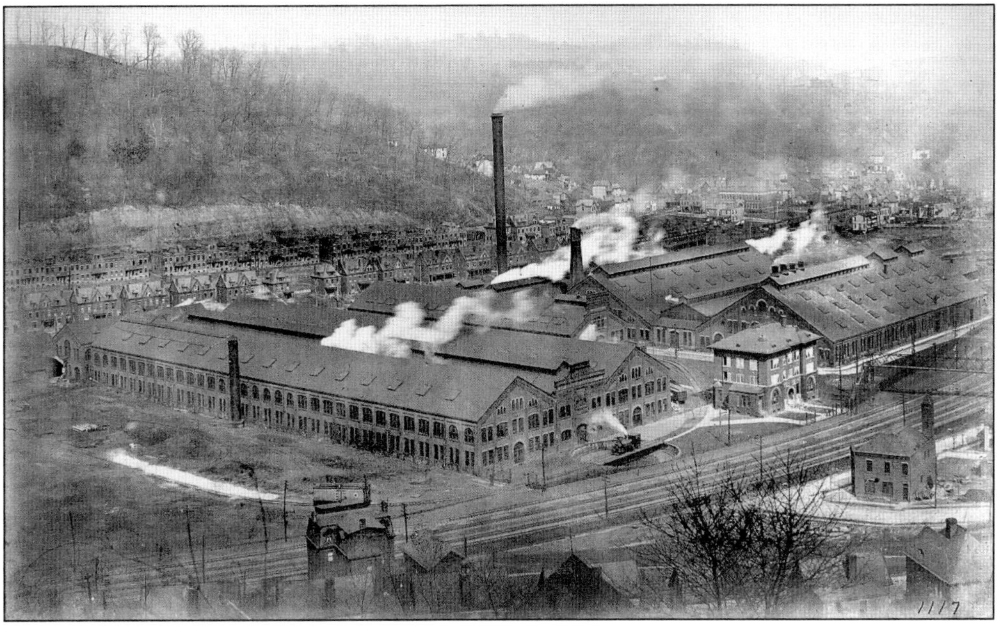

This photograph shows a general view of the Westinghouse Air Brake Company plant as it appeared c. 1900. Points of interest are, from left to right, the main machine shop, warehouse, foundry building, and newly enlarged superintendent's building. Construction of the "flats" can be seen behind the plant. The company's first steam locomotive is seen on the turntable in front of the machine shop.

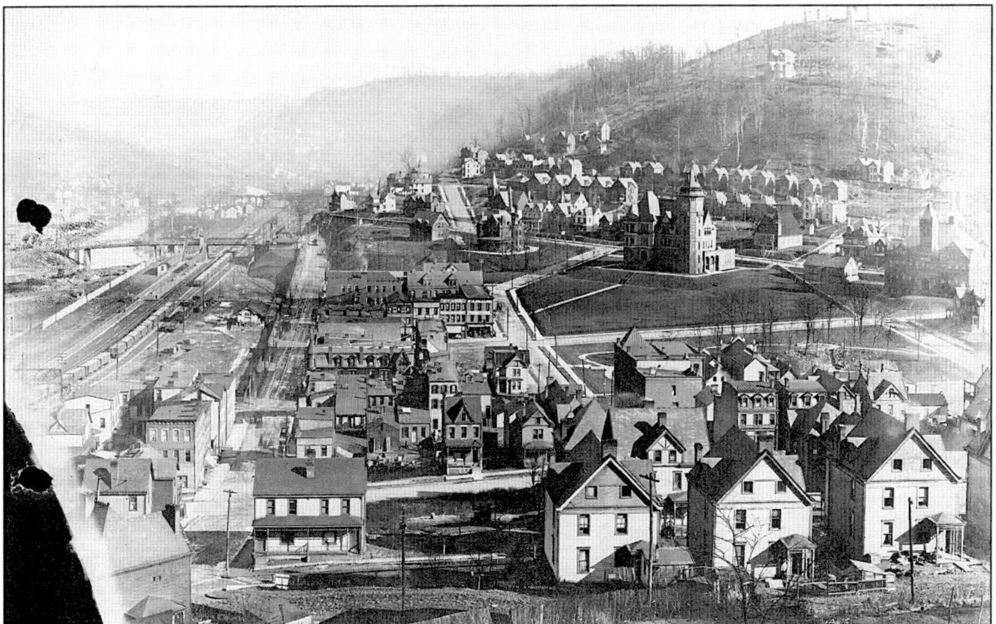

Here is a central view of Wilmerding, looking east c. 1897. The new general office building can be seen to the right of center. To its right are the temporary school building and the school. To the left of the general office building is the home of the plant superintendent, T.W. Welsh. All of these buildings were on Marguerite Avenue.

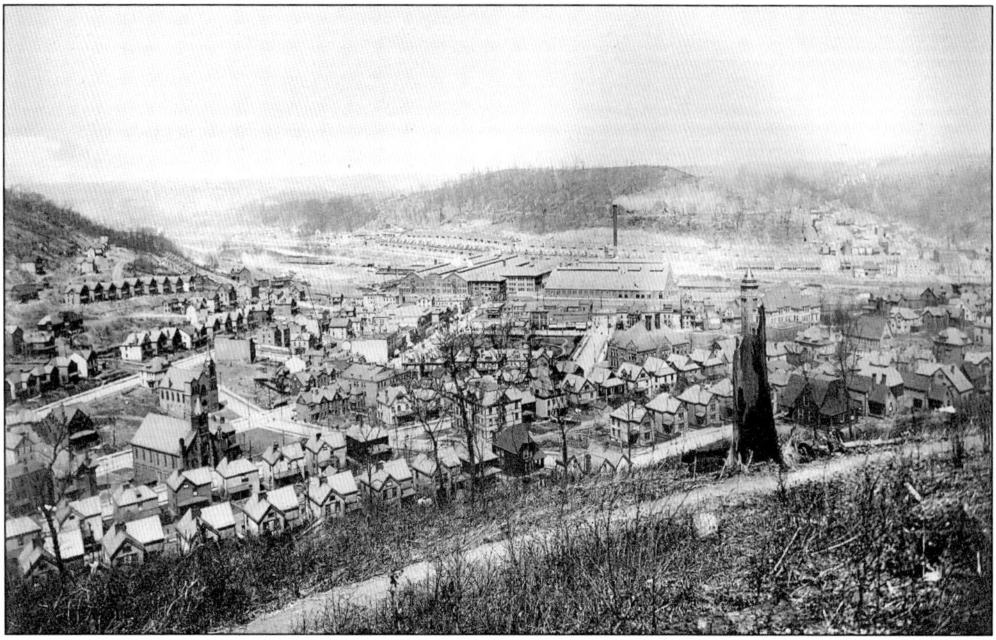

In a view Looking north, the entire borough of Wilmerding can be seen in this general photograph. The building in the center foreground is the Glen Hotel, located on Marguerite Avenue. To the right are the school and the Westinghouse Air Brake Company's general office building. This view was taken in late 1903.

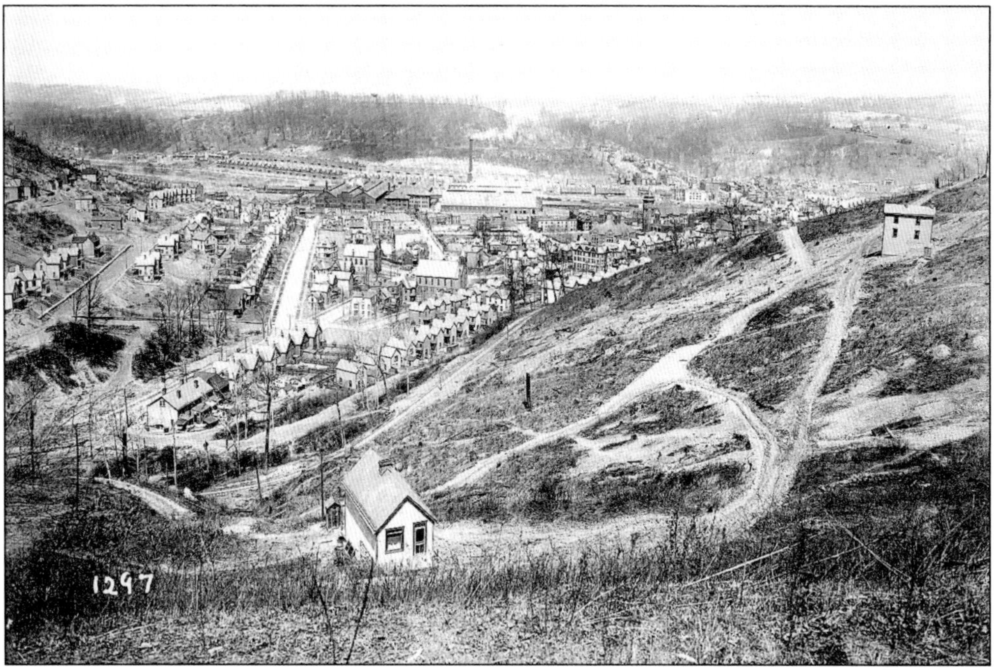

The upper part of the borough of Wilmerding can be seen in this photograph. The trolley tracks coming from East McKeesport are clearly visible in the foreground. Although from this perspective Wilmerding appears stark, notice the neatly constructed rows of homes. Can you find the Castle? This photograph was taken *c.* 1903.

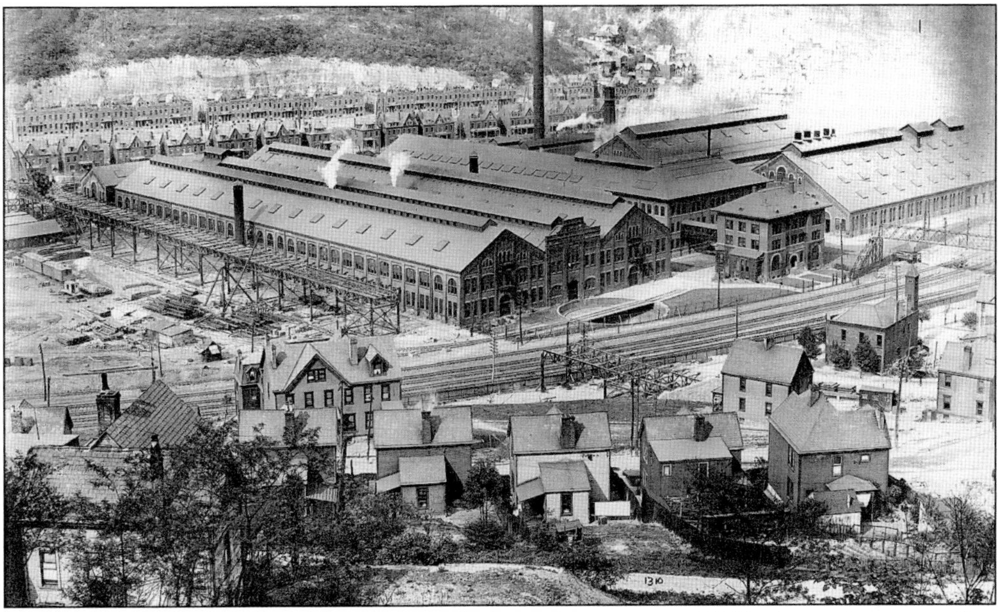

This view of the Westinghouse Air Brake plant, in the summer of 1903, shows the new trolley bridge (the viaduct) under construction. Also note the new extension to the warehouse and bridge connecting to the superintendent's building. At the far right is the initial construction of the personal tunnel entrance, which replaced the old footbridge.

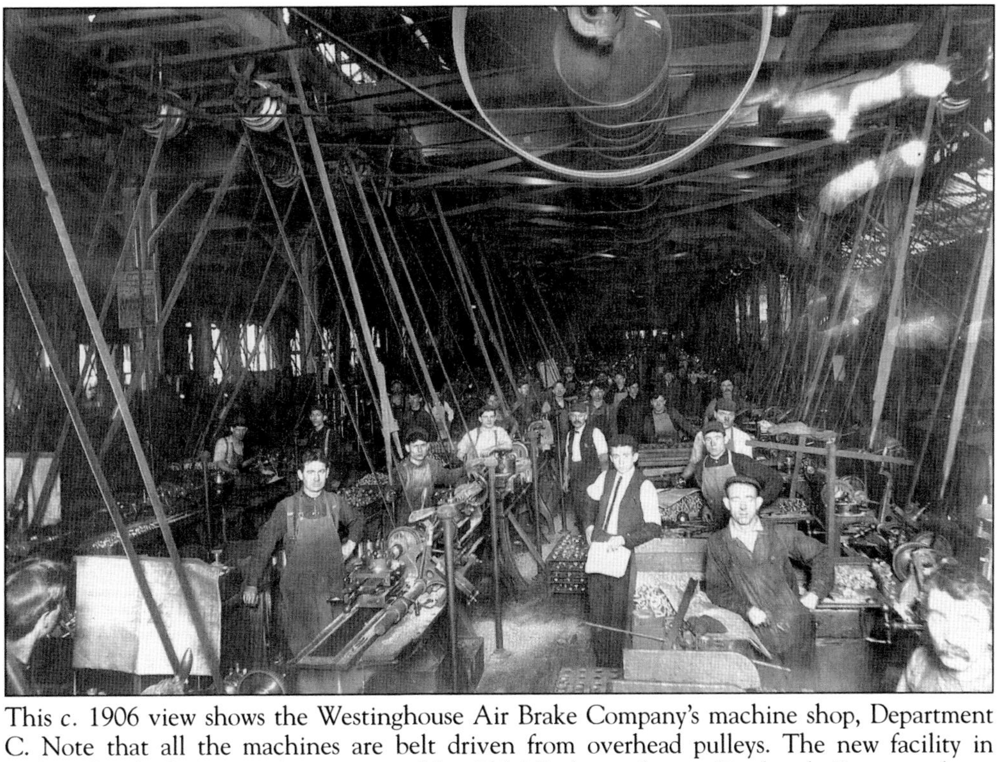

This *c.* 1906 view shows the Westinghouse Air Brake Company's machine shop, Department C. Note that all the machines are belt driven from overhead pulleys. The new facility in Wilmerding had 10 times the capacity of the Old Allegheny plant in Pittsburgh. Every employee has been asked to look at the camera.

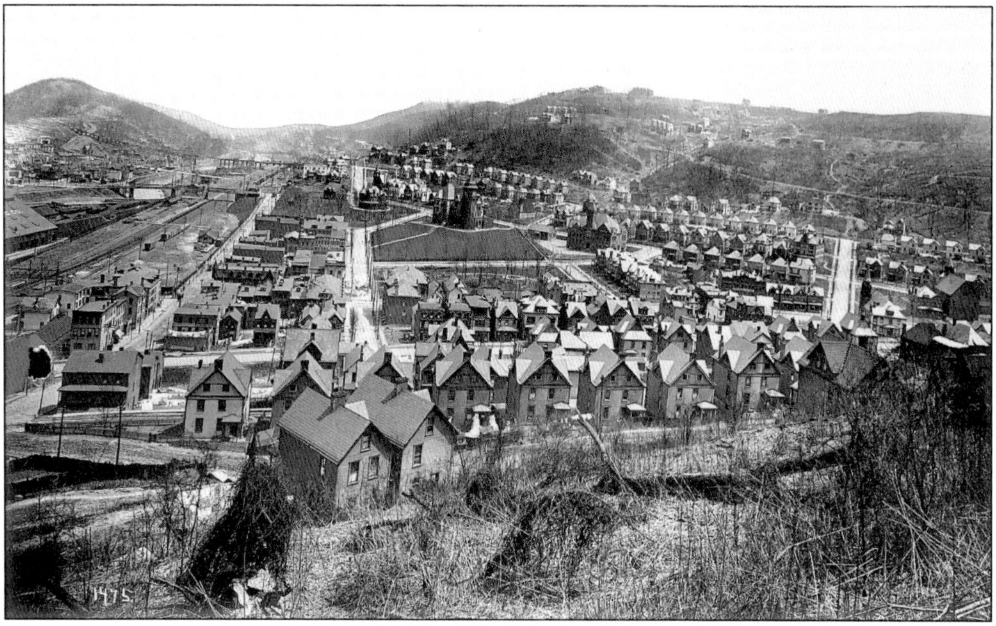

Another panoramic photograph of Wilmerding looks east toward the little town of Wall. When compared with a similar, earlier photograph (taken in 1897), the increase in the number of homes is quite evident. As the years rolled on, the population skyrocketed to 6,441 and remained high for many years.

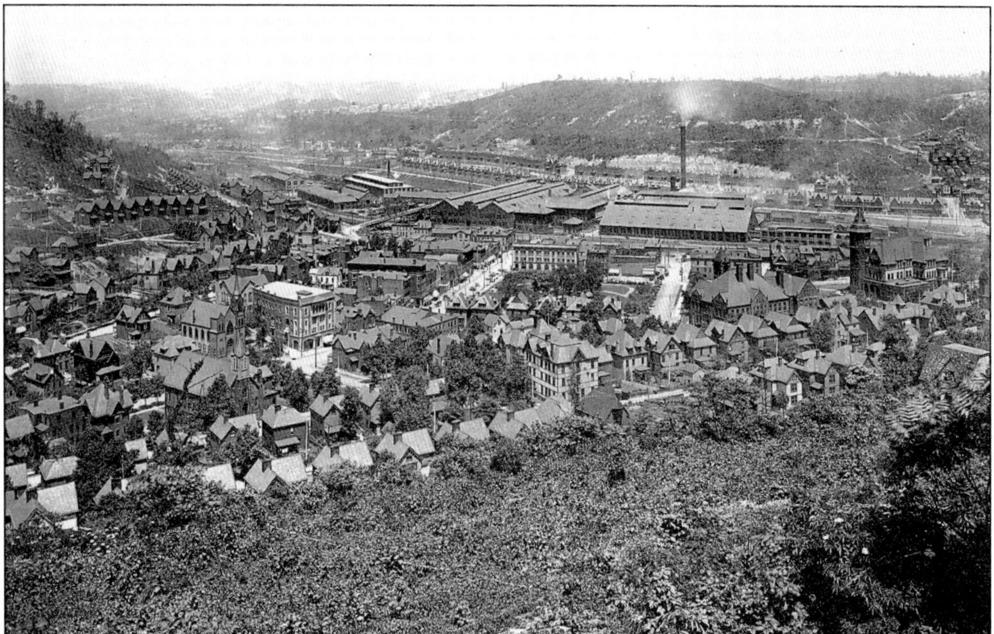

Considering the year is 1915, this panoramic view of Wilmerding was shot from a rather lofty perch. It shows the plant's size increasing west of the trolley viaduct. New innovations and engineering kept improving the already world-leading production of railroad equipment and related components, making expansion necessary. Note the neat row of homes to the left and how they differ in position from the row of homes directly below.

Three

A Community and Company Prosper

Wilmerding is situated some 13 miles east of Pittsburgh along the Turtle Creek and the main line of the Pennsylvania Railroad. The borough became the home of the ever-expanding Westinghouse Air Brake Company, gaining worldwide recognition thanks to George Westinghouse Jr.

Wilmerding derived its name not from George Westinghouse but mainly from Robert Pitcairn, superintendent of the Pittsburgh division of the Pennsylvania Railroad. Pitcairn was a friend of Major William B. Negley. Major Negley, in partnership with a Mr. Bruce, owned the farmland soon to become Wilmerding. Major Negley was married to the former Joanna Wilmerding Bruce. Robert Pitcairn suggested naming the new borough Wilmerding after Mrs. Negley's middle name.

Thanks to the phenomenal demand for air brakes and related railroad equipment, the Westinghouse Air Brake Company plant was immense, with 1,000 employees almost immediately. Wilmerding grew as quickly. No sooner were homes constructed than they were occupied. Most homes were company owned, built singly or in connected rows known as "flats." Stores of all sorts opened, including the H.G. Croushore drugstore, the Redfern and Glen Hotels, the post office, railroad station, bank, and schools—Public School No. 1, or Horrocks School, on the south side and Public School No. 2, or Gottwals School, on the north side. The first church was the First Methodist Church on Westinghouse Avenue. Police and fire departments were formed. The company also built the general office building (called the G.O.) and the park as recreational facilities for the townspeople. From the company's boiler house, steam heat was supplied to the plant, the G.O., and the YMCA (the second largest in Pennsylvania). Trolley lines were installed. A movie theater opened. Life was good and business flourished in Wilmerding.

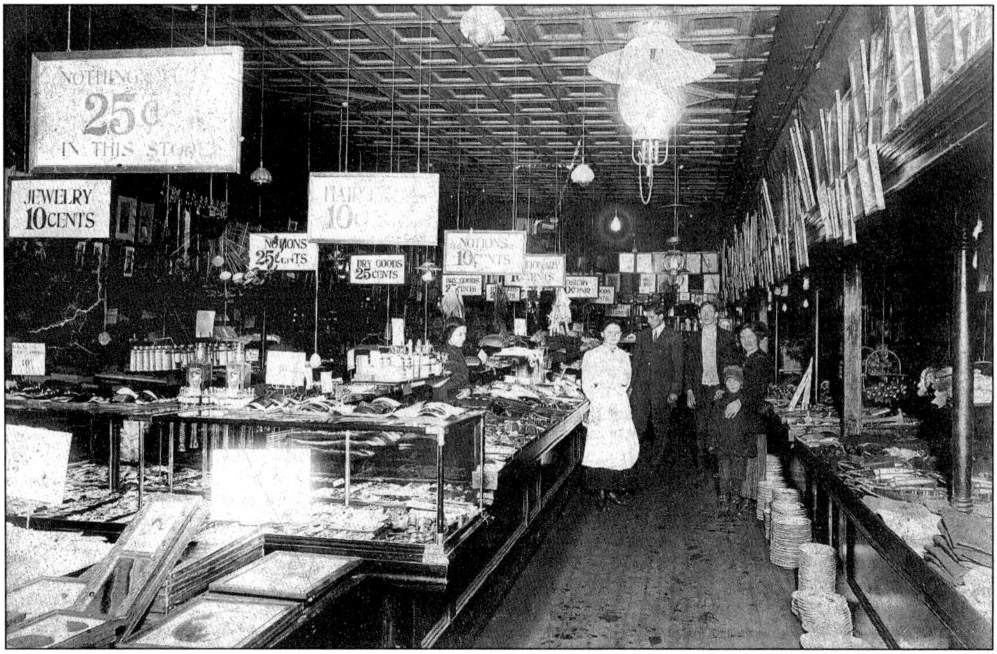

This *c.* 1900 view shows the inside of Murphy's Five and Ten Cent Store on Station Street. The floors are wood, merchandise prices are quite visible, and products for sale are stacked. Prices of 10¢ and 25¢ seem to be the rule. The man in the suit is likely the store manager.

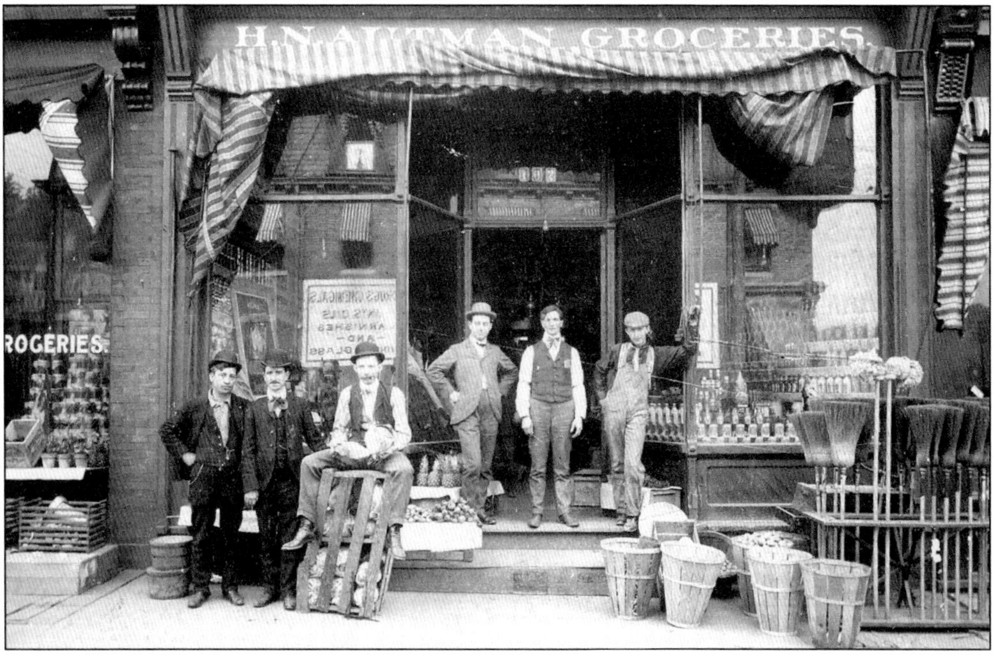

Brooms and vegetables are sold at a sidewalk sale in front of Autman Groceries on Westinghouse Avenue. The grocery store is located on the opposite side of the W.L. Stewart drugstore, which can be seen in the reflection on the windows. Back then, men sported ties and hats; vests were popular. Cloth awnings adorned many shops downtown. This photograph was taken in the early 1900s.

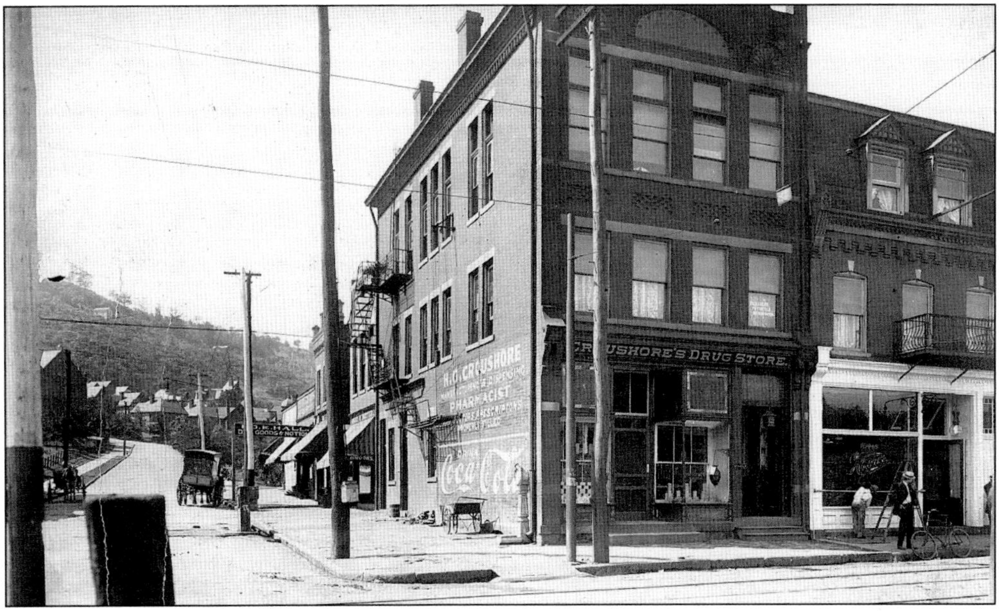

The H.G. Croushore drugstore was at the corner of Station Street and Herman Avenue. The trolley tracks ran as far as Bridge Street. In later years, this building was known as Mazur's Hotel. Most of these buildings in the downtown area were razed during the Model Cities Program of the 1960s.

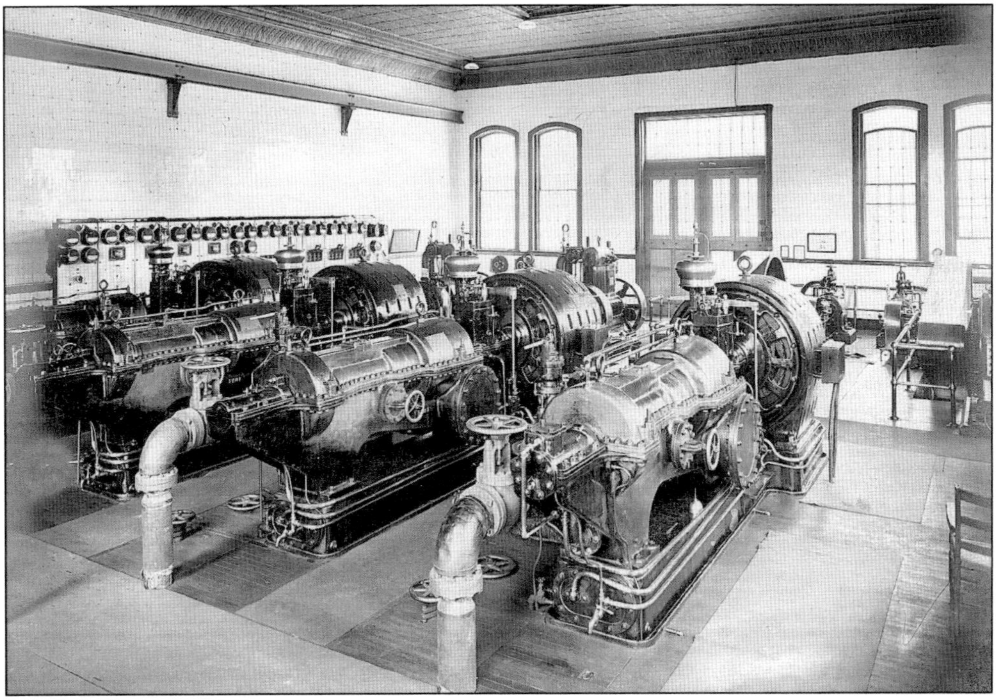

This is an interior view of the Westinghouse Air Brake Company's light station c. 1904. Carpet runners have been placed on the floor around the perimeter of the generators, perhaps to protect the floor or perhaps as a safety precaution to prevent workmen from slipping. The light station was torn down in the 1960s.

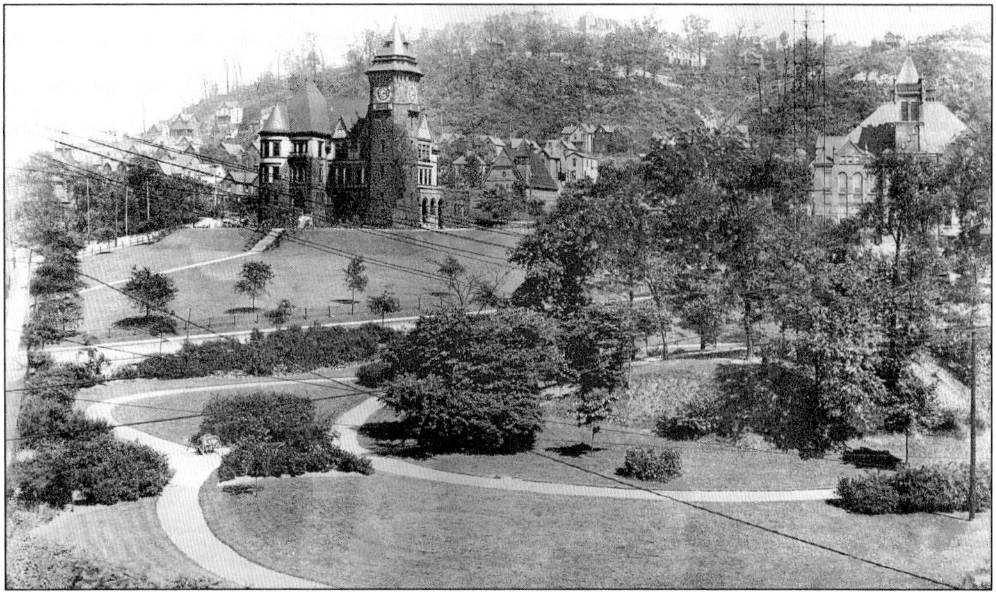

Shown here is an early view of the park in front of the Westinghouse Air Brake Company's general office building. To the right is a steel tower that held three arc lights used to illuminate the borough. Workers had to change carbons daily to ensure operations. The trees were removed and the ground leveled in later years to eliminate problems with the homeless sleeping there.

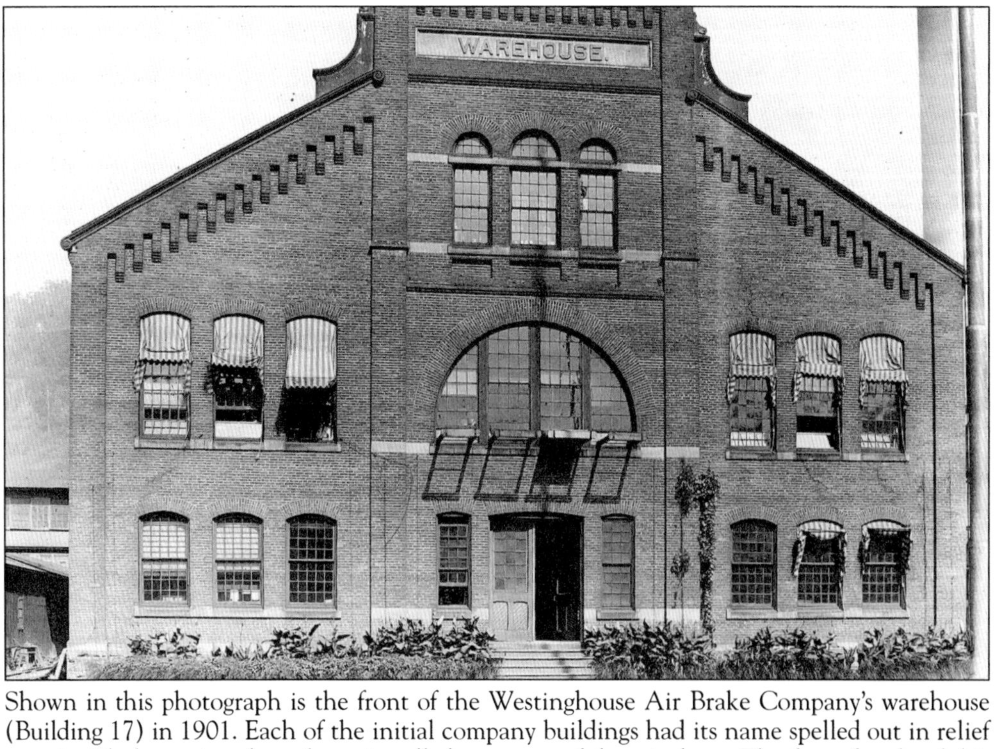

Shown in this photograph is the front of the Westinghouse Air Brake Company's warehouse (Building 17) in 1901. Each of the initial company buildings had its name spelled out in relief atop it. Cloth awnings have been installed on many of the windows. The front facade of this particular building was removed to permit an addition in 1902.

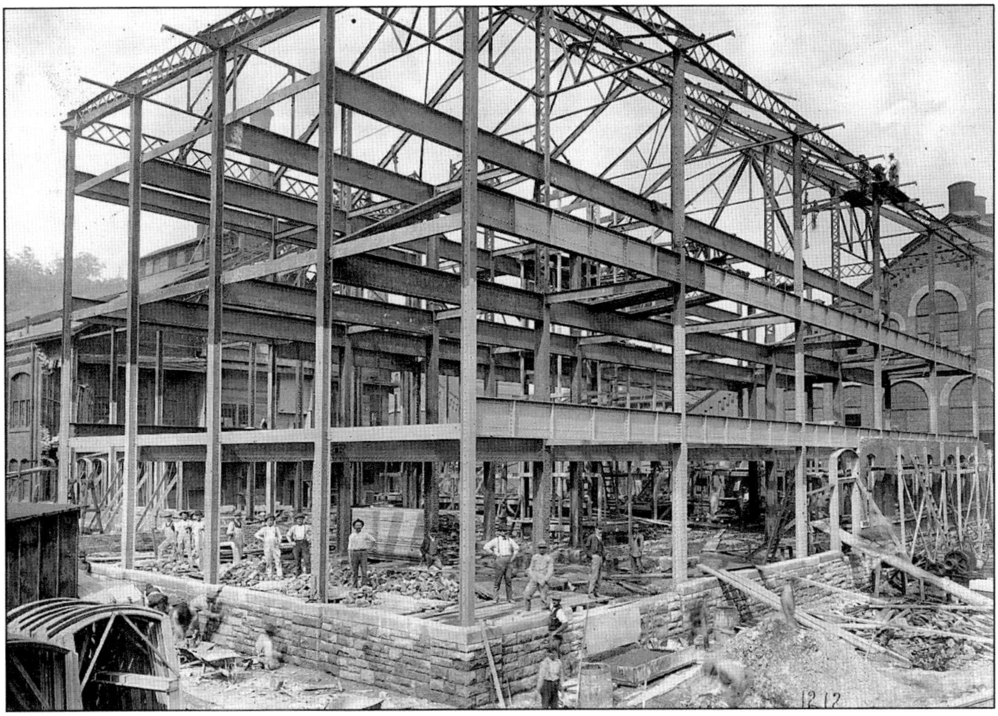

Steel construction begins on the addition to the warehouse building, 17A. The Westinghouse Air Brake Company's engineering department would be located on the third floor. Although George Westinghouse's office was in the Castle (the G.O.), he spent much time here with his engineers and workers developing air brake equipment. George Westinghouse often strode through the plant conversing with employees, no matter their rank or position.

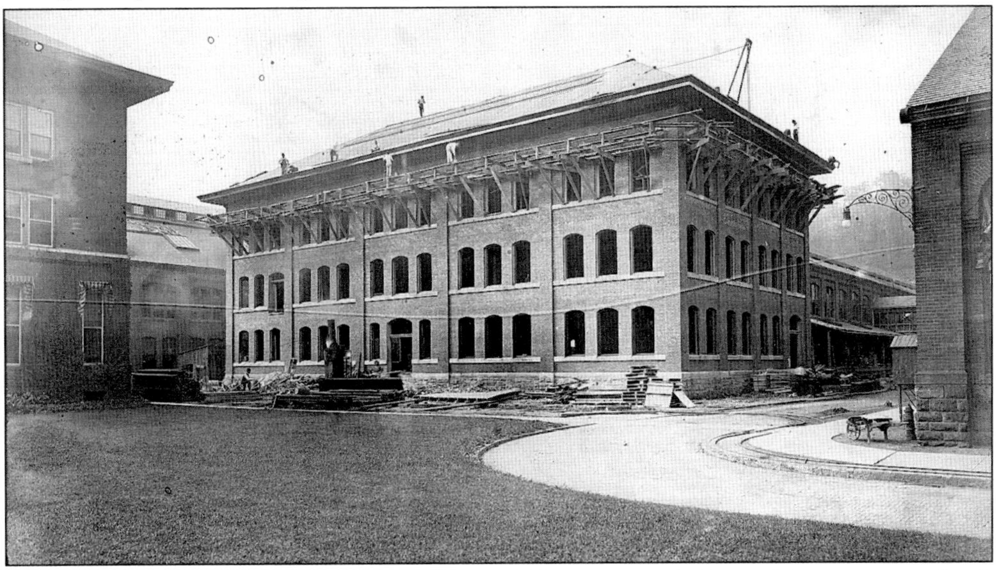

This view shows the brickwork of Building 17A one month later. The superintendent's building is on the left and the foundry is on the far right. The machine shop is behind the superintendent's building. Note the tracks for the 18-inch-gauge plant industrial transportation system seen between the buildings.

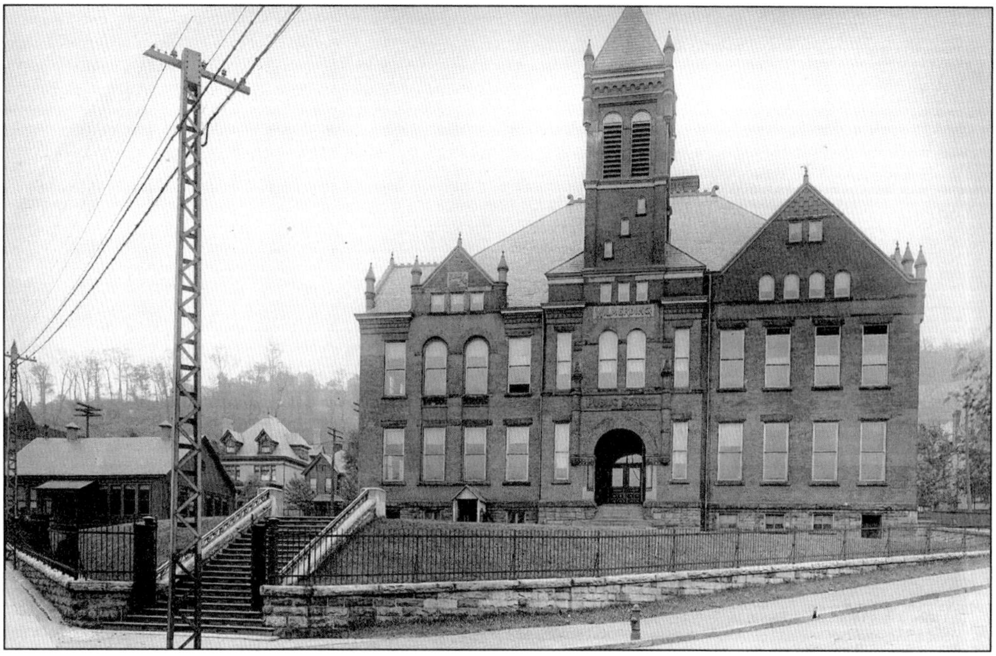

Wilmerding Public School No. 1, known as the Horrocks School, was built on Herman Avenue c. 1903. The school was named for Christopher Horrocks, who had been instrumental in forming the first church in Wilmerding, the Methodist church located on Westinghouse Avenue. The building to the left is a temporary schoolhouse.

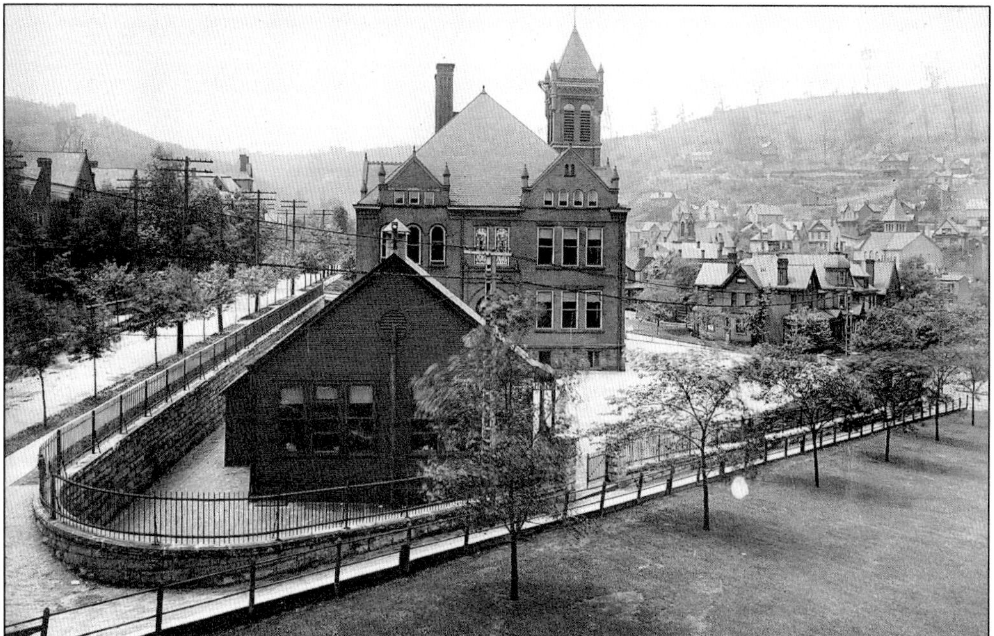

Shown here is another view of Public School No. 1, this time looking south from the vantage point of the Westinghouse Air Brake Company's general office building. Can you see the retaining wall built around the school property? The sloping topography of Wilmerding made retaining walls a common sight. The nicely treed road on the left is Marguerite Avenue.

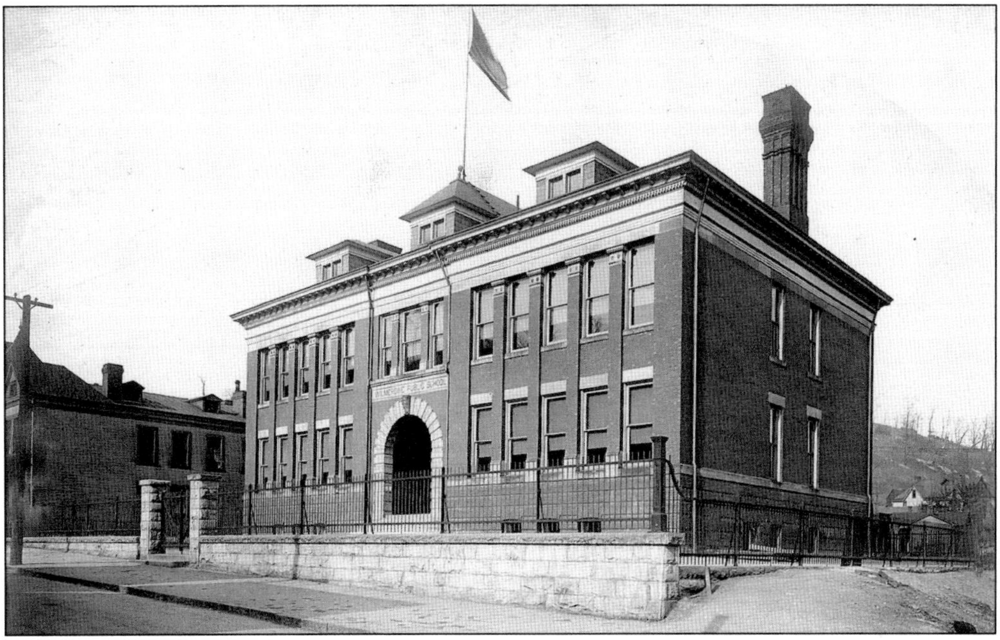

Here is a photograph of Wilmerding Public School No. 2, or the Gottwals School. Completed in 1899, it was named for a former member of the school board. It was located on Bridge Street on the north side of Wilmerding, serving kindergarten through third grade. The building was razed in the late 1960s. The former Italian Club of Wilmerding was built on this location. Today, it is the home of Banquets Unlimited.

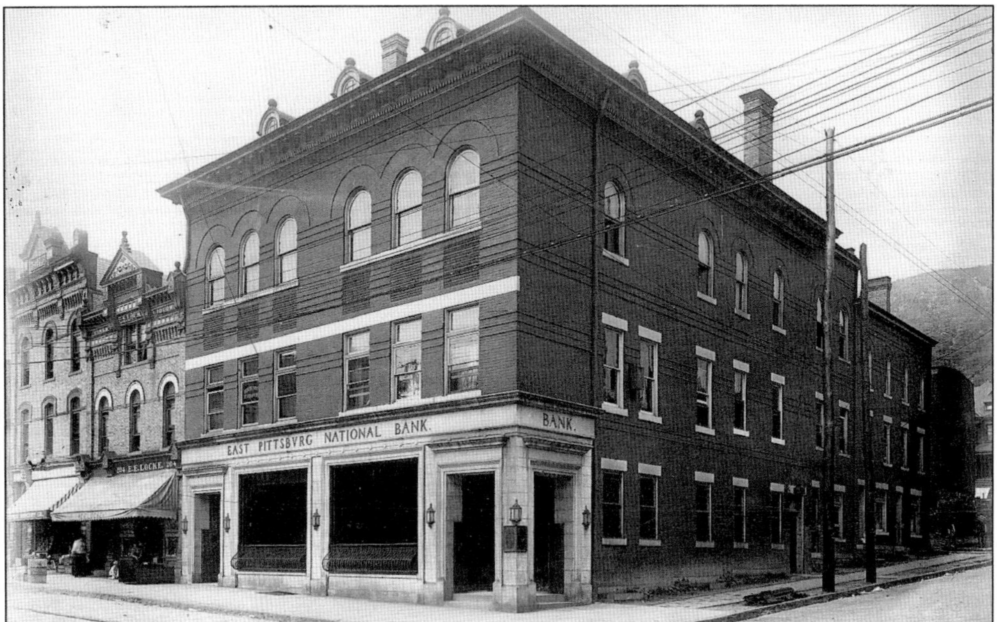

In 1905, the East Pittsburgh National Bank was located at the corner of Westinghouse Avenue and Commerce Street. Over the years, this bank building has undergone many revisions and name changes, including the First National Bank of Wilmerding and Mellon Bank Branch of Wilmerding. The two top stories would eventually be removed.

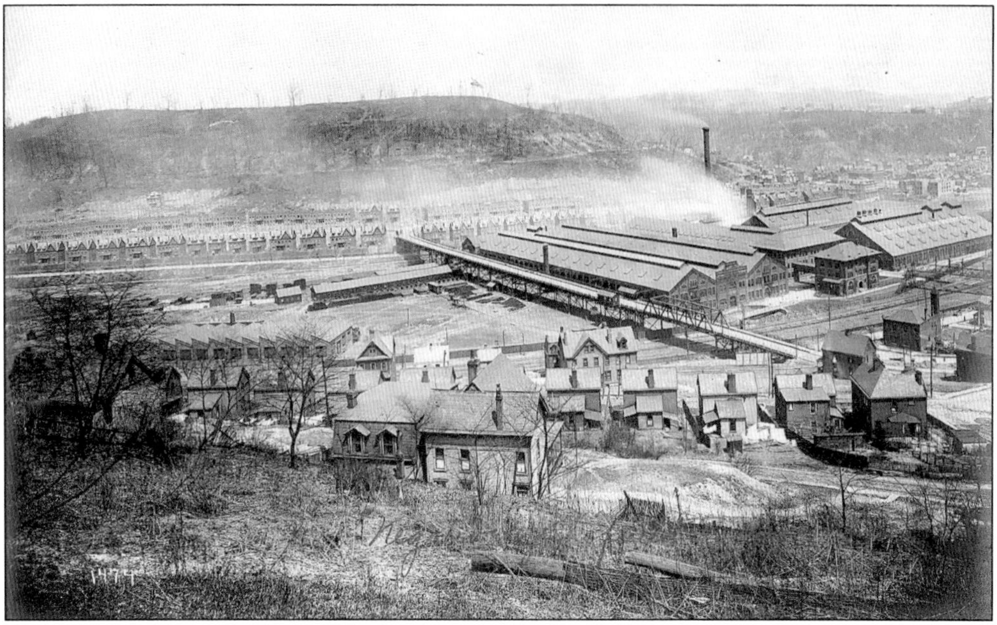

This panoramic view of the Westinghouse Air Brake Company was taken *c.* 1910. Note the completed trolley viaduct, Building 17A, and the bridge connecting to the superintendent's building. Note also that the hillside has very few trees. Can you see the tidy row of "flats" at the foot of the hill to the rear?

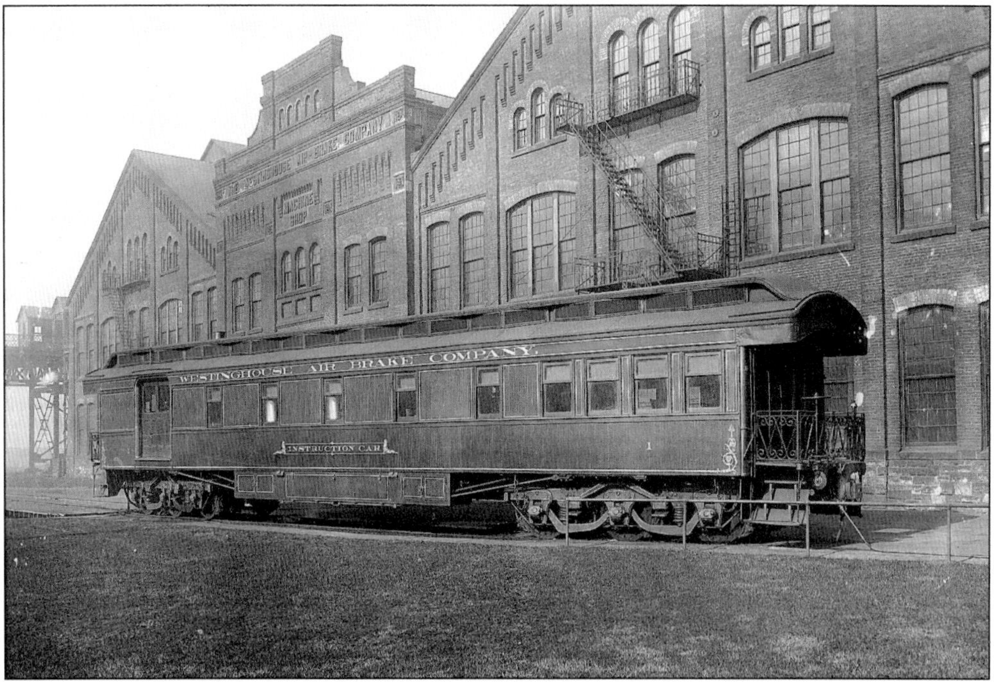

Instruction Car No. 1 of the Westinghouse Air Brake Company is seen *c.* 1915 in front of the machine shop. This car was placed in service in 1888 and, for 30 years, wandered over the continent giving free education to the men who handled the air brakes in service. Inside, there were operating test racks of air brake devices used on locomotive, passenger, and freight equipment.

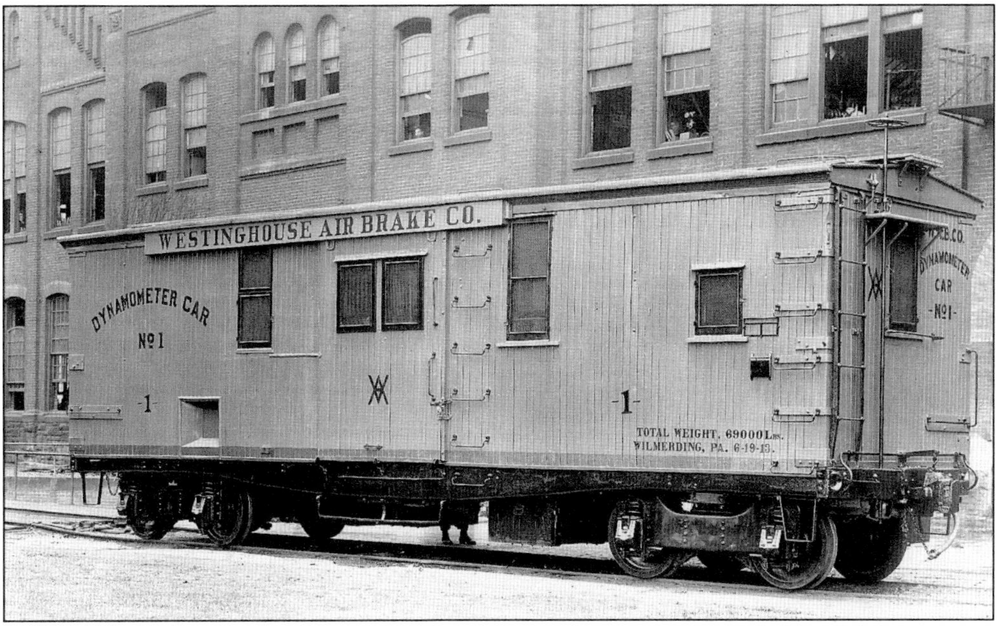

The Westinghouse Air Brake Company's first dynamometer car is shown on the track in front of the machine shop in 1913. Dynamometer cars were placed in a test train of railroad cars between the locomotive and train of cars. Inside these dynamometer cars were various recording instruments to measure air brake and train performance.

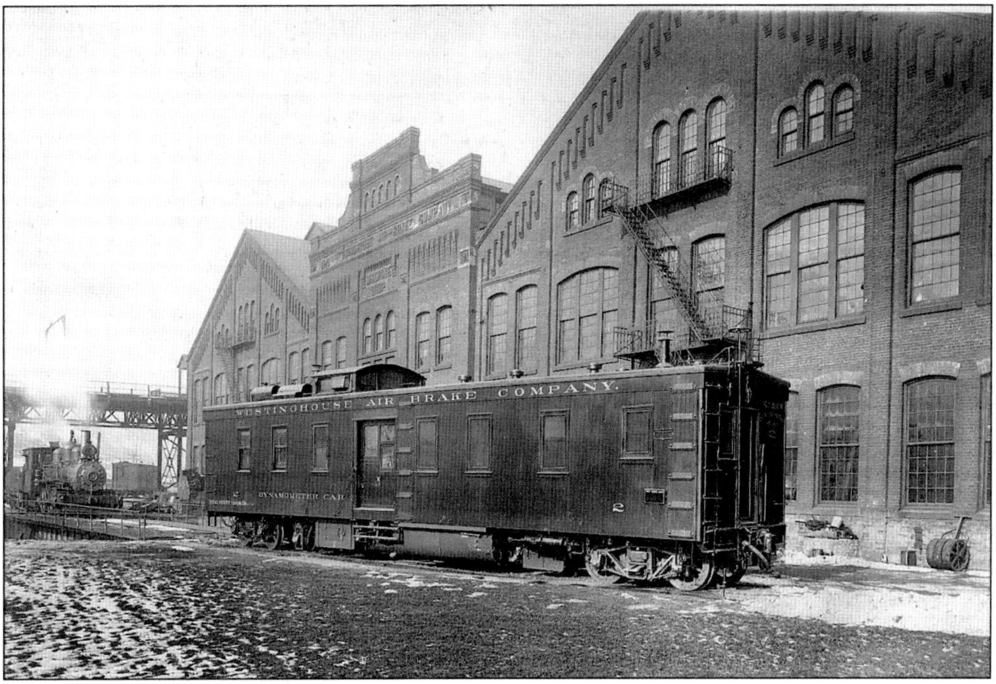

The Westinghouse Air Brake Company's Dynamometer Car No. 2 is shown in front of the machine shop. The name of the machine shop can be seen at the top center of this view. At the left, the new trolley viaduct appears, as well as an early plant locomotive. This locomotive is a 0-6-0 switcher with a separate tender, the only one of this type used in the plant.

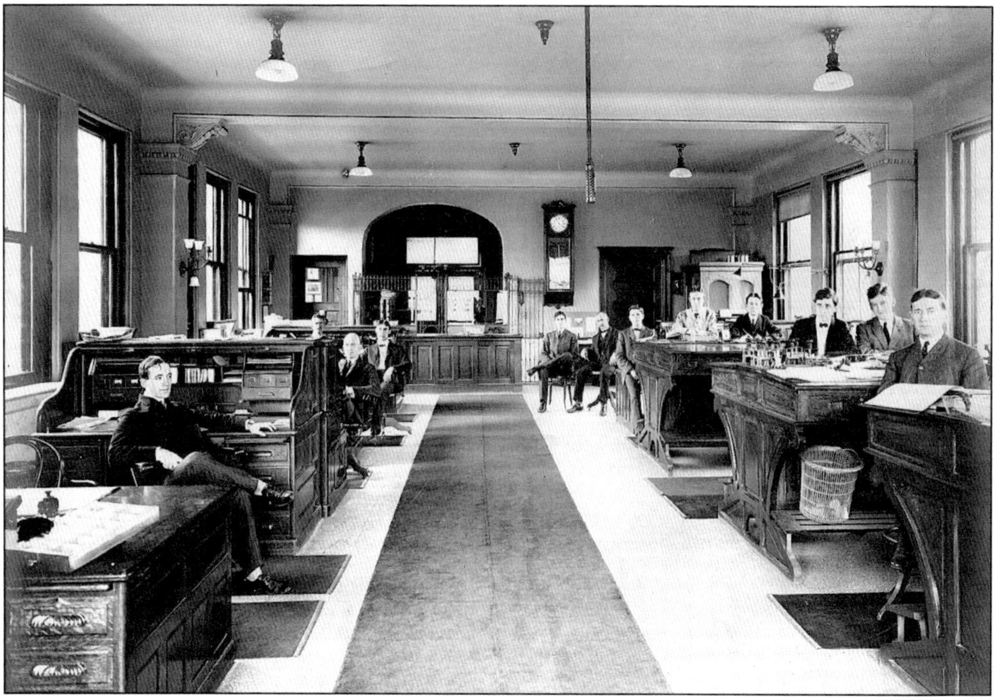

This *c.* 1906 view shows the interior of Mr. Craig's office (Westinghouse's secretary) in the finance department of the Westinghouse Air Brake Company. The office was located on the third floor of the general office building. The staff is all male, dressed in suits, and has been directed to pose for the camera.

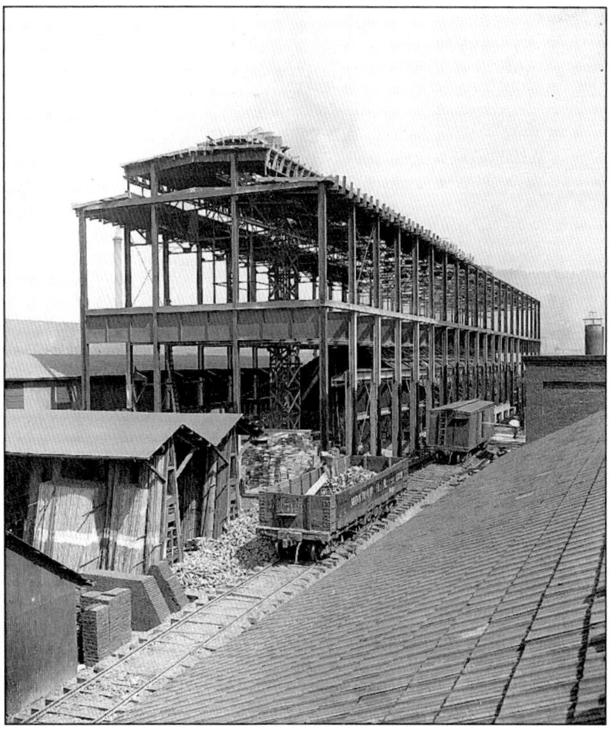

The photograph clearly shows the construction of Foundry No. 3 in July 1913. Note that the erection process is taking place on top of an existing building. Foundry No. 3 was located west of the viaduct. A worker removes materials from a sitting boxcar. Behind the boxcar, a gondola car rests, perhaps collecting waste.

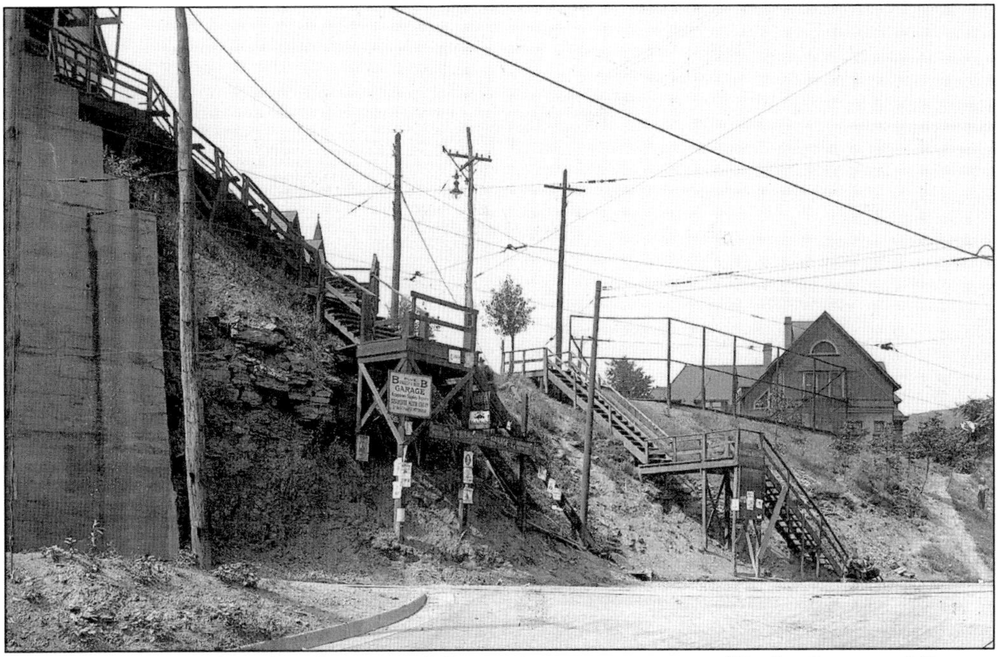

In 1916, a photographer shot this view while standing at one corner of Bridge Street and Station Street, looking south. The building to the right is the Wilmerding YWCA, located on Marguerite Avenue. A hodgepodge of utility poles and wooden steps fills the picture. To the upper left is a broken wood fence used to protect passersby from slipping over the steep embankment.

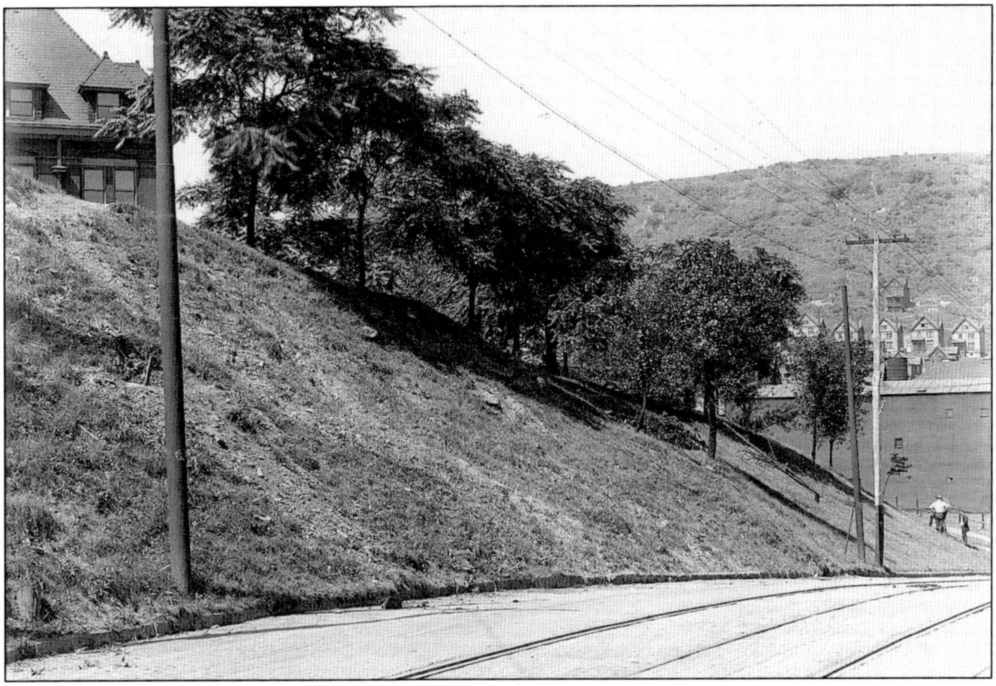

This c. 1916 view, taken at the end of Station Street, looks west. The building at the far left is the Wilmerding YMCA. Note the homes built on the hillside at the right center of the photograph. Three men are talking on the lower right-hand corner.

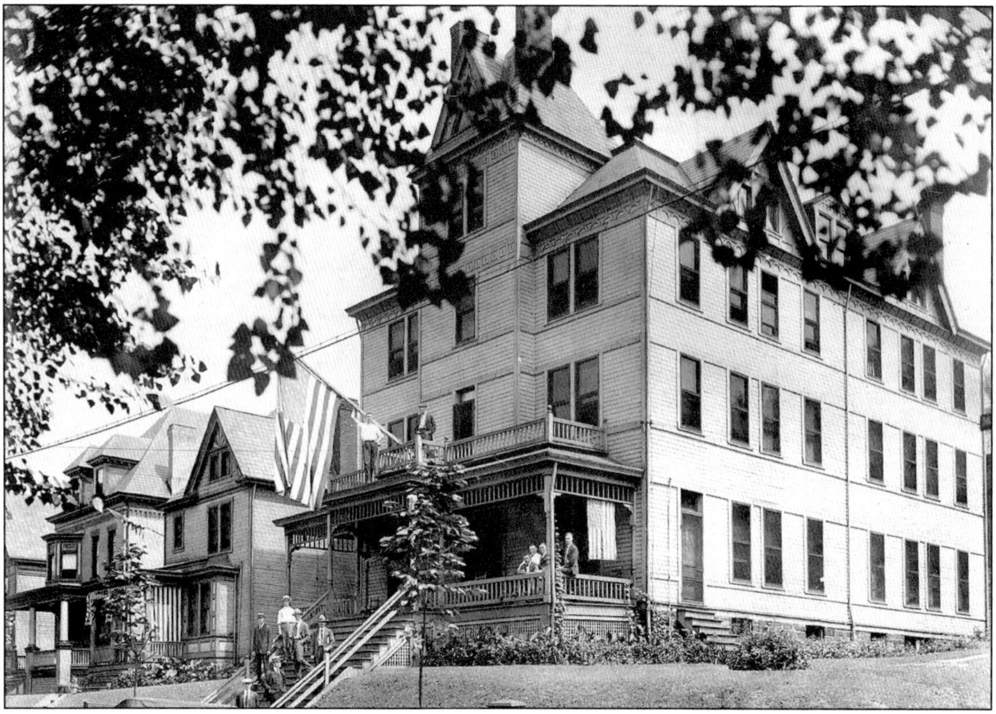

The Tonnaleuka Club (formerly the Glen Hotel), located at the corner of Marguerite Avenue and Clara Street, is pictured *c.* 1917. The Westinghouse Air Brake Company purchased the hotel to house traveling engineers who trained in the plant. In later years, the club housed single, male Westinghouse Air Brake engineers.

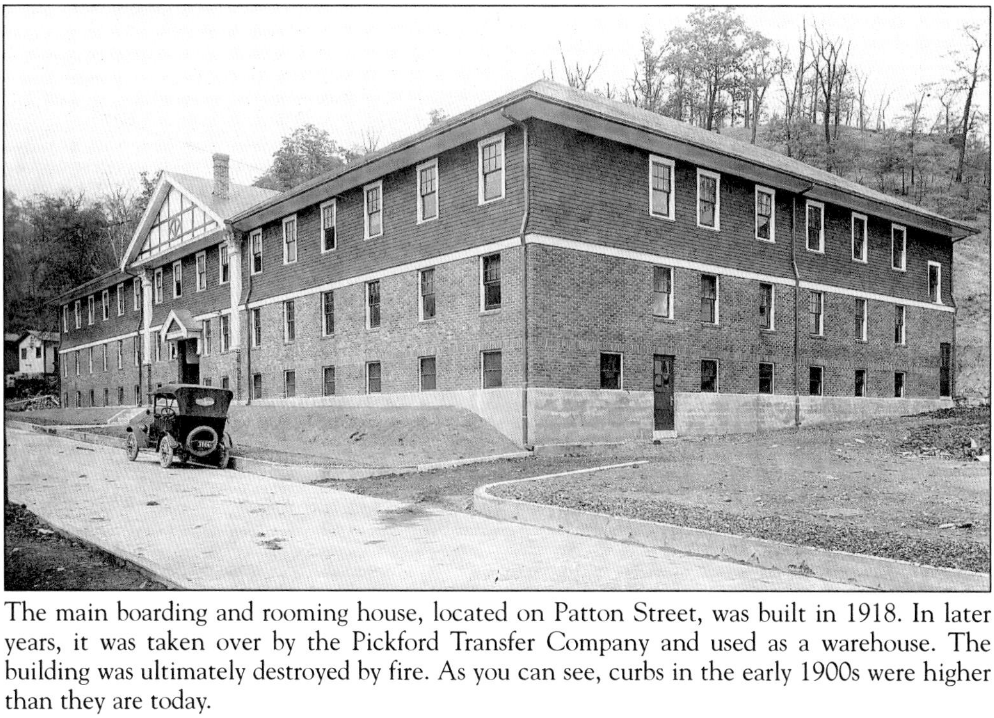

The main boarding and rooming house, located on Patton Street, was built in 1918. In later years, it was taken over by the Pickford Transfer Company and used as a warehouse. The building was ultimately destroyed by fire. As you can see, curbs in the early 1900s were higher than they are today.

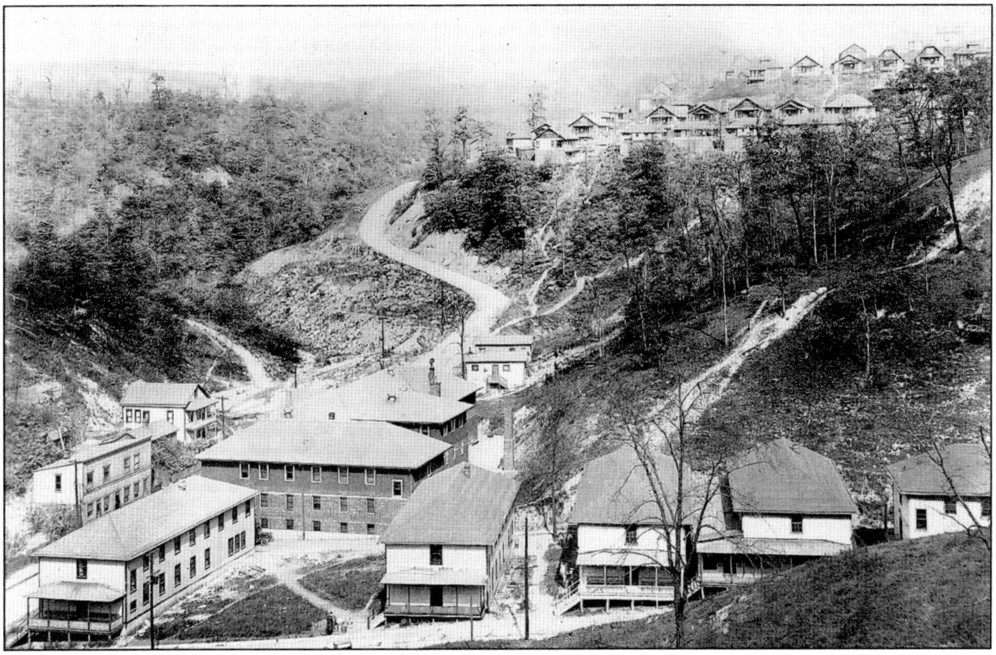

This *c.* 1923 view of upper Patton Street shows a rear view of the main boardinghouse to the left and other rooming houses in the foreground. The 24 cottages at the top of Patton Street were erected for black foundry help who had migrated to the North in search of better working conditions.

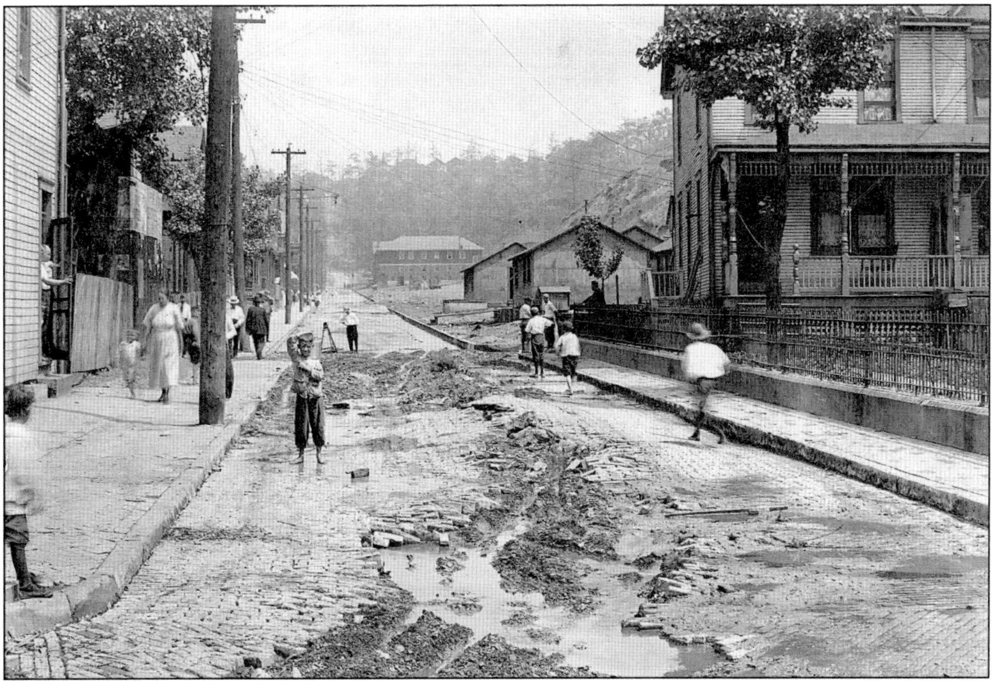

Shown here is a view of lower Patton Street from State Street, looking north. The photograph was taken shortly after heavy rains had fallen in June 1919. Wilmerding Borough was constantly repairing brick streets. The new boardinghouse can be seen in the distance.

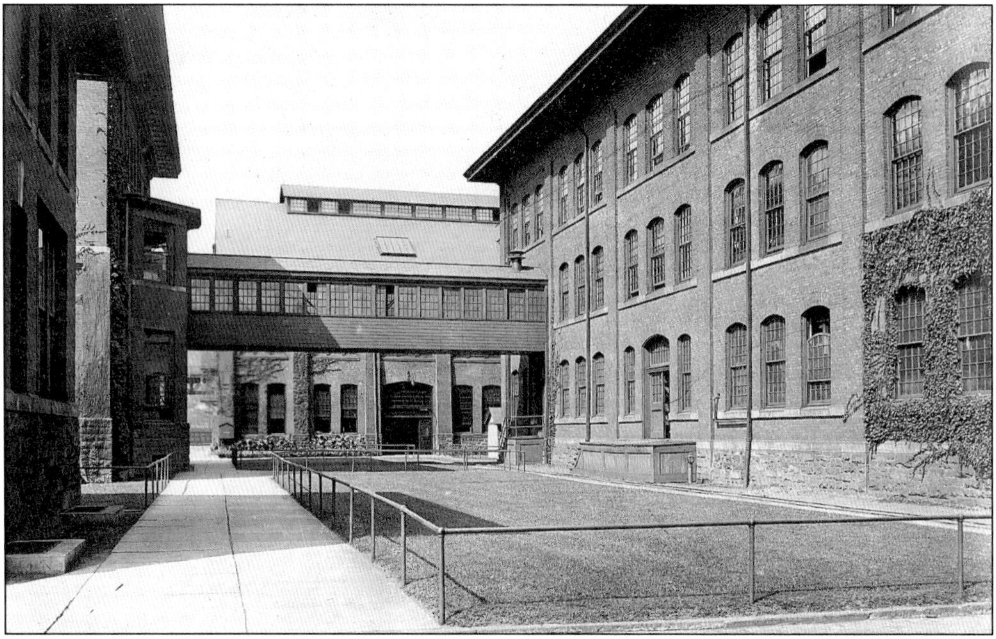

Shown here is an overhead bridge between Building 17A and the superintendent's building. In 1915, when this photograph was taken, Building 17A was a storeroom. Notice the grass in the open area and the vines growing up the front of the building on the far right. The machine shop is in the rear.

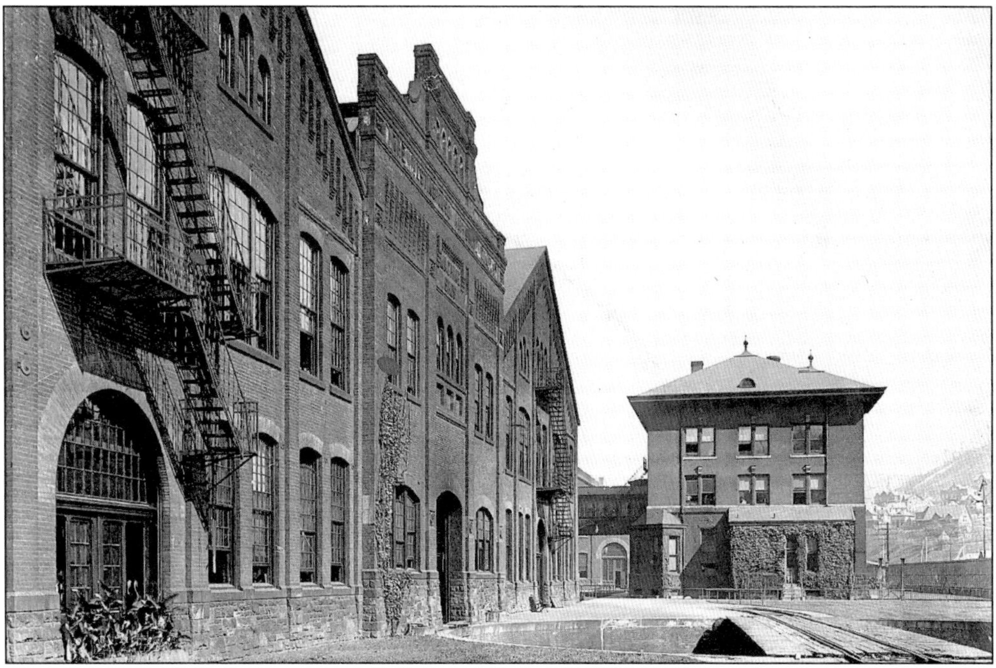

The machine shop and the superintendent's building looked like this in 1915. Notice the old turntable in the foreground, which was gone by the early 1920s. When the table turned, the engine entered directly into the shop area. A small section of Wilmerding can be seen over the wall on the far right-hand side of the photograph.

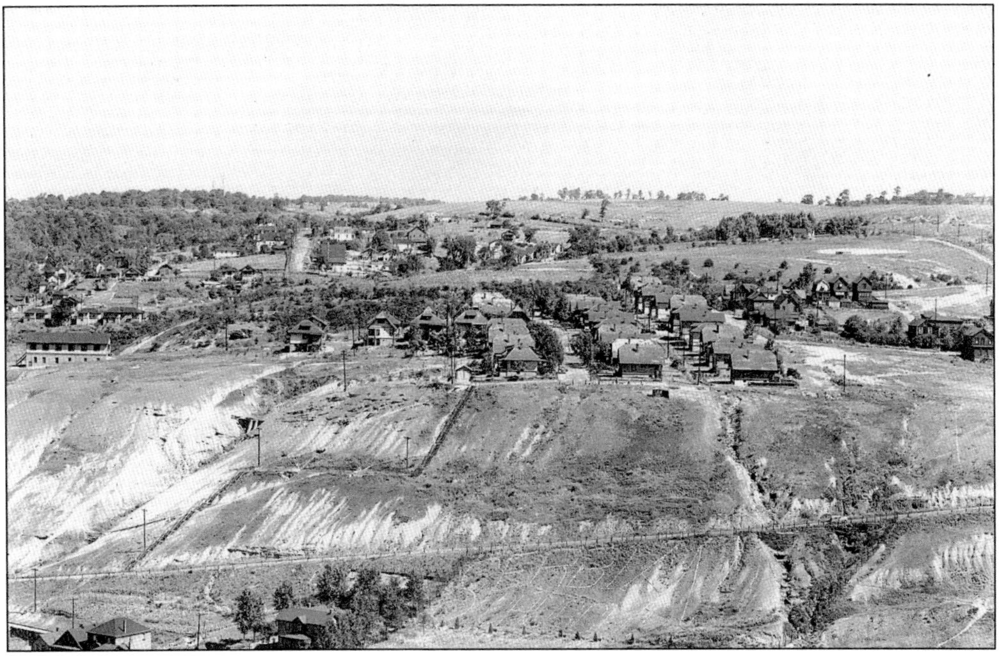

This photograph shows the community settlement of Fort Wildin, taken from Victor Avenue in East McKeesport. Fort Wildin was built in the early 1920s and named for G.W. Wildin, who was the general manager of the Westinghouse Air Brake Company at the time. Someone had gone to a great deal of trouble to plant trees.

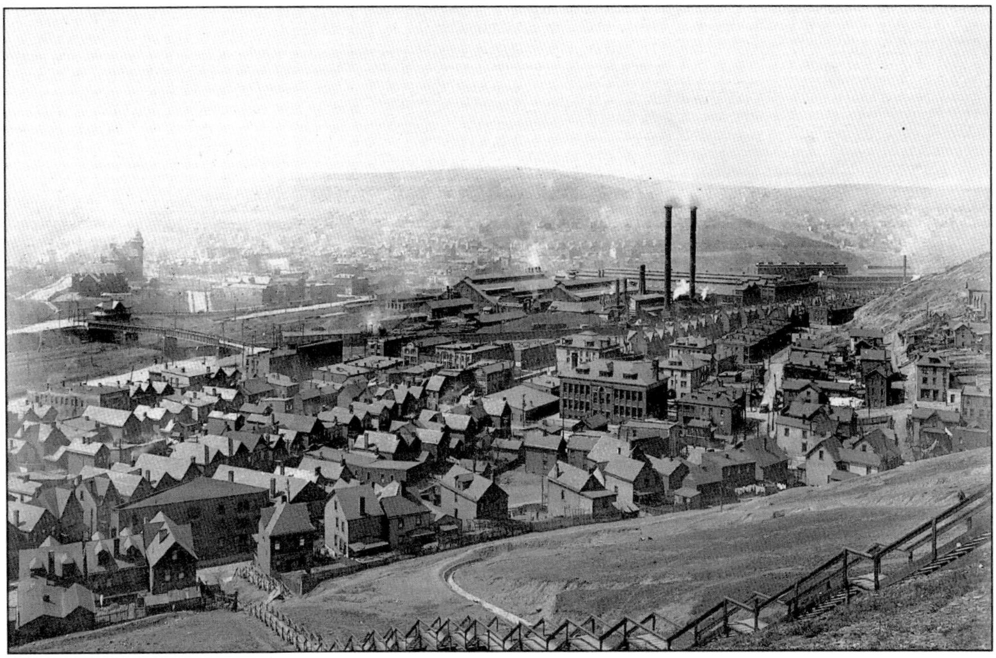

From Fort Wildin, here is a view of Wilmerding showing the steps from the top of the hill facing State Street. The Gottwals School can be seen in the center, and the Westinghouse Air Brake plant is in the background. If you lived in Fort Wildin and worked at the plant, you would surely get a lot of exercise. Most employees, at that time, walked to work.

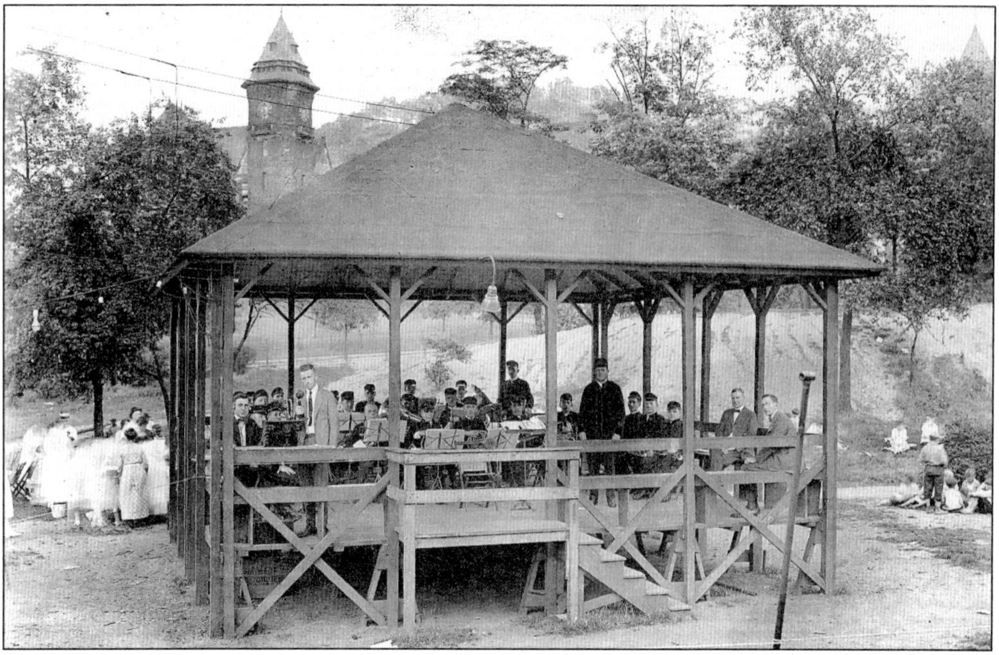

The Westinghouse Air Brake Band, under the direction of Joseph Nirella, broadcast the first concert by wireless over the world's first radio station, KDKA. The Westinghouse Air Brake bandstand was located in the park in Wilmerding. The clock tower on the company's general office building (the Castle) can be seen in the background.

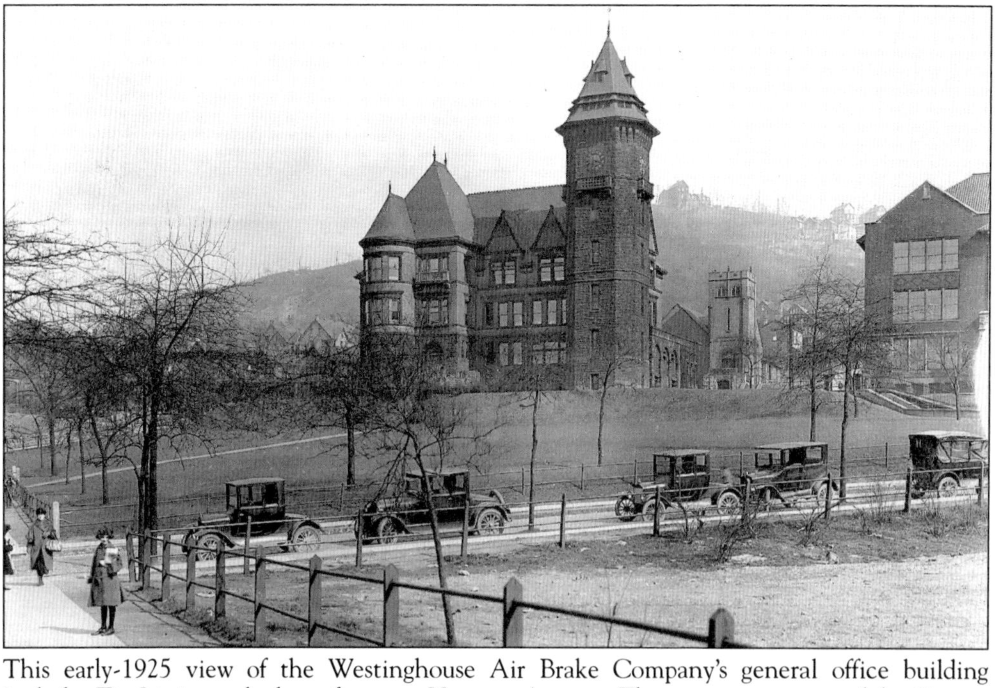

This early-1925 view of the Westinghouse Air Brake Company's general office building includes Tin Lizzies parked out front on Herman Avenue. The avenue was named for George Westinghouse's brother Herman, who became the general manager of the company after the death of George Westinghouse in 1914.

Here is an exterior view of the Westinghouse Air Brake Company's boiler house and light station. In addition to supplying steam and power to the plant and general office building, the company furnished steam to various businesses in Wilmerding, including the Wilmerding YMCA. The plant's industrial railway can be seen in the foreground.

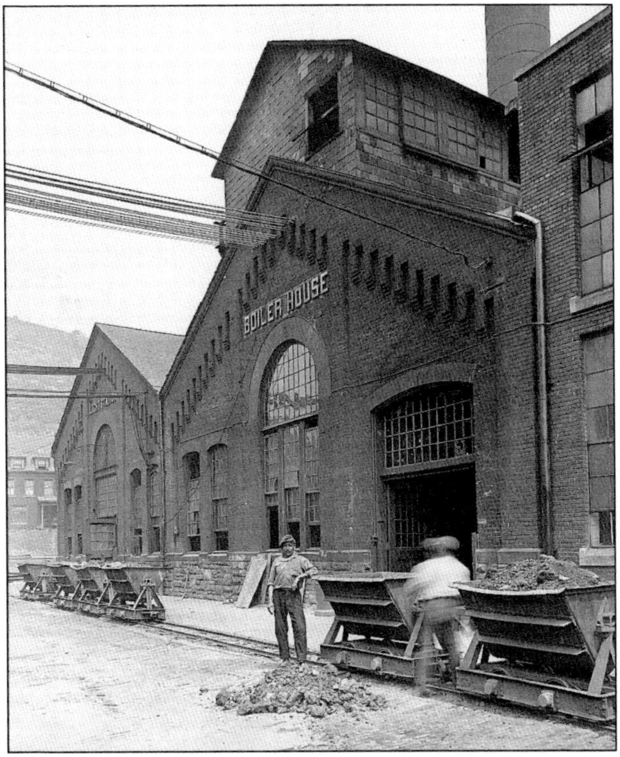

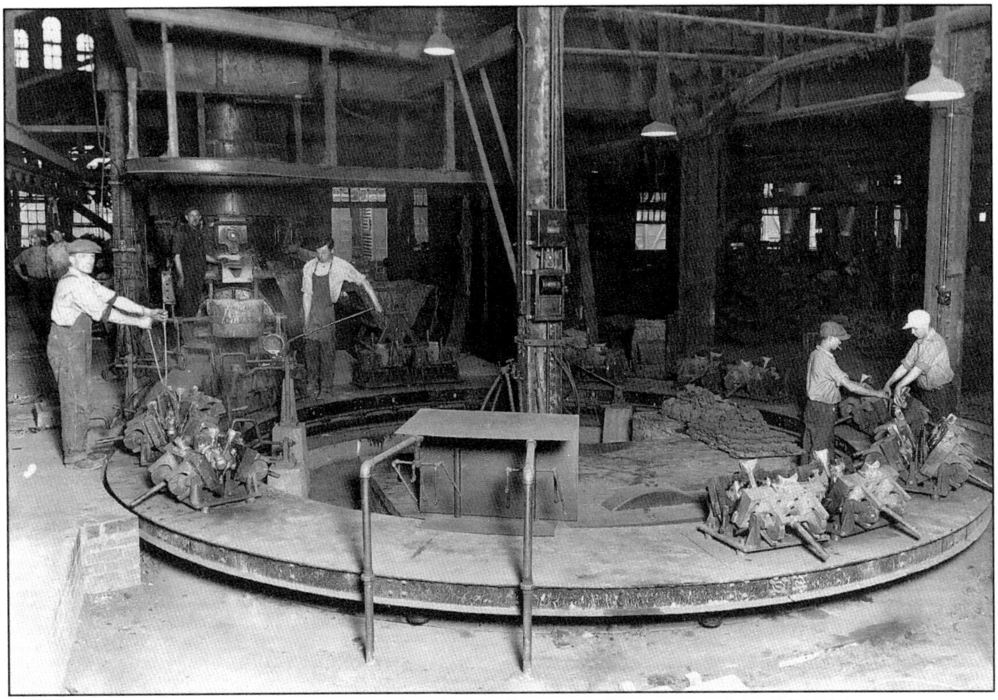

This c. 1925 photograph of the foundry shows the Pettis Repetition Mould Table in operation (an advanced form of molding castings). The table helped make the process of manufacturing more efficient. Notice the man to the rear pouring molten liquid into a mold.

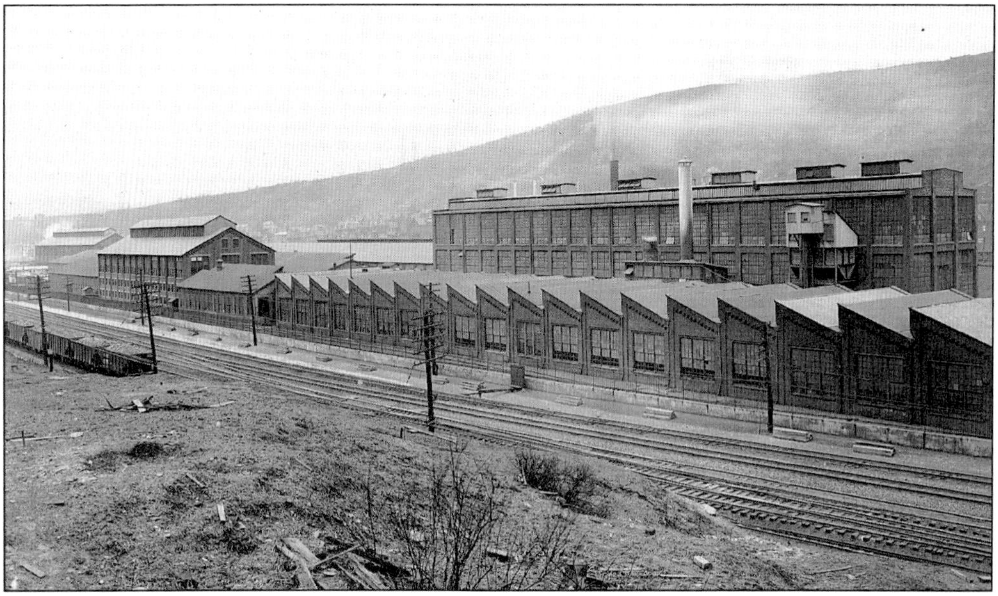

Shown in a view looking west in 1924, these Westinghouse Air Brake buildings sat at the west end of the plant. The Sawtooth Building (designed to bring in an abundance of light) is at the front, with Foundry Building No. 3 behind it. The brick building to the left housed the pattern shop. The new carpenters shop is at the far left. The main line of the Pennsylvania Railroad is in the foreground.

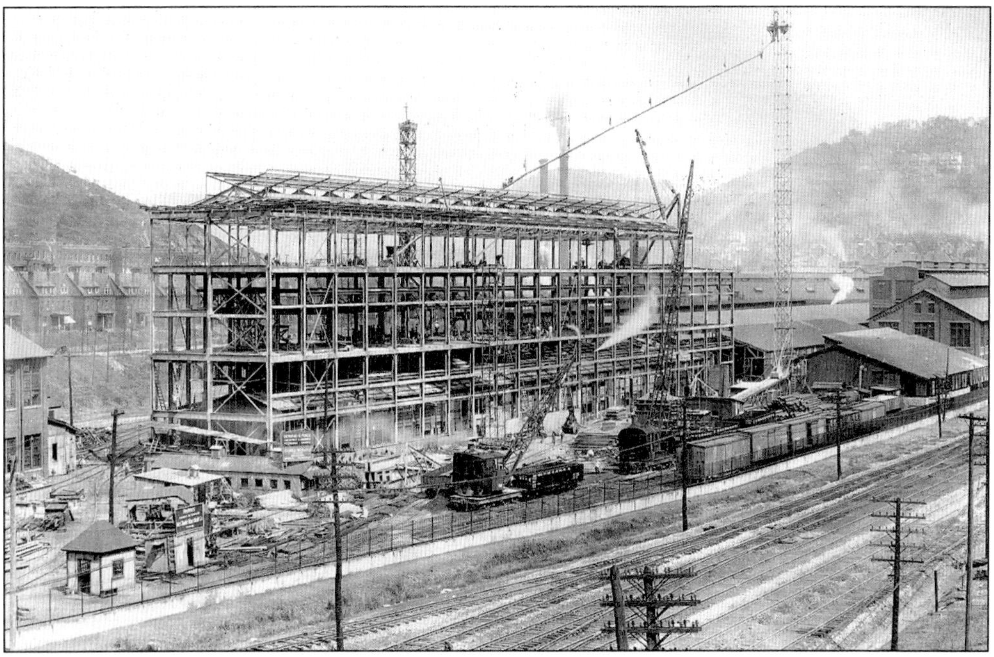

The Westinghouse Air Brake Company's new rubber plant building went up in 1924. McClintoch-Marshall Company of Pittsburgh constructed the new factory building for the Air Brake Company. A portion of the new carpenters shop can be seen at the far left. The No. 3 Foundry is at the far right. Once completed, the new building was connected with No. 3 Foundry to increase its capacity.

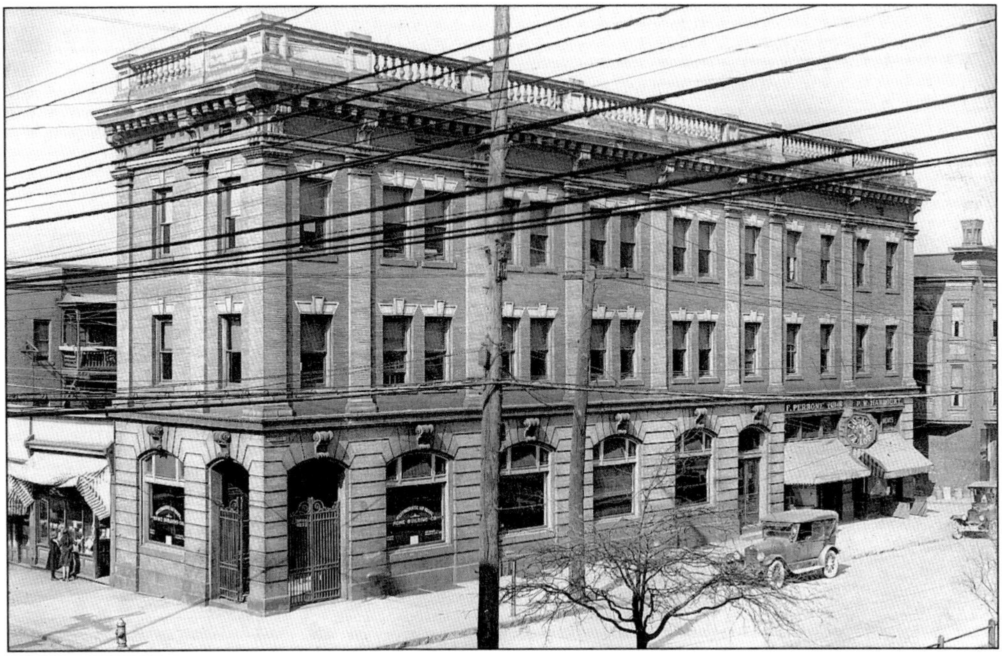

The general office annex building, which was located on Commerce Street at the corner of Westinghouse Avenue, was owned by the Westinghouse Air Brake Company and was primarily used by their publicity department. At the time of this photograph, the Air Brake Company's home-building division used the first floor. The building was razed in the 1960s, when redevelopment came to Wilmerding.

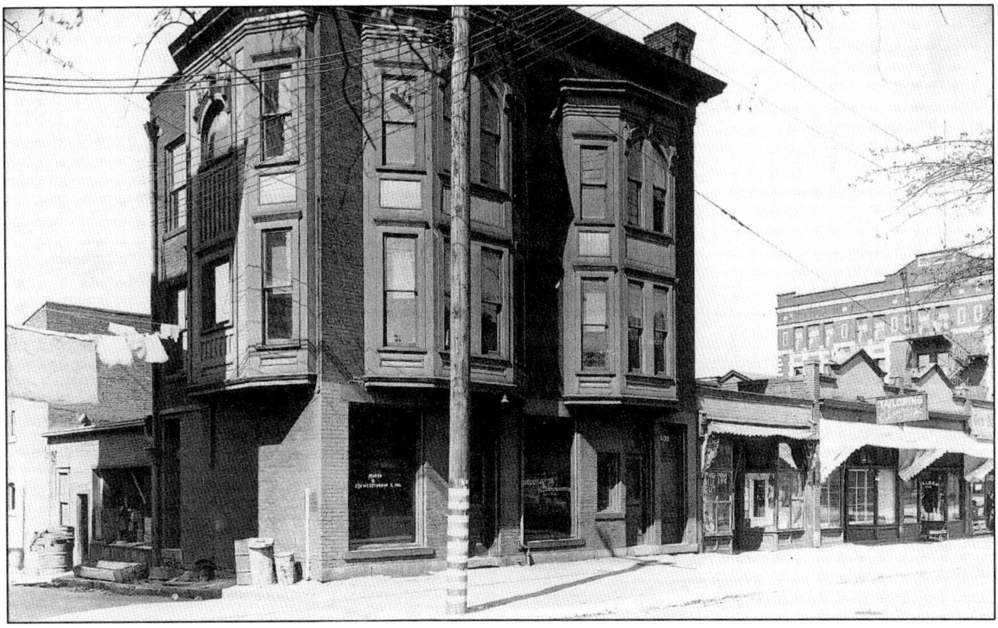

This is the present site of an apartment building on Commerce Street. The photograph was taken of the building located on the site before demolition. Several storefronts operate to the right of the building, each with awnings to protect from the sun's heat. There were no air conditioners at the time. Note the clothes drying on a line to the left.

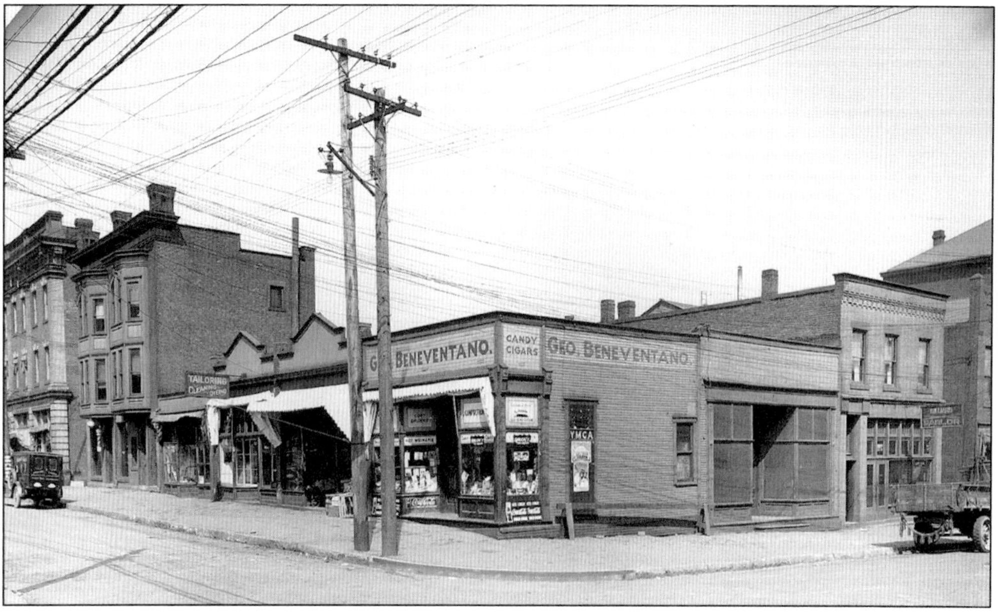

Here are some businesses located at the corner of Commerce Street and Herman Avenue. Several of the storefronts are obviously in poor repair and are closed. The tailor shop up the street from "Geo. Beneventano" is open. The photograph was taken in 1926 prior to the razing of the buildings in order to build a new apartment house.

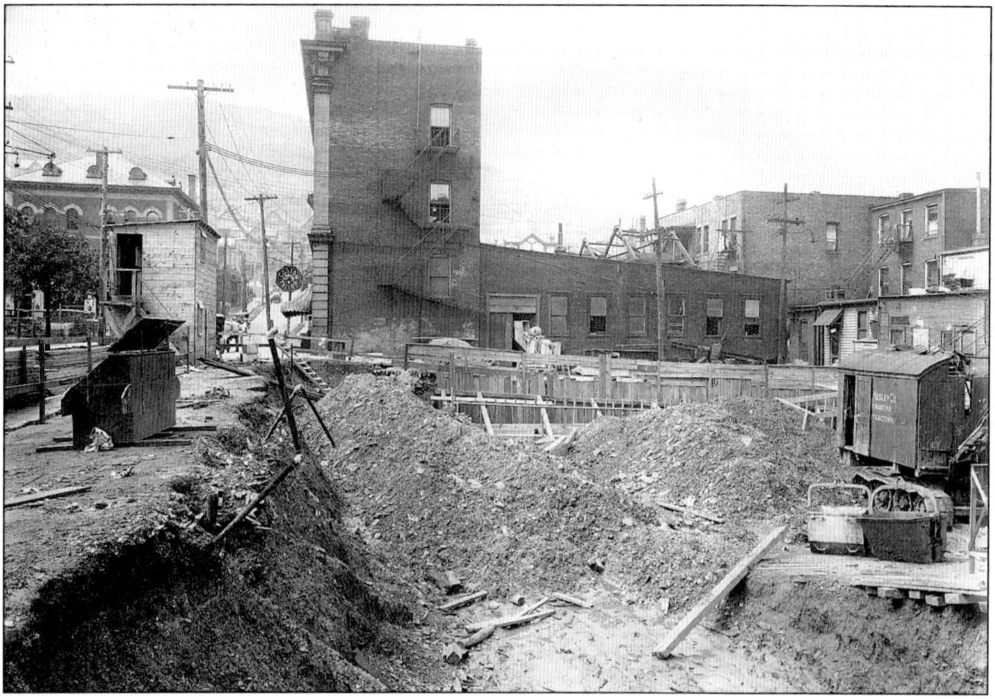

Ground was broken in 1926 for the construction of a new apartment building located on Commerce Street in Wilmerding. The lot is across from the park in Wilmerding. This view was taken in 1926, looking west. Most of the remaining buildings shown in this photograph would also be torn down and replaced by modern structures.

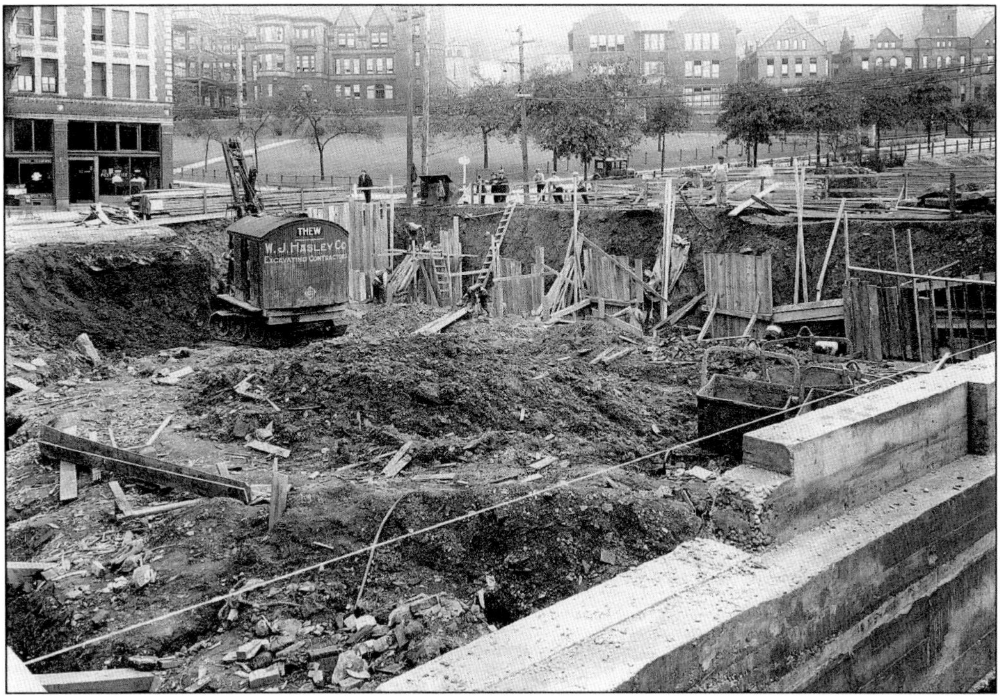

Shown in 1926 is the foundation construction of a new apartment building to be erected at the corner of Commerce Street and Herman Avenue. Construction of an addition to the Westinghouse Air Brake Company's general office can be seen in the distance. The Wilmerding Post Office can be seen at the far left.

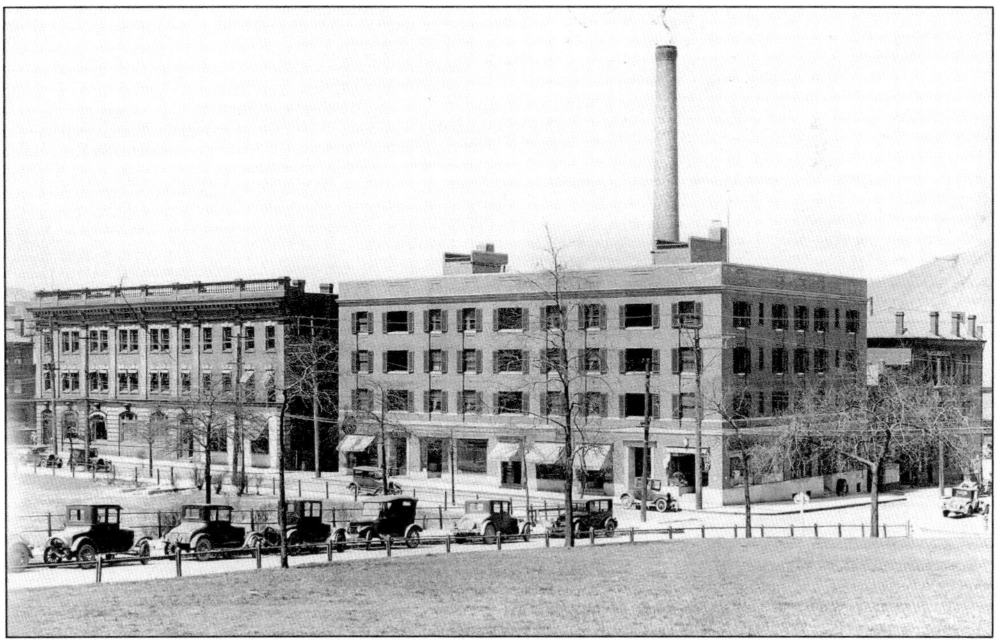

This photograph, taken in 1928, shows the new apartment building at the corner of Commerce Street and Herman Avenue. The general office annex is to the left. The building to the far right on Herman Avenue is the seventh location of the Wilmerding Post Office.

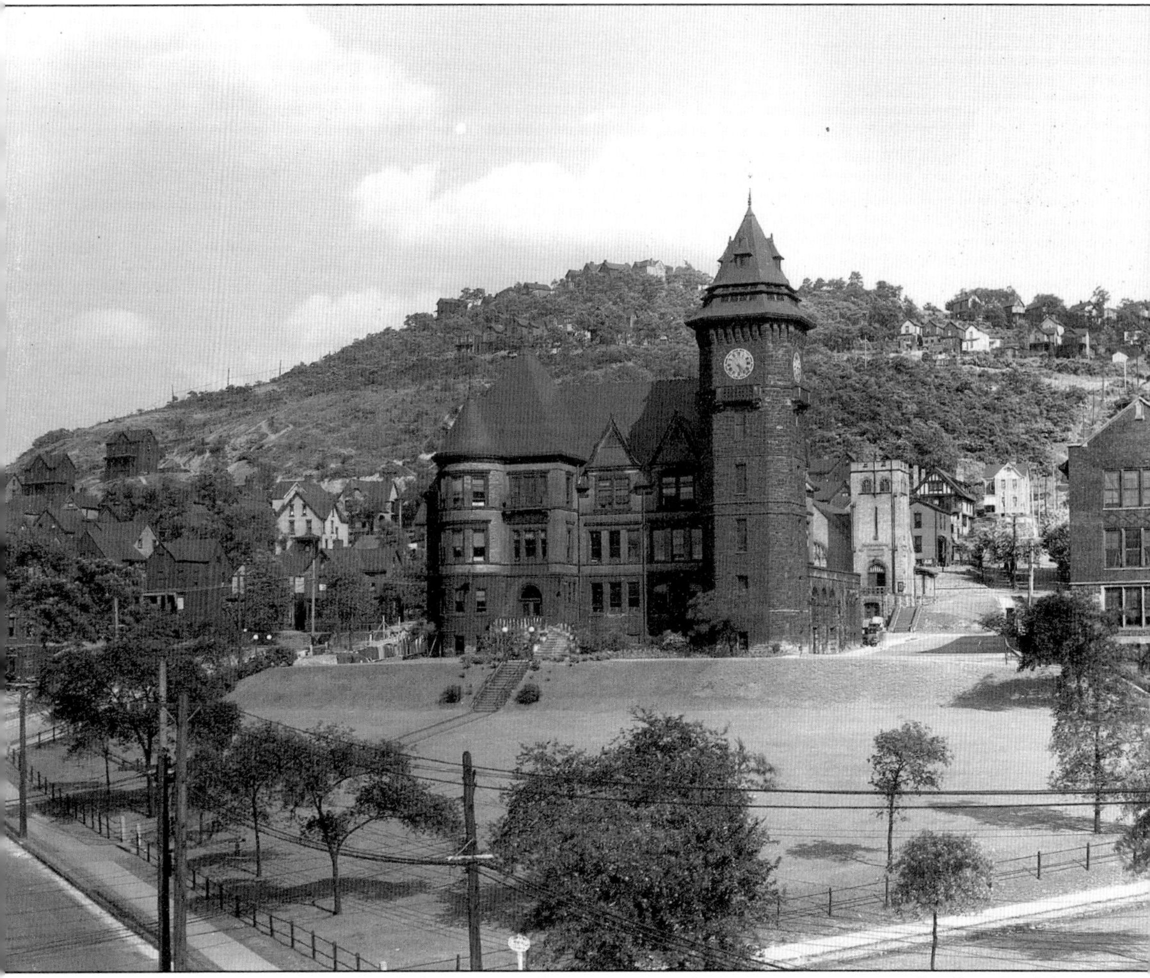

Here is a July 1926 image of the Westinghouse Air Brake Company's general office building before the extension was added to its left side. The building is black from smoke and coal dust. A fence surrounds the property. To the right of the general office building stands the old school building. To the right rear of the castlelike structure on Marguerite Avenue is the Presbyterian church. George Westinghouse's old office was in the turret on the left of the building, three sets of windows up from the bottom. The clock in the turret to the right chimed on the hour and again on the half-hour. As it is today, the Castle is the centerpiece of the borough.

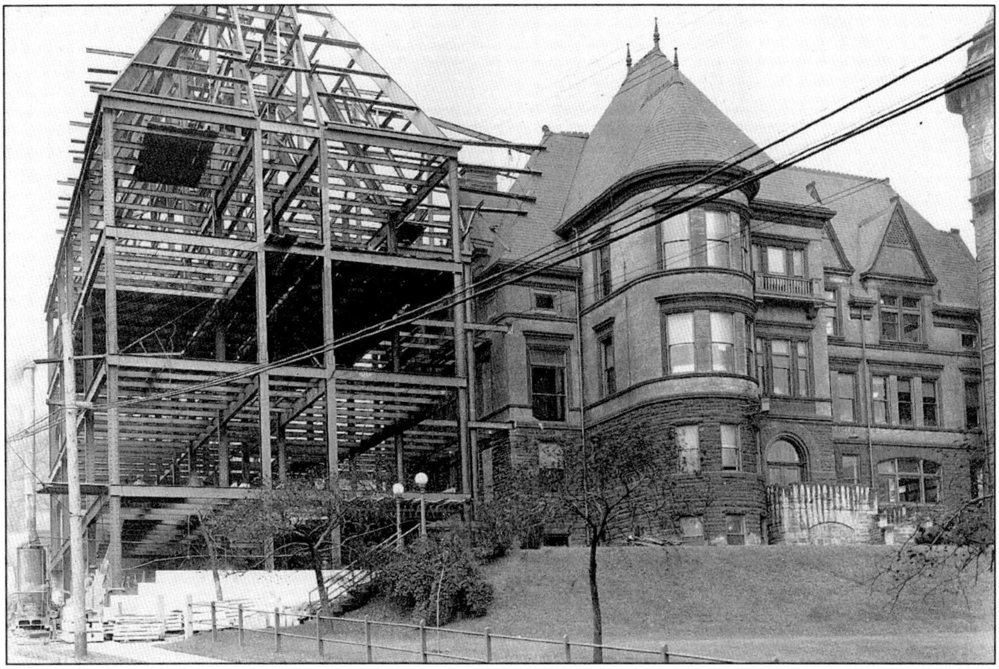

Taken in December 1926, this view shows the progress of the new addition to the Westinghouse Air Brake Company's general office building. This new addition has no turrets and represents a more simplistic design. Later, the steps seen at the left would be removed and a parking area would be added across the front.

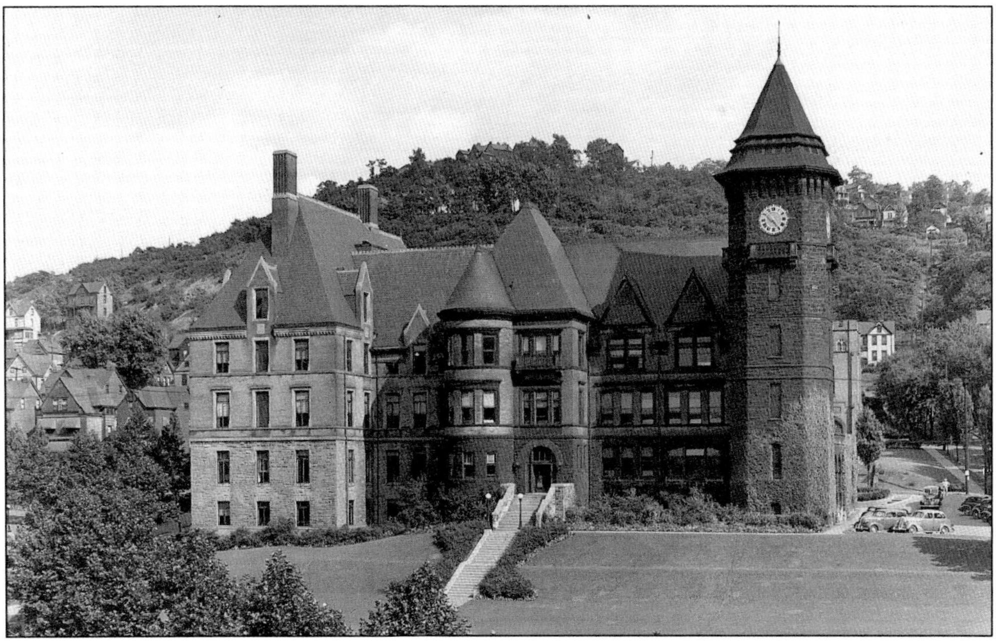

The completed addition to the Westinghouse Air Brake Company's general office building was known as the "Executive Wing" of the building, housing executive offices, conference rooms (including the boardroom for the board of directors), dining rooms, and an elevator. The building to the right is the School Annex.

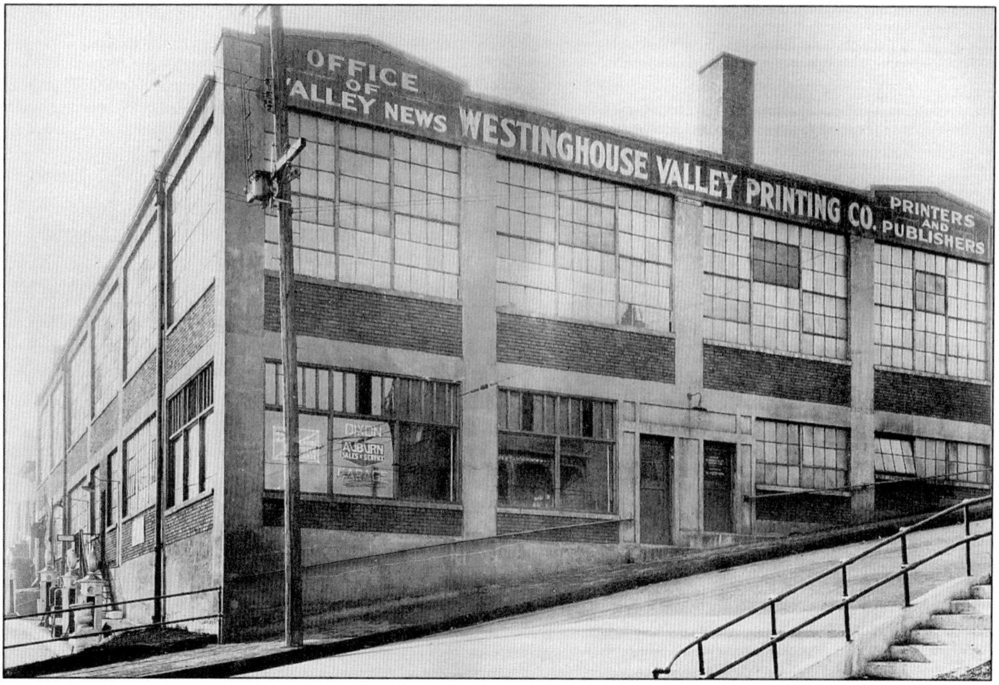

Beginning operations in 1917, the Westinghouse Valley Printing Company was located at the corner of Station Street and Caldwell Avenue. Because of the steep hill (Station Street) to the right of the building, it was necessary to install handrails on the building for pedestrian safety. Coming down the sidewalk in the winter was a treacherous trek.

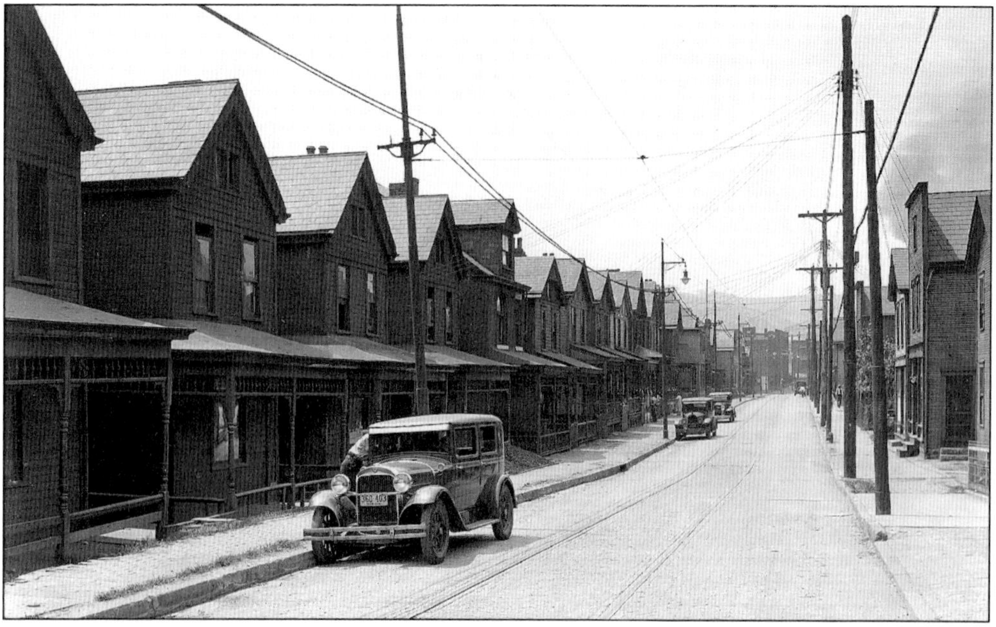

On the north side of Wilmerding, this shot looks west down Watkins, or Middle, Avenue. The trolley line ran past Wilmerding to Pitcairn and Trafford. In the sky, note the overhead trolley wire used to power the streetcars. In 1931, when this photograph was taken, not many cars ran on Wilmerding streets.

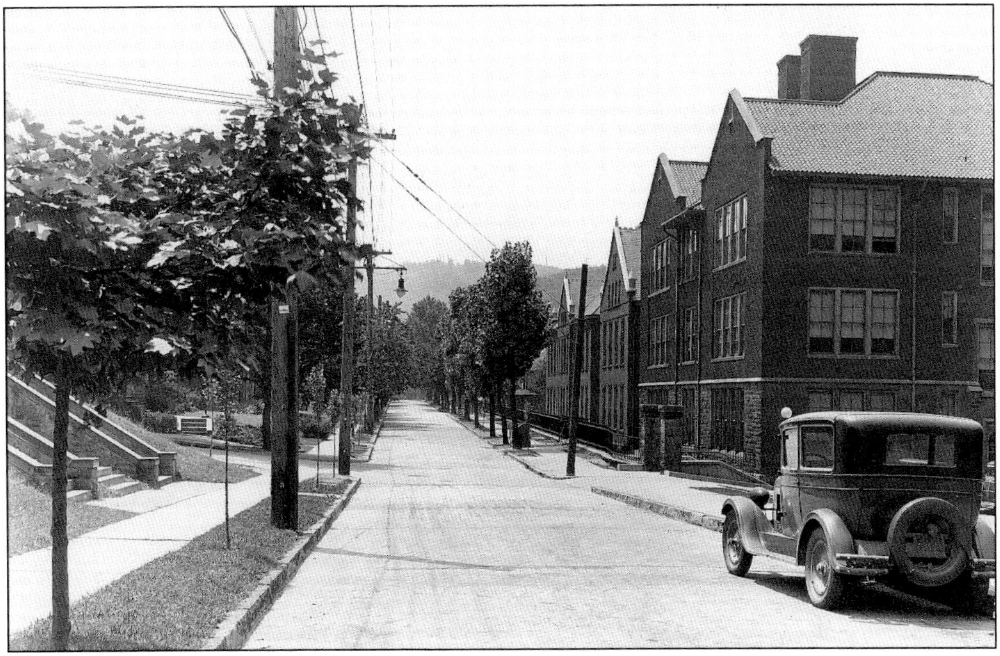

This view looks south on Marguerite Avenue, showing the Westinghouse Elementary School, Horrocks School, and annex in 1931. The concrete steps on the left side lead to the Presbyterian church. An opening into the parking lot of the Westinghouse general office building can be seen directly in front of the parked car.

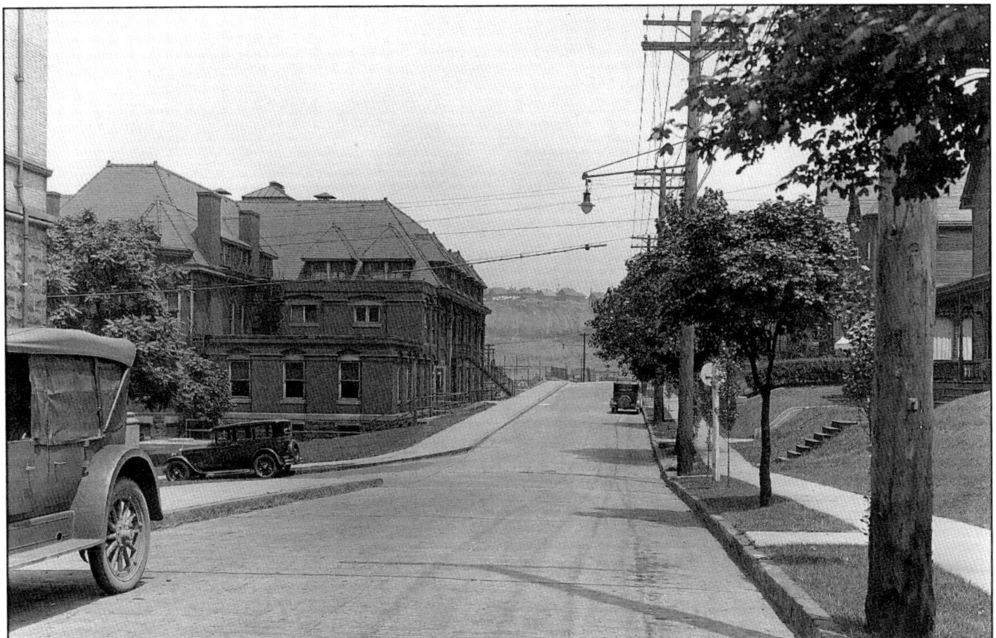

Looking north on Marguerite Avenue, this view shows the Wilmerding YMCA on the left at the corner of Bluff Street. One corner of the Westinghouse Air Brake general office building can be seen above the parked car. Streets and most sidewalks were made of brick. There were sidewalks in front of most properties in the borough.

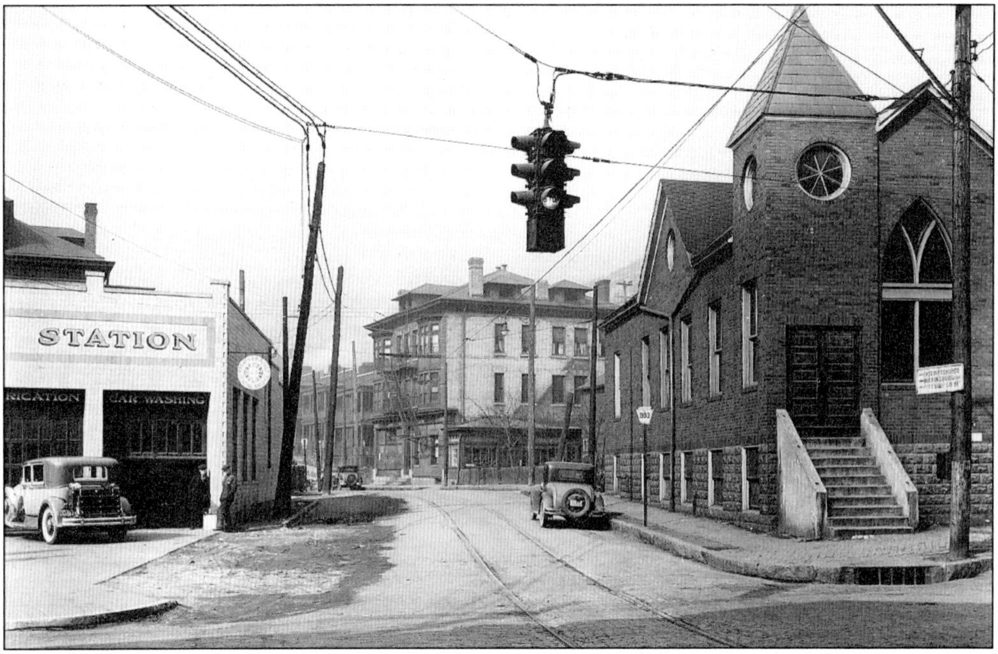

Taken in the 1930s, this is an interesting view of the north side of Wilmerding. The building on the right is St. John Baptist Church, formed in 1918. The photograph was taken at the corner of Bridge Street and Middle Avenue (Route 993). St. John Baptist Church is still located on this corner much the way it looked in the photograph.

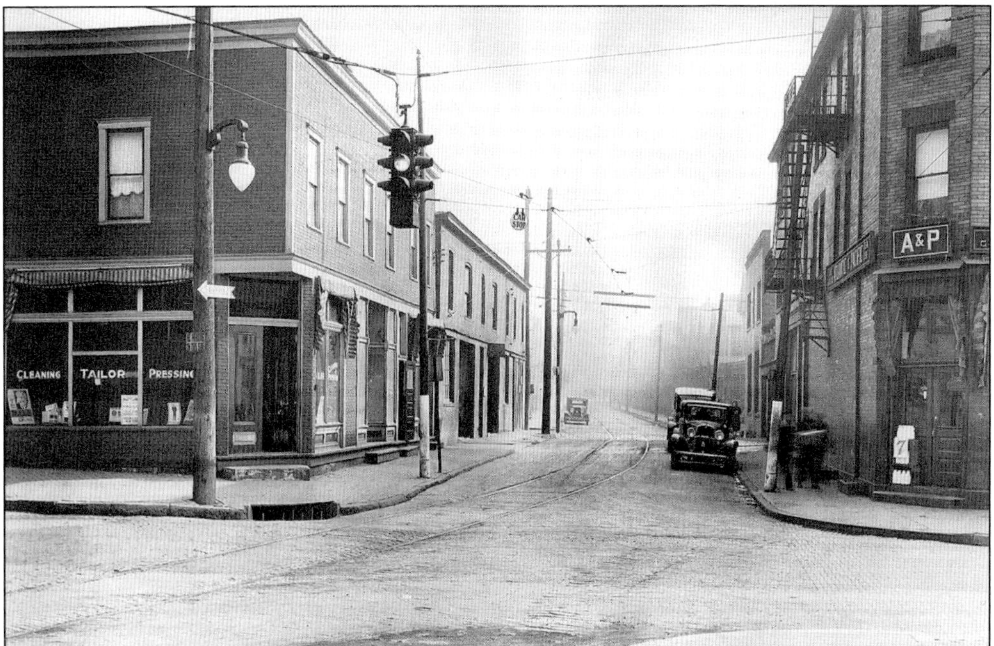

This view looks east from the corner of Bridge Street and Middle Avenue. Note the A & P grocery store on the right, the streetcar tracks down the center of the street, and a simple traffic light hanging over the center of the intersection. The streets are brick and appear damaged.

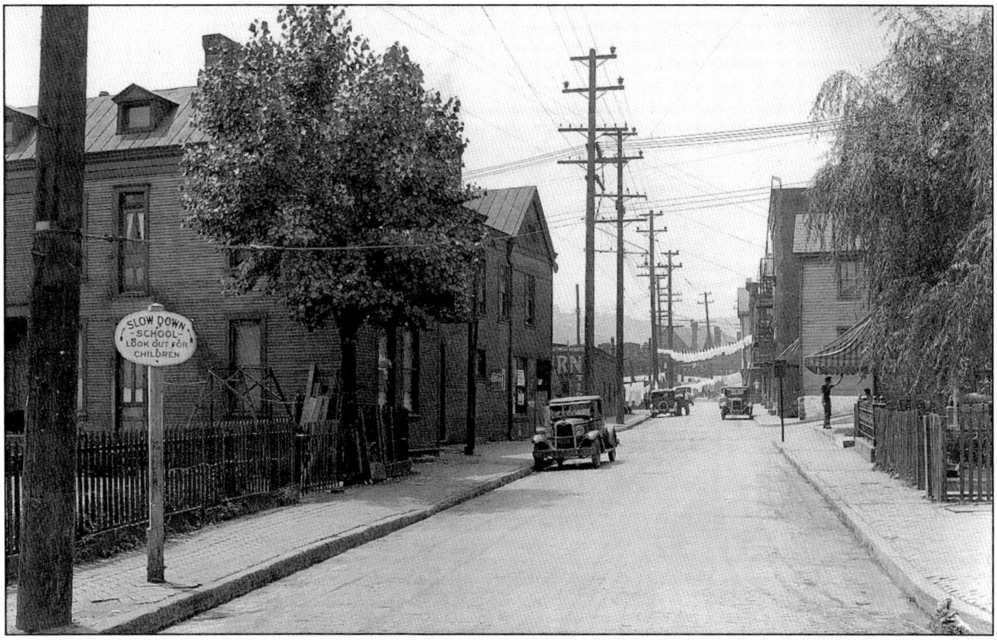

This photograph peers west on State Street on the north side of Wilmerding. It must have been Monday or wash day, for clothes hang on lines strung across the street. During this time, residential properties were constructed next to the sidewalk and very near the road. The Gottwals School is to the left of the building on the left.

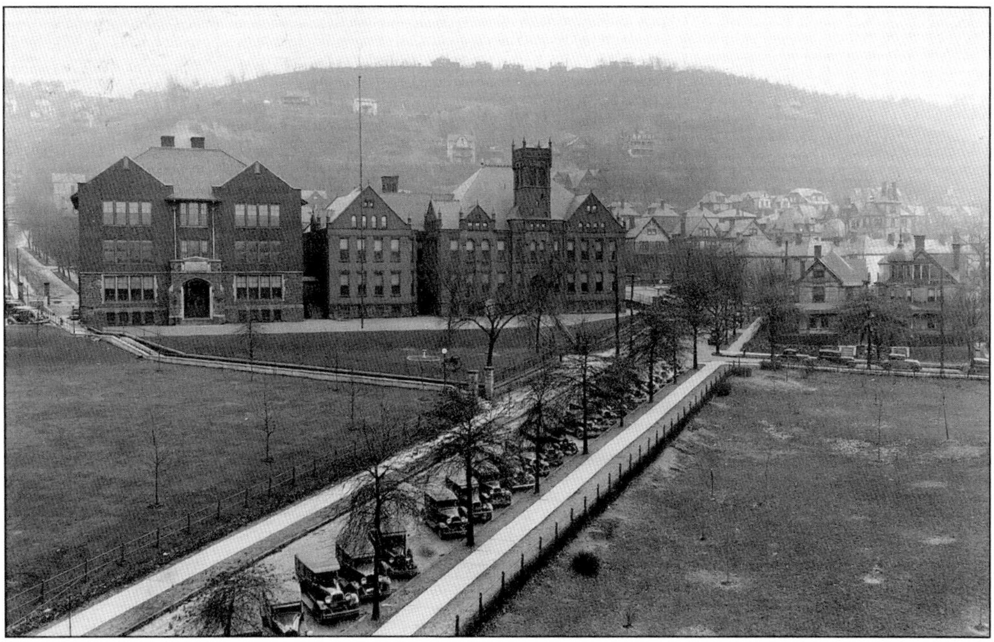

The Westinghouse Elementary and Horrocks Schools are clearly seen in this photograph looking up Herman Avenue. Horrocks School was named for Christopher Horrocks, who in 1870 was the first man employed by George Westinghouse in his plant in Pittsburgh. He worked at the Westinghouse Air Brake Company for 49 years, retiring in Wilmerding in 1919. He proved to be a valuable friend to George Westinghouse.

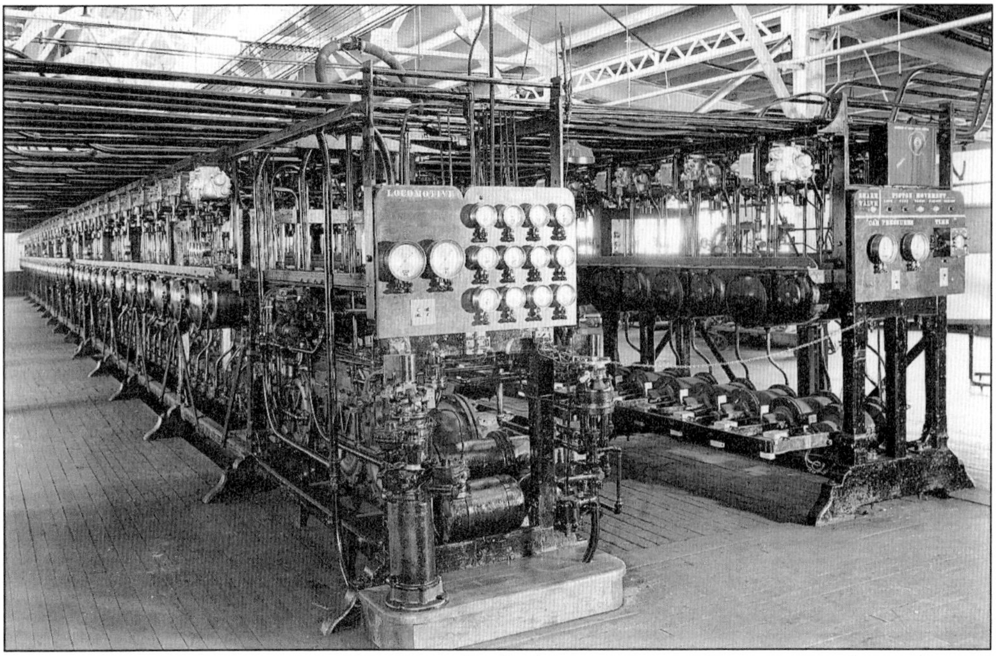

Westinghouse Air Brake Company's AB and K brake equipment 150-car test rack was located at the company's test division on the third floor of Building 17. The engineering department test racks were used to evaluate and demonstrate the operation of railway air brakes. This was just one of several test racks used by the Westinghouse Air Brake Company.

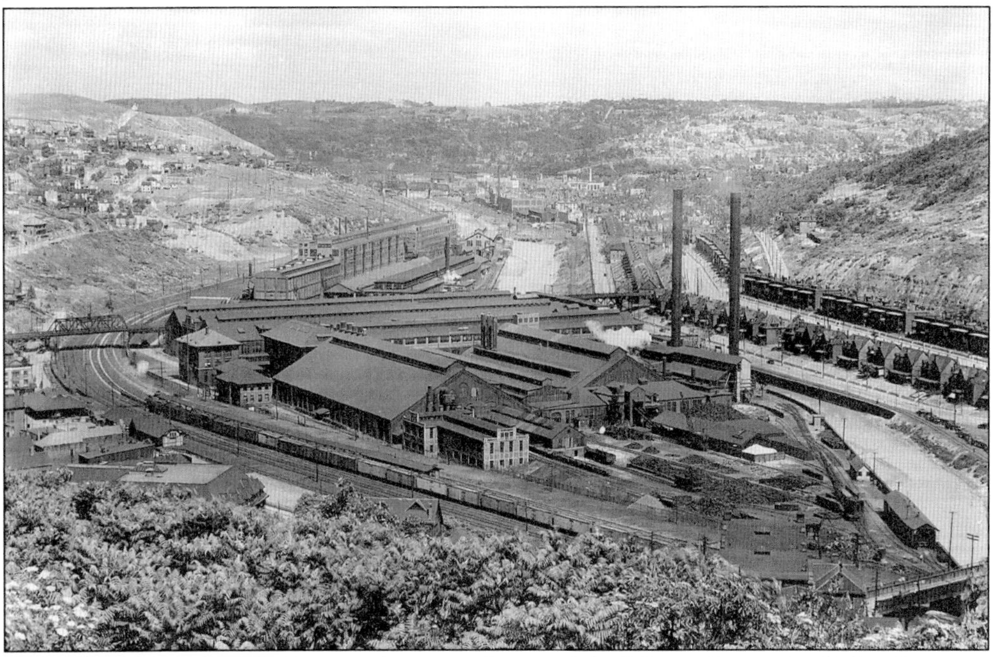

Looking west from Styling Terrace, this general view of the Westinghouse Air Brake Company plant was taken in the early 1930s. Note the plenitude of greenery in the foreground. Moving west toward Pittsburgh past the passenger loading platform is a steam locomotive pulling freight. Turtle Creek is visible in the lower part of the photograph.

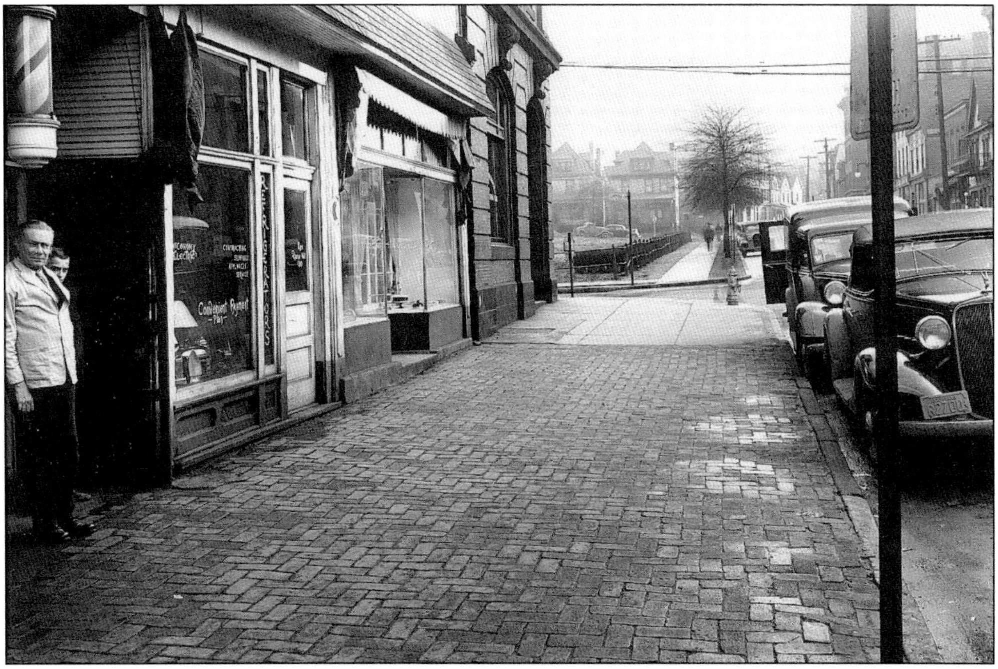

Pictured is a view looking south on Westinghouse Avenue near the corner of Commerce Street on February 8, 1937. Very few of the structures in this view have survived. It must not be too cold; the barber is standing outside without the traditional overcoat of the period. On the left, under the awning, is a bake shop. To the rear, the park can be seen, encircled by an old iron fence.

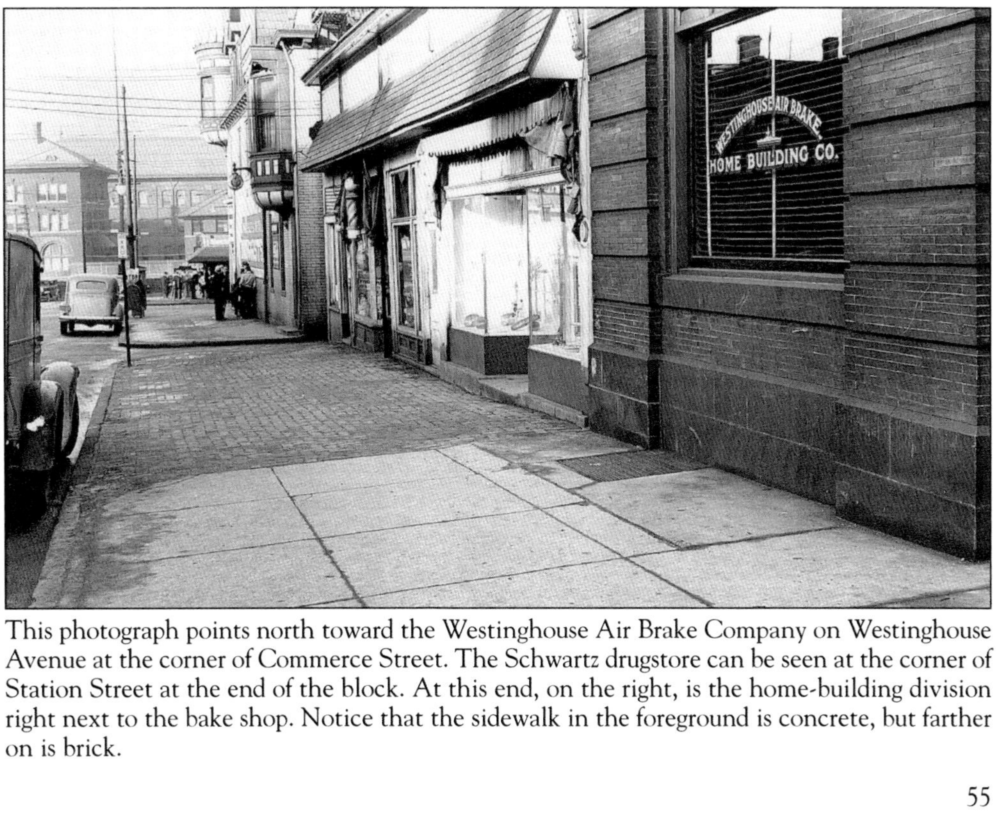

This photograph points north toward the Westinghouse Air Brake Company on Westinghouse Avenue at the corner of Commerce Street. The Schwartz drugstore can be seen at the corner of Station Street at the end of the block. At this end, on the right, is the home-building division right next to the bake shop. Notice that the sidewalk in the foreground is concrete, but farther on is brick.

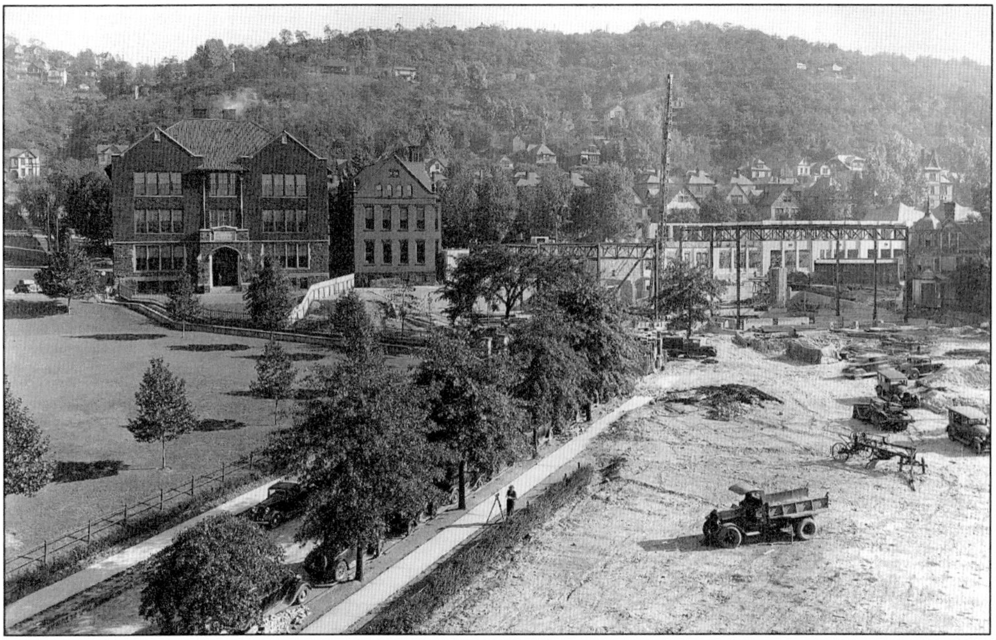

Wilmerding decided to erect a modern high school on the site of the Horrocks School and Annex. In September 1936, construction began on the Westinghouse Memorial High School. Up until this time, Wilmerding students acquired their secondary education at Turtle Creek Union High School in Turtle Creek. The Westinghouse Elementary School can be seen on the left of the Horrocks School Annex.

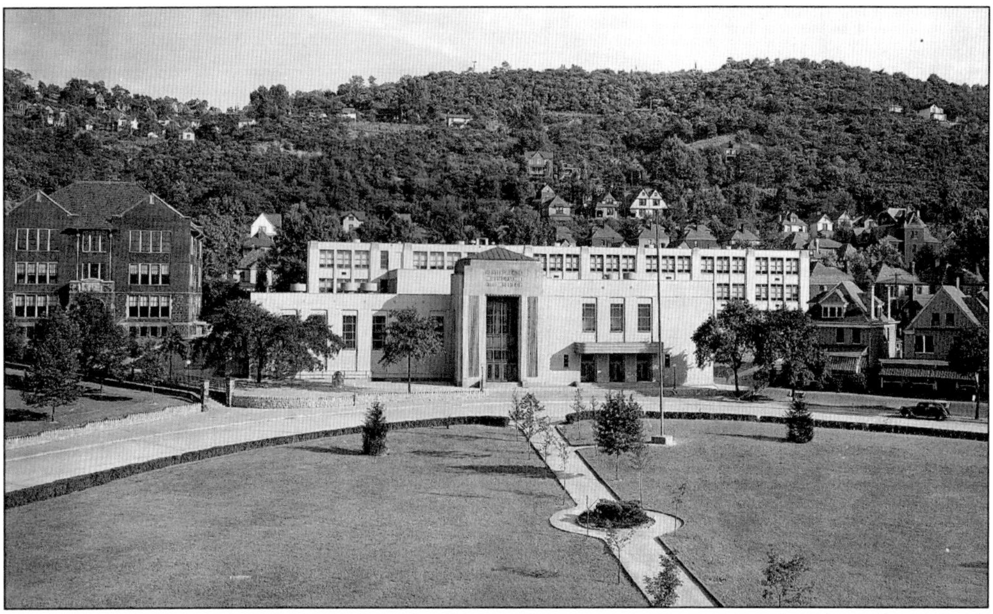

The Westinghouse Memorial High School, seen here in 1937, remained Wilmerding's high school until 1969. Thereafter, Wilmerding became part of the East Allegheny School District in North Versailles. Now the Westinghouse Memorial High School building is the Wilmerding Middle School. Local high school students have to travel to school, whereas before 1969, most could walk.

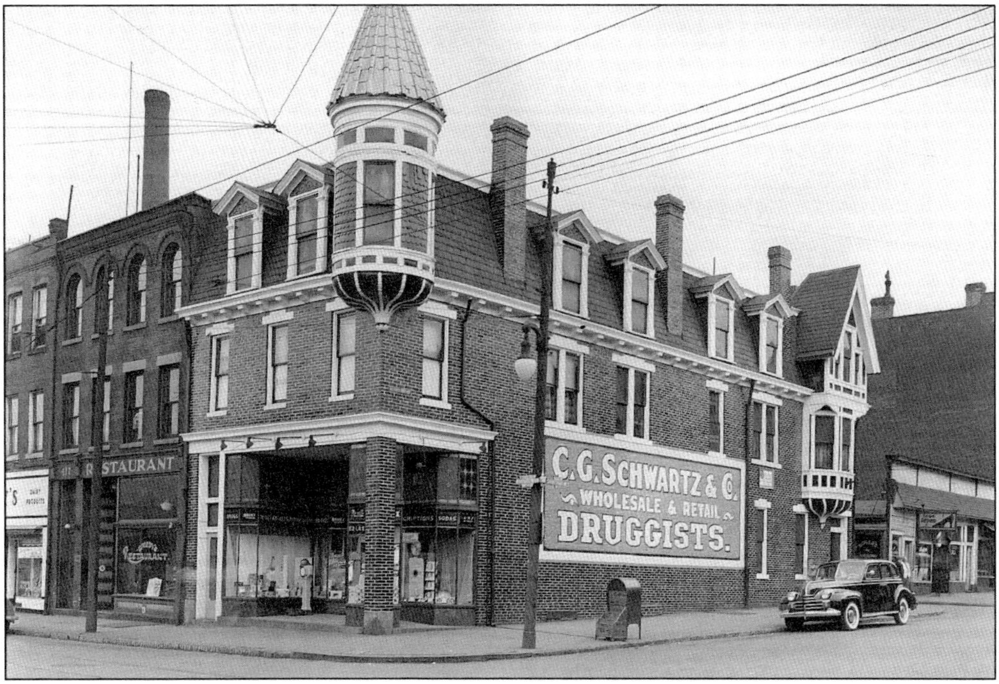

The C.G. Schwartz & Company drugstore was located at the corner of Westinghouse Avenue and Station Street in Wilmerding. Originally the W.L. Stewart drugstore, the building was remodeled after a fire in 1912. In later years, the store became Grimm's Drug Store, remaining so until a fire caused the building's destruction in 1967. Isaly's (dairy specialists), shown at the far left next to Speedy's Restaurant, later built a new store on this site.

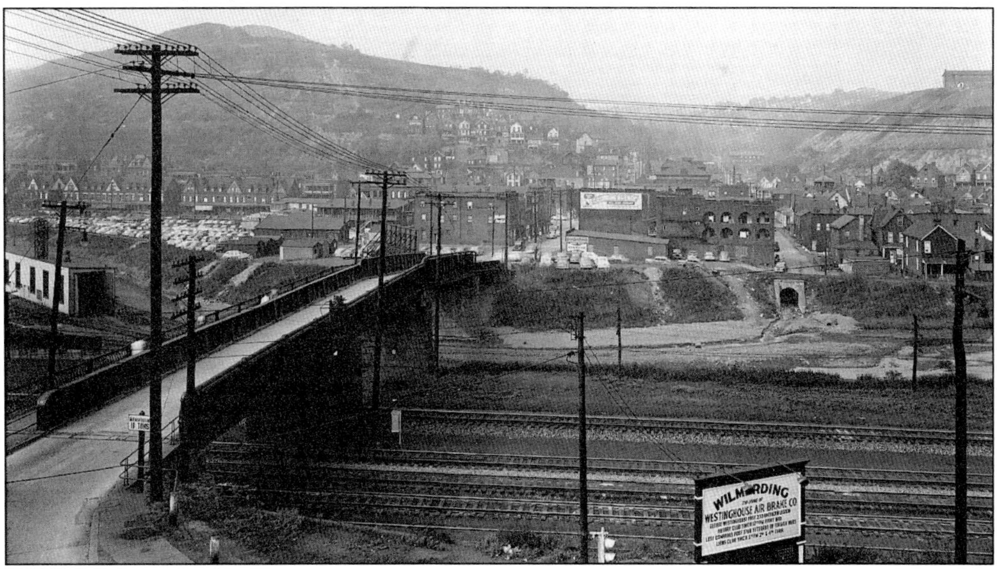

The Old Bridge Street Bridge connected the north and south sections of Wilmerding. The Westinghouse Air Brake Company Engine House appears at the far left. Many of the homes and businesses on the north side of the Pennsylvania Railroad, including the bridge, were torn down during the redevelopment era. A new bridge was built just east of this bridge. The photograph was taken in 1951.

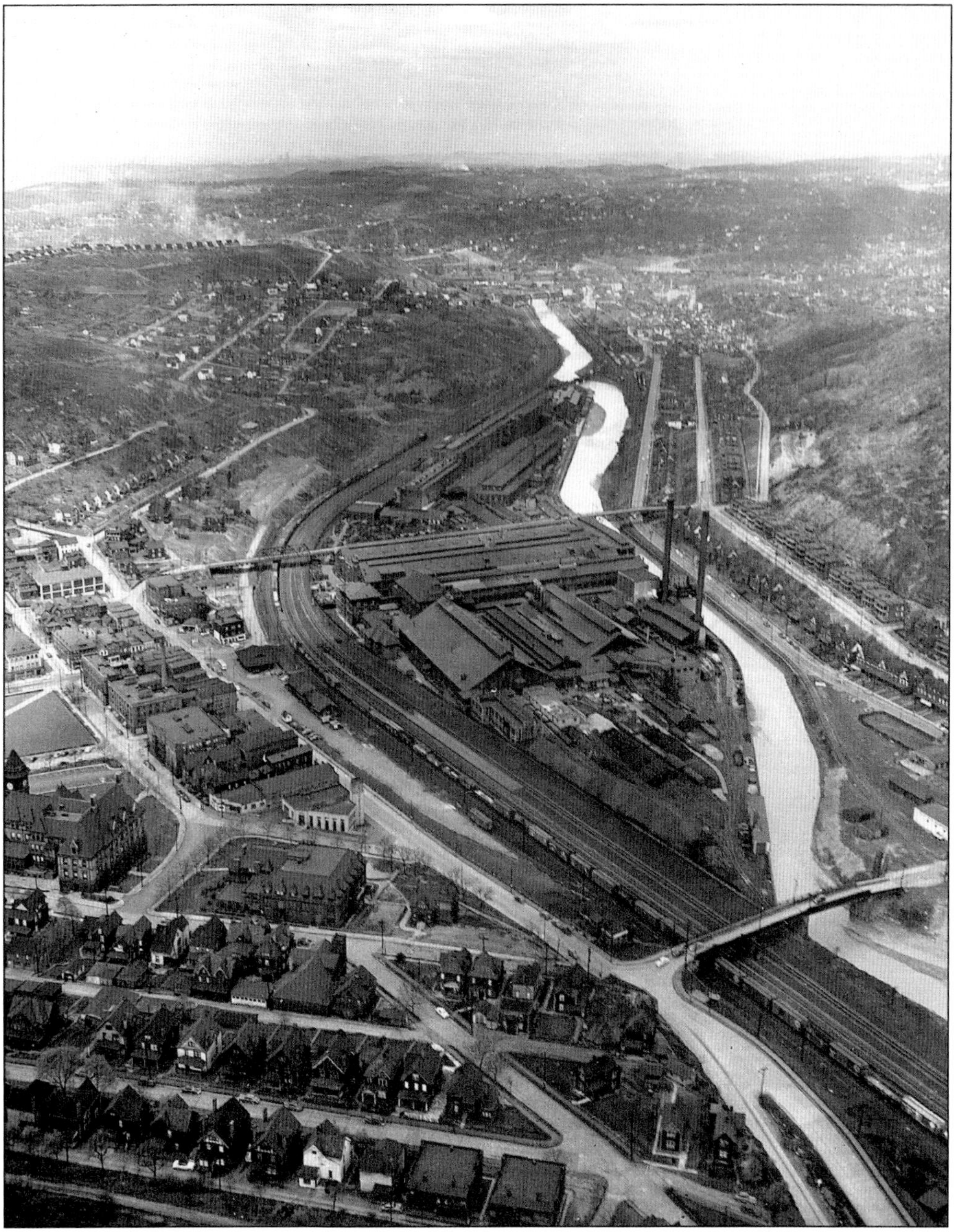

In this rather detailed picture of the borough, the focal point is the Westinghouse Air Brake Company, nestled between Turtle Creek and the railroad tracks. Station Street is to the left of the plant, and Airbrake Avenue is to the right. Smoke can be seen coming from the Edgar Thompson Works of the U.S. Steel Company in the upper portion of the photograph. Bridges on each end of the plant are clearly visible. A lengthy freight train winds its way through the borough on its way to the Pittsburgh area. The "flats" are seen to the right of Airbrake Avenue. Notice the roofs of the business district left of Station Street. Can you spot the general offices of the Westinghouse Air Brake Company?

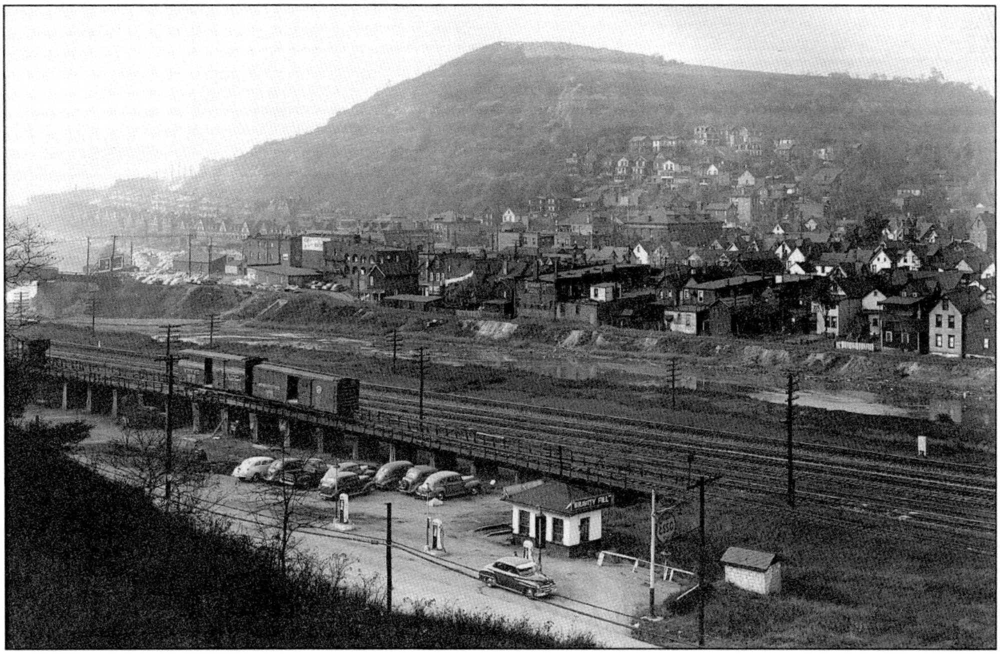

Here is a view showing the north side of Wilmerding. The Gravity Fill gas station is seen in the foreground. Behind the Gravity Fill is the coal ramp for the Barnes Coal Company. Behind the railroad tracks lies Turtle Creek. The gas station is long gone, but today there are still some old remains of the Barnes Coal Company.

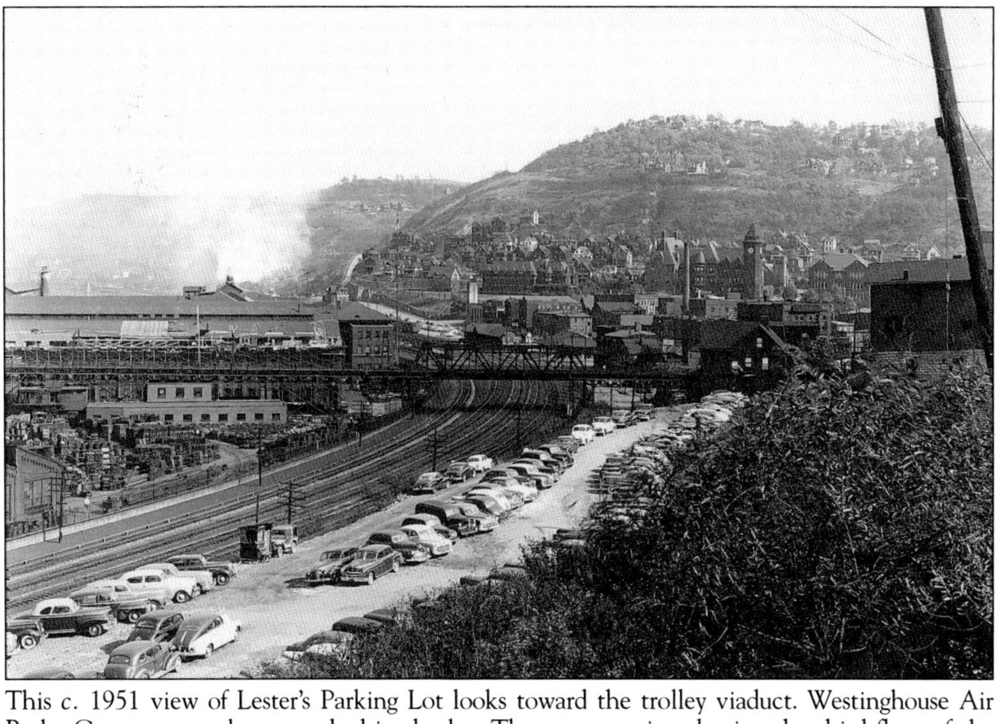

This *c.* 1951 view of Lester's Parking Lot looks toward the trolley viaduct. Westinghouse Air Brake Company employees parked in the lot. The company is enlarging the third floor of the main machine shop. The Castle can be seen in the background. To its right is the grade school.

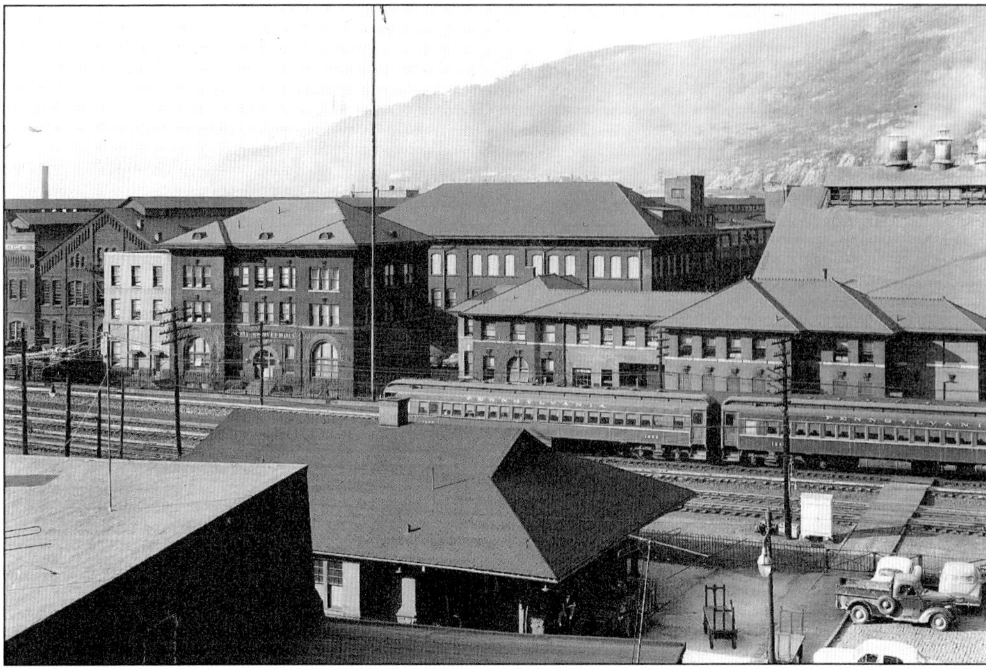

This view shows the main entrance to the Westinghouse Air Brake Company, the superintendent's office, and the engineering department. The Pennsylvania Railroad station and the station platform can be seen in the foreground between the east and west tracks. Several passenger cars await arrivals. This photograph was taken *c.* 1951 from across Station Street.

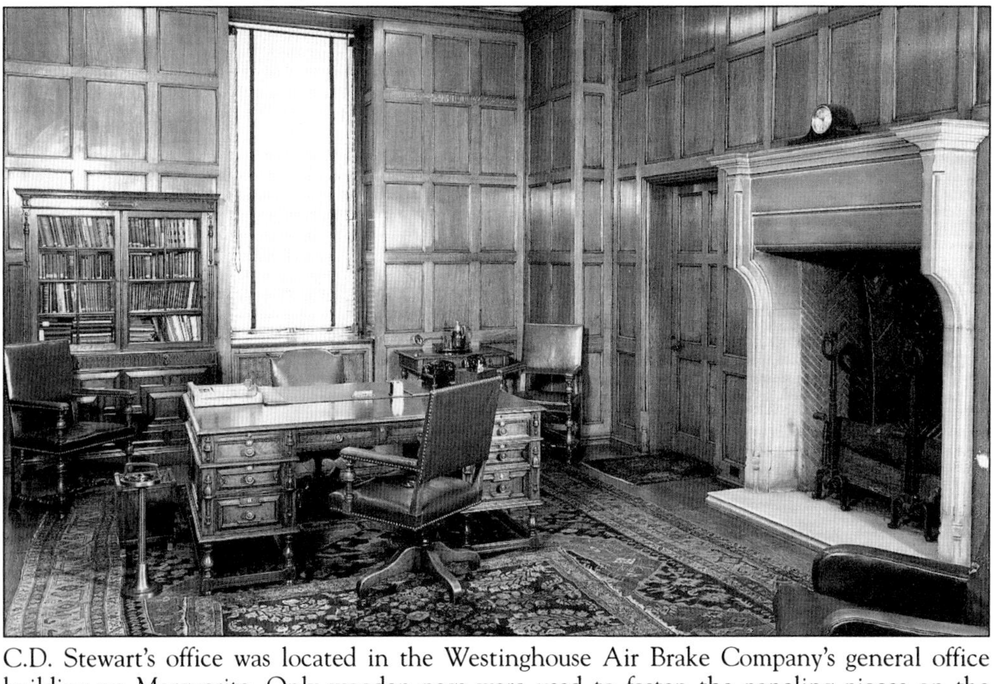

C.D. Stewart's office was located in the Westinghouse Air Brake Company's general office building on Marguerite. Only wooden pegs were used to fasten the paneling pieces on the walls, no nails or screws. The fireplace material came from Italy. Today, the building is known as the Castle.

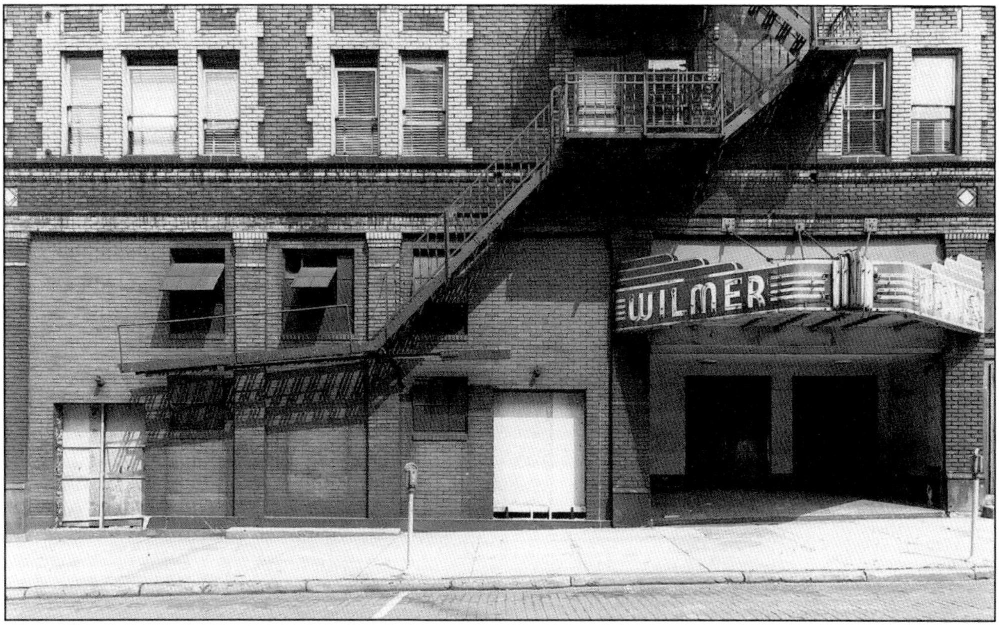

Shown here is the Wilmer Theater on Herman Avenue in the Faller Building. At the time, the Wilmer was one of two theaters located in Wilmerding. The other was in the YMCA auditorium. In previous years, there was also a theater on Station Street—the first one in town—called the Liberty and yet another on Westinghouse Avenue. The Wilmer Theater closed in 1953 with the advent of television.

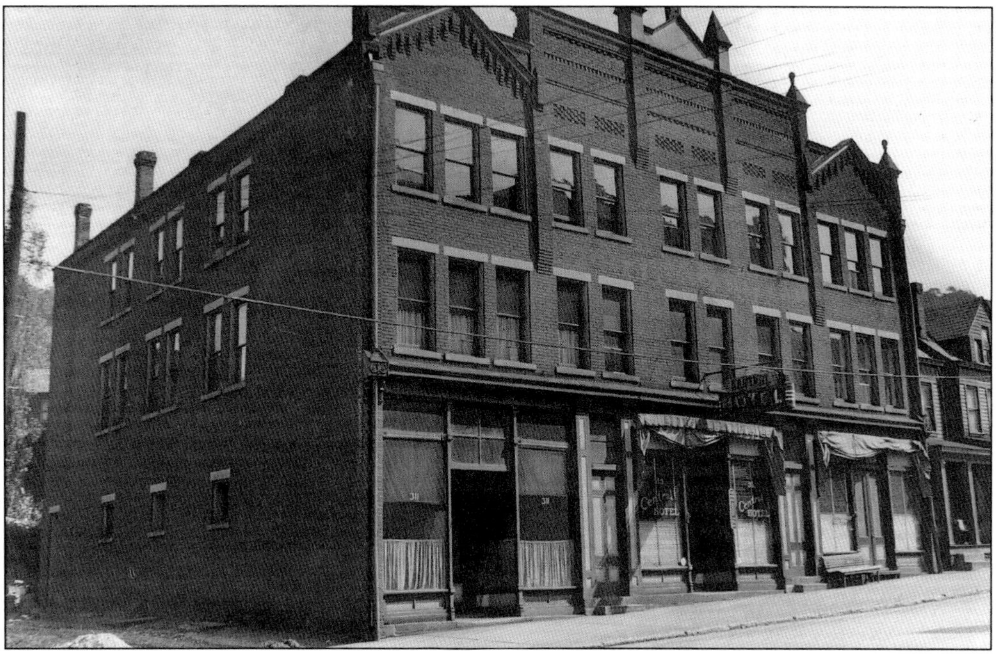

Wilmerding was a hub of sorts in the early days, and because of this, there were a number of hotels. The Central Hotel, located on Westinghouse Avenue and known for its "longest back bar," remained until the late 1960s, when it was torn down as part of the Model Cities Program. The building was then occupied by LaGorga's Restaurant.

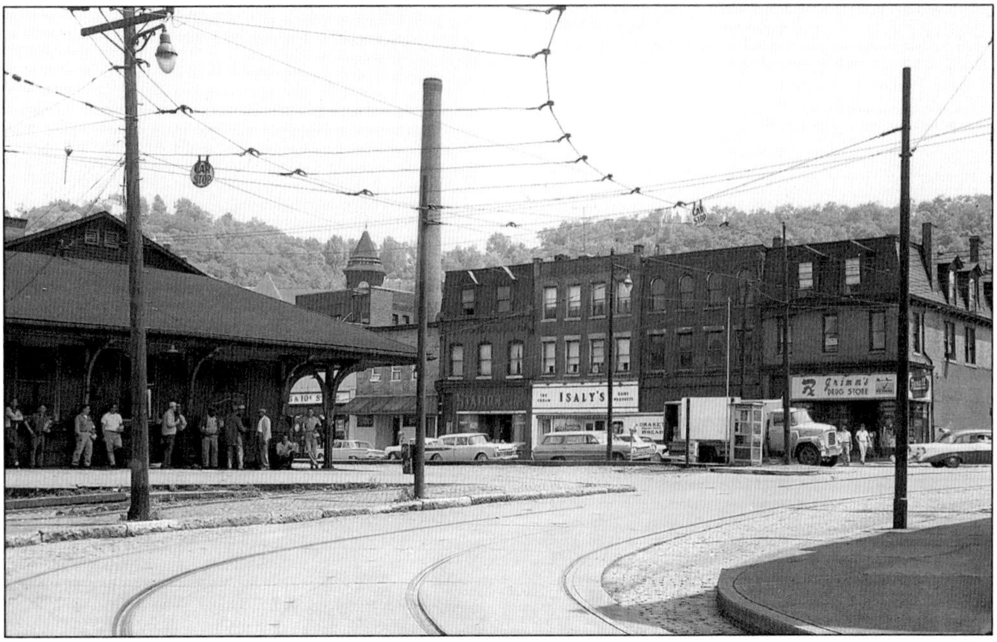

This view shows the trolley loop, railroad station, and stores on Station Street c. 1964. On the corner of Westinghouse Avenue is Grimm's Drug Store, formerly the Schwartz and Stewart drugstores. The original Isaly's Dairy Store was in this same block of stores. These businesses were all located in buildings that housed tenants on upper floors. The large smokestack belonged to the apartment building on Commerce Street behind Station Street.

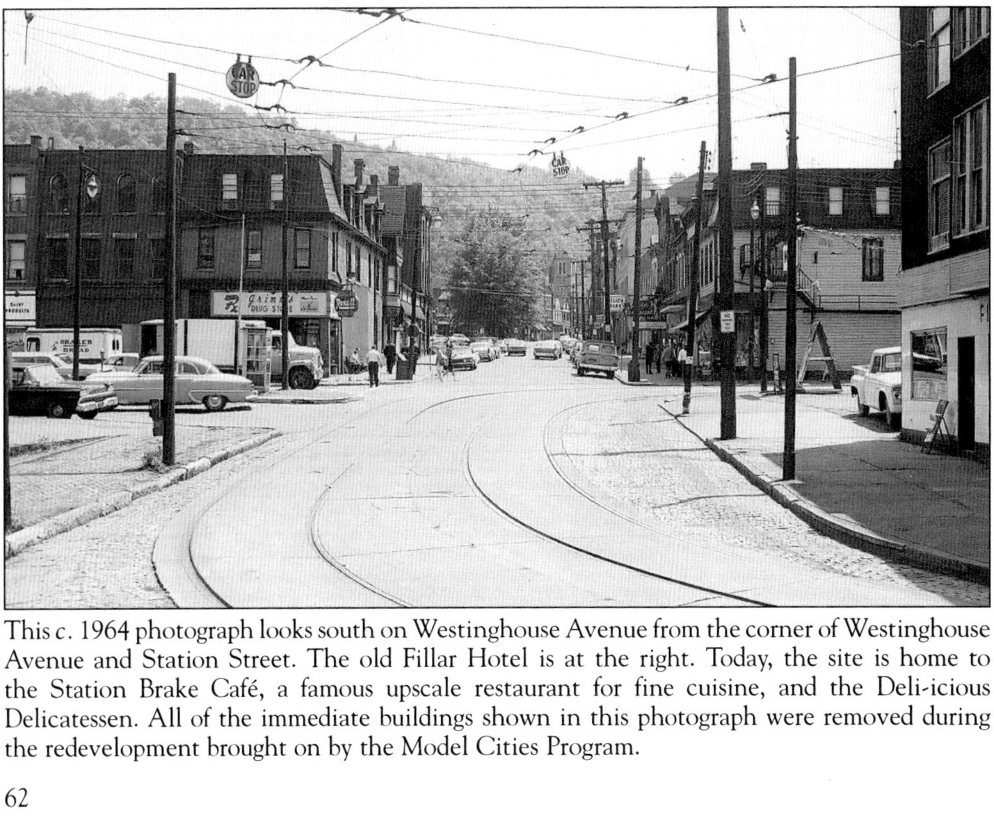

This c. 1964 photograph looks south on Westinghouse Avenue from the corner of Westinghouse Avenue and Station Street. The old Fillar Hotel is at the right. Today, the site is home to the Station Brake Café, a famous upscale restaurant for fine cuisine, and the Deli-icious Delicatessen. All of the immediate buildings shown in this photograph were removed during the redevelopment brought on by the Model Cities Program.

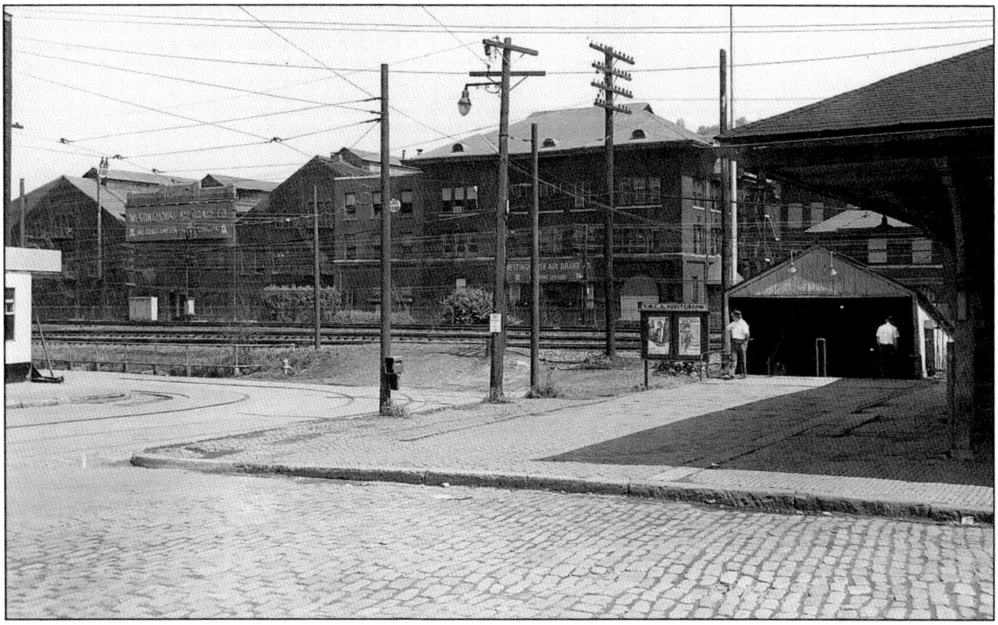

Looking across Station Street, this 1964 photograph shows the main tunnel entrance to the Westinghouse Air Brake Company. The Pennsylvania Railroad station is at the far right, entered via the brick road in the foreground. The tunnel was also the entrance for westbound passengers on the Pennsylvania Railroad. Can you spot two sets of streetcar tracks in the left center of the photograph?

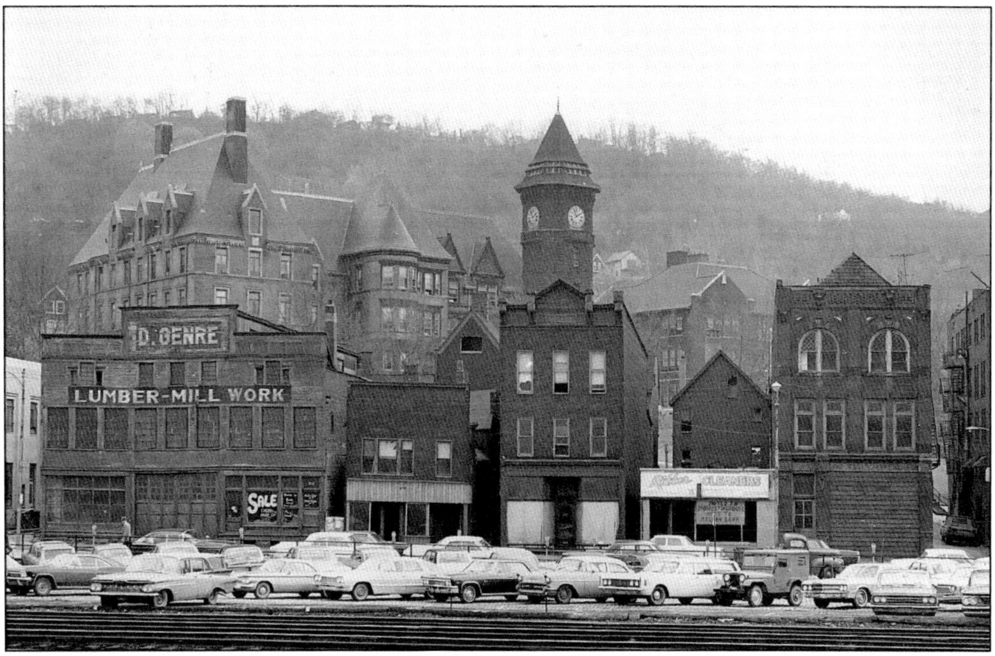

The Genre Lumber Company and other local businesses are seen as they once existed on Station Street. On the far left, the municipal building is partially seen. The Westinghouse Air Brake general office looms in the background. The photograph was taken in the 1960s before demolition by the Model Cities Program.

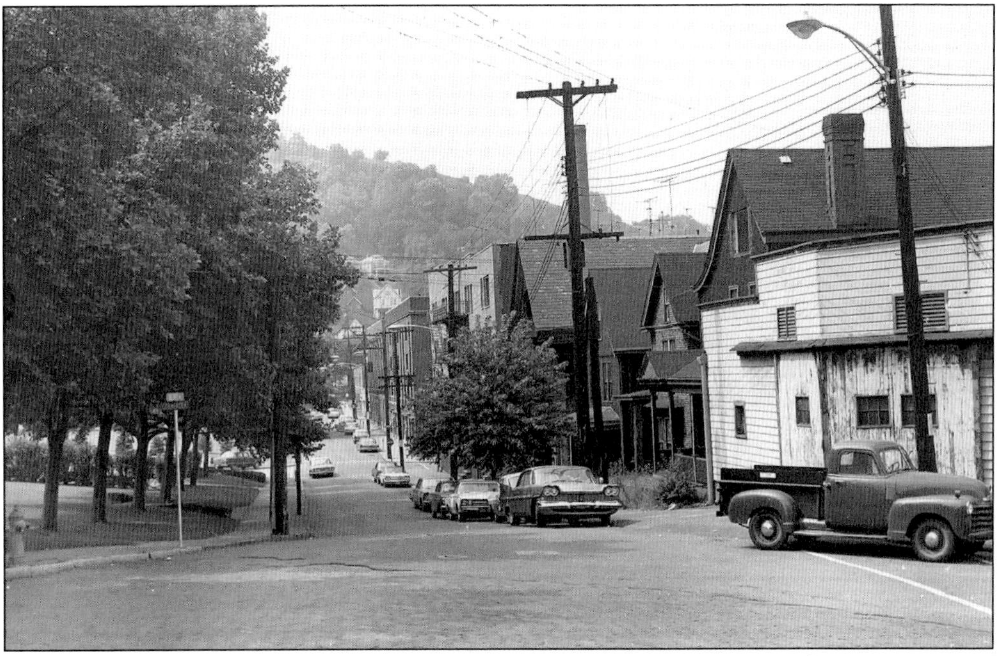

Shown here is a view looking west on Commerce Street during the 1960s at the intersection of Bluff Street. The houses on the right were torn down in order to build the new senior citizens' high rise. The Castle is on the left, the municipal building on the right. Straight ahead one block on the right side is an apartment building.

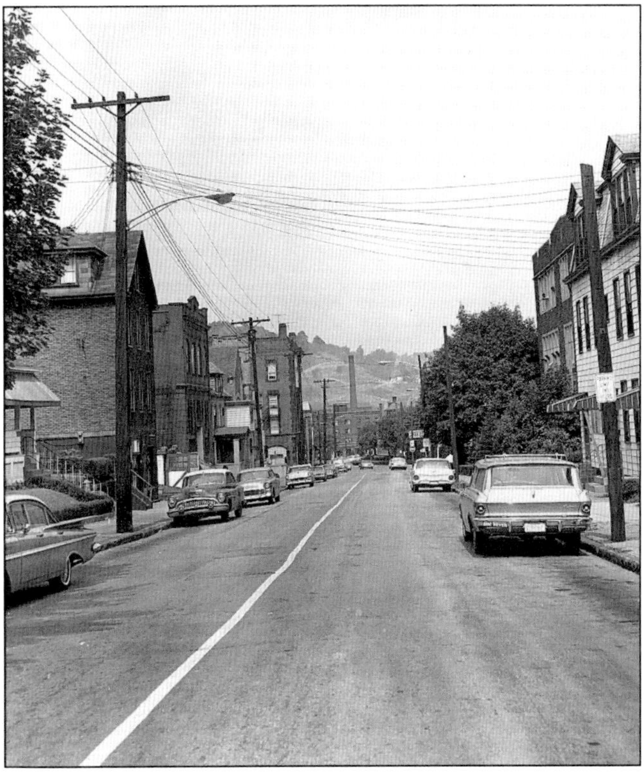

In this view looking north on Westinghouse Avenue in 1966, the former Elks building is on the left. On the right is St. Aloysius Parochial School. A small confectionery once occupied the storefront directly behind the pole on the left. The smokestack in the distance belongs to the apartment house on Commerce Street.

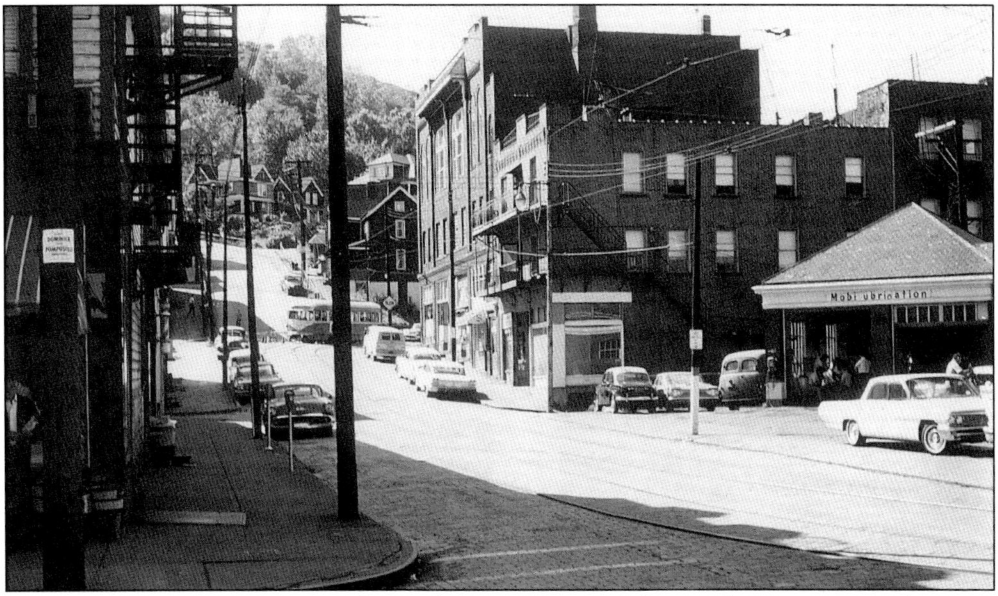

Looking west on Station Street, this mid-1960s view was taken at the intersection of Station Street and Westinghouse Avenue. A Pittsburgh Railways PCC trolley is about to enter town. The building near the trolley, at the end of the block, belongs to the Philaretic Society. Built in 1926, the building housed the Philaretic Hall on the top floor, which comprised a huge dance floor and stage with a state-of-the-art sound system.

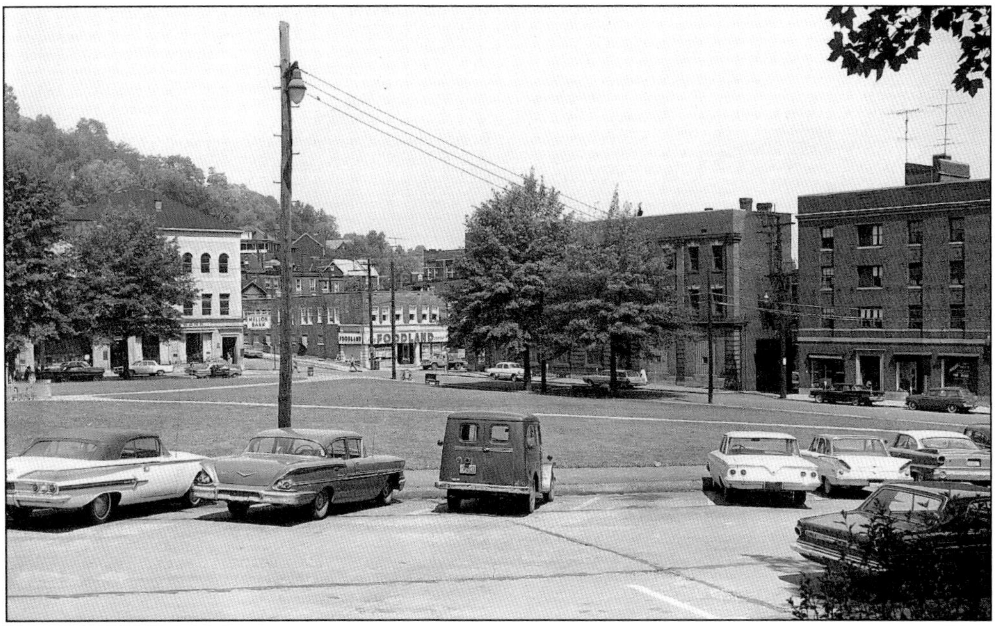

This photograph of Wilmerding Park, looking northwest toward Mellon Bank and the Foodland grocery store, was taken in the mid-1960s. The bank building was one of the earliest buildings in Wilmerding. Originally, it housed the East Pittsburgh Bank, which later merged with the Wilmerding National Bank to become the First National Bank of Wilmerding. The building consisted of three floors of offices. Local churches held meetings there while their buildings were being constructed.

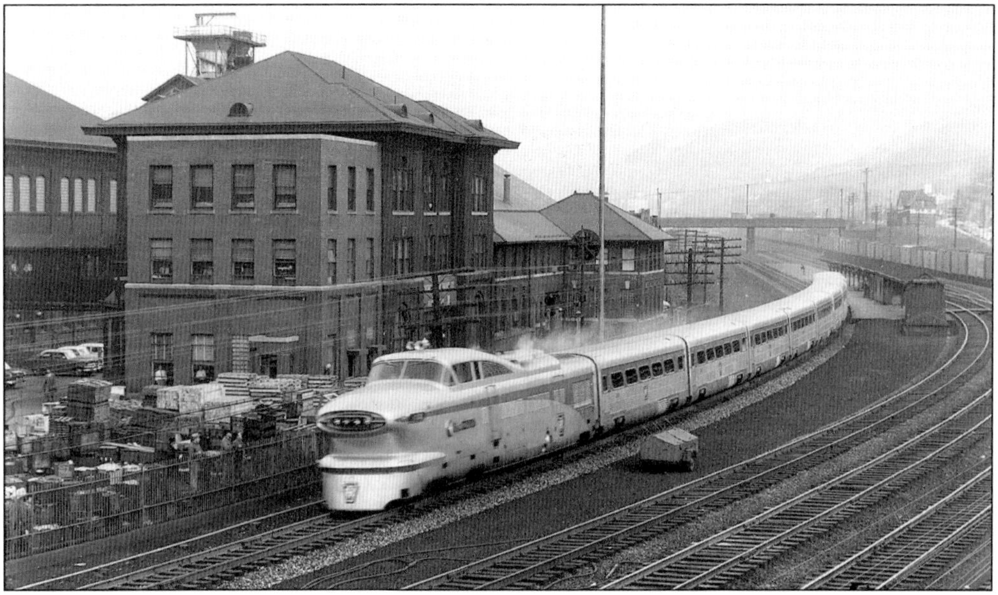

The Pennsylvania Railroad's Aero Train is seen here traveling west through Wilmerding in the mid-1950s. The Pennsylvania Railroad ran the General Motors–built experimental passenger train for about two years in an effort to regain lost passenger traffic. One of these trains still exists at the Museum of Transportation in St. Louis, Missouri.

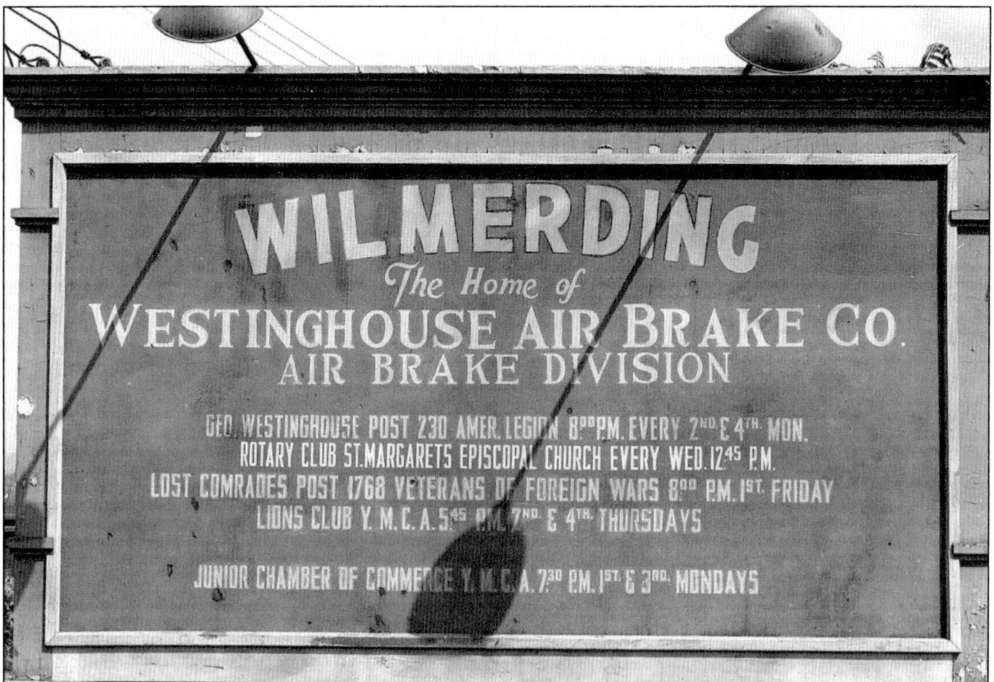

This familiar sign stood at the corner of Bridge Street and Wall Avenue: "Wilmerding, the Home of the Westinghouse Air Brake Co., Air Brake Division." Meeting times were displayed for several local clubs and organizations. The sign remained there until construction of the Patton Street Bridge began in the mid-1960s.

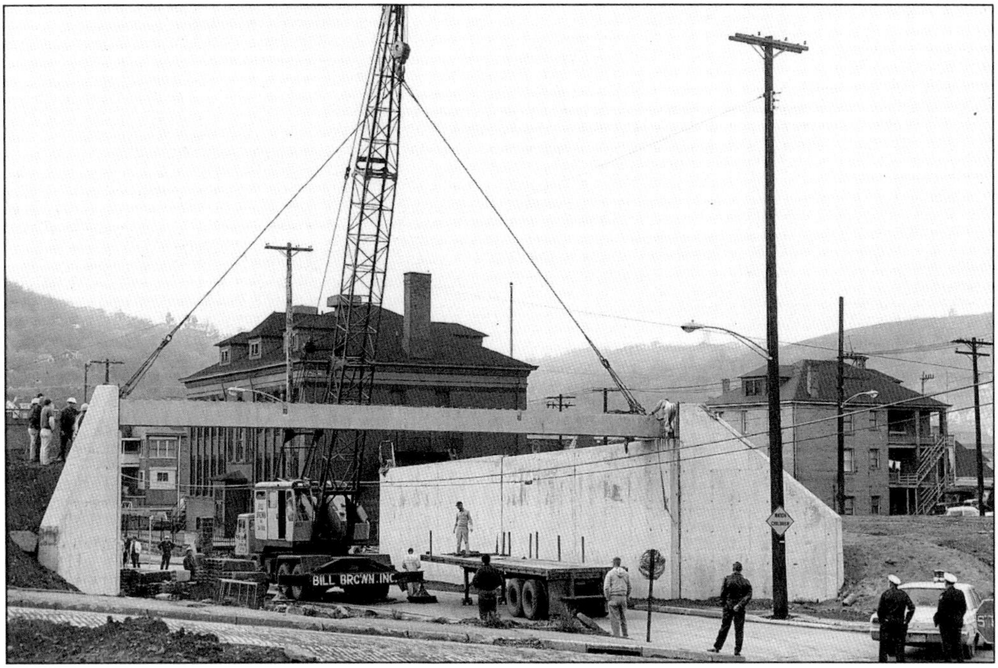

This steel beam has just been set in place over Patton Street, beginning the construction of the Tri-Boro Expressway on the north side of Wilmerding. The back of the Gottwals School is visible behind the beam. Wilmerding police block traffic as the workers fasten the beam. This photograph was taken in 1968.

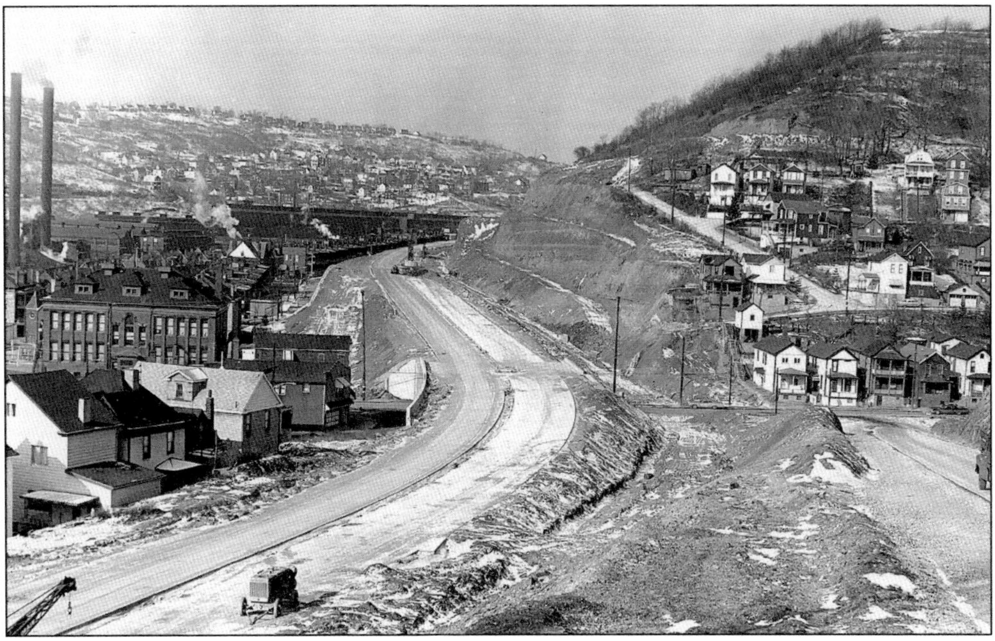

The initial construction of the Tri-Boro Expressway cut into Russian Hill, shown on the right in 1968. The three streets known collectively as Russian Hill were Howard, Bella, and Laveen. Patton Street can be seen in the right center of the photograph, directly in front of a row of homes.

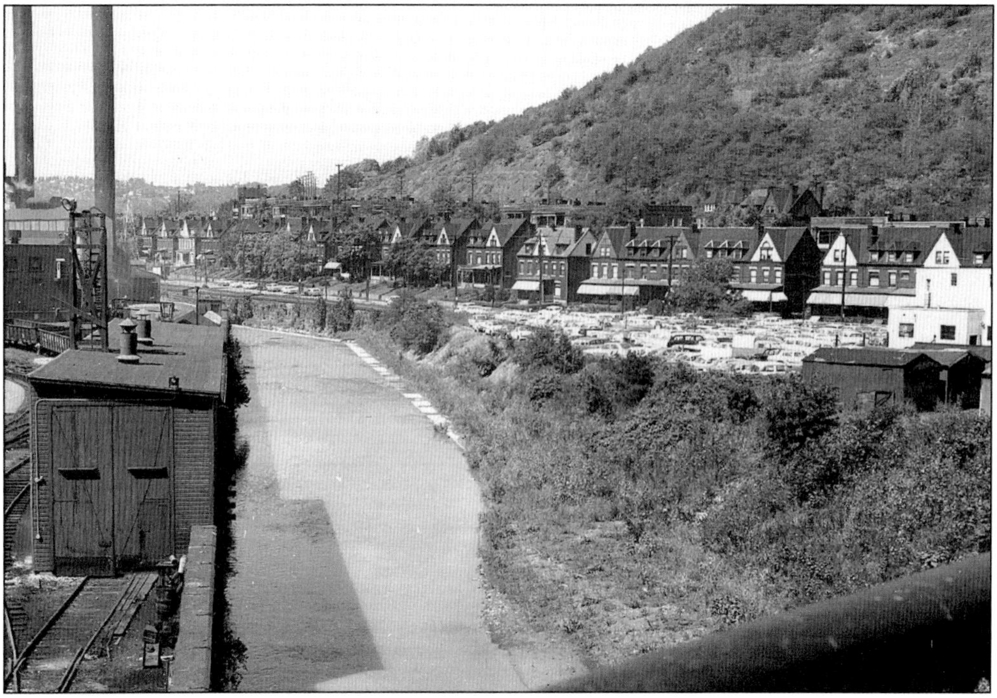

This photograph, taken from the bridge connecting the north and south sections of Wilmerding, shows a typical scene prior to flood control. Turtle Creek flows under this bridge. After having been plagued with floods since 1888, the Turtle Creek Flood Protection Project was born. Work began to correct the flooding problem on November 20, 1963.

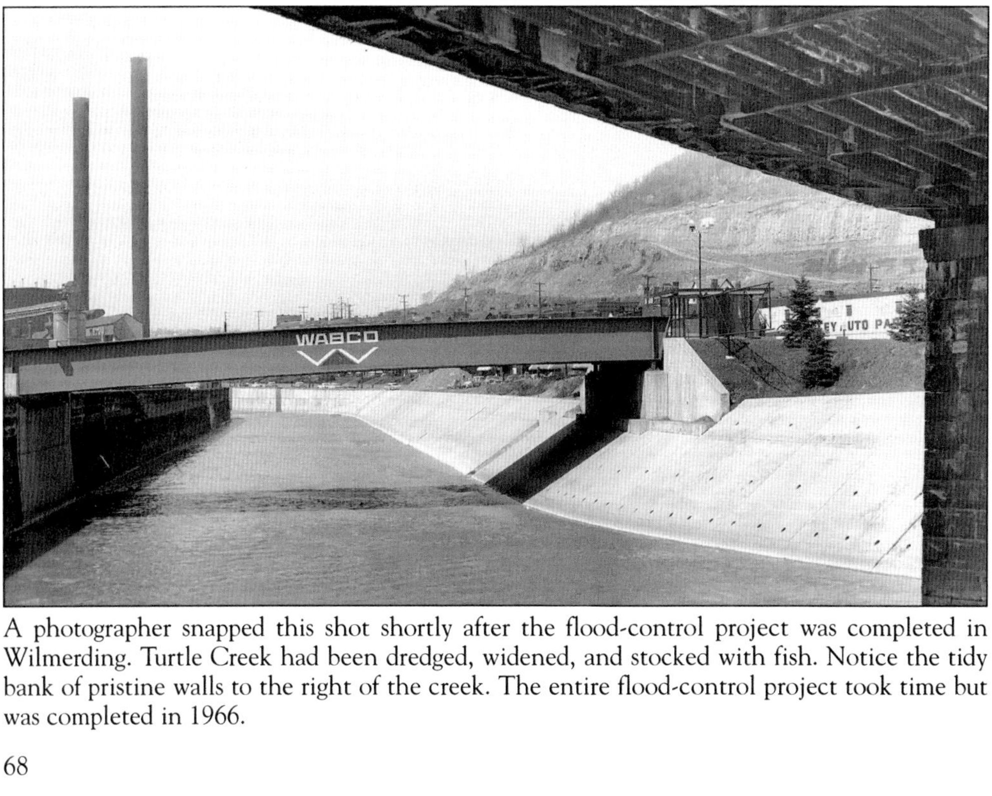

A photographer snapped this shot shortly after the flood-control project was completed in Wilmerding. Turtle Creek had been dredged, widened, and stocked with fish. Notice the tidy bank of pristine walls to the right of the creek. The entire flood-control project took time but was completed in 1966.

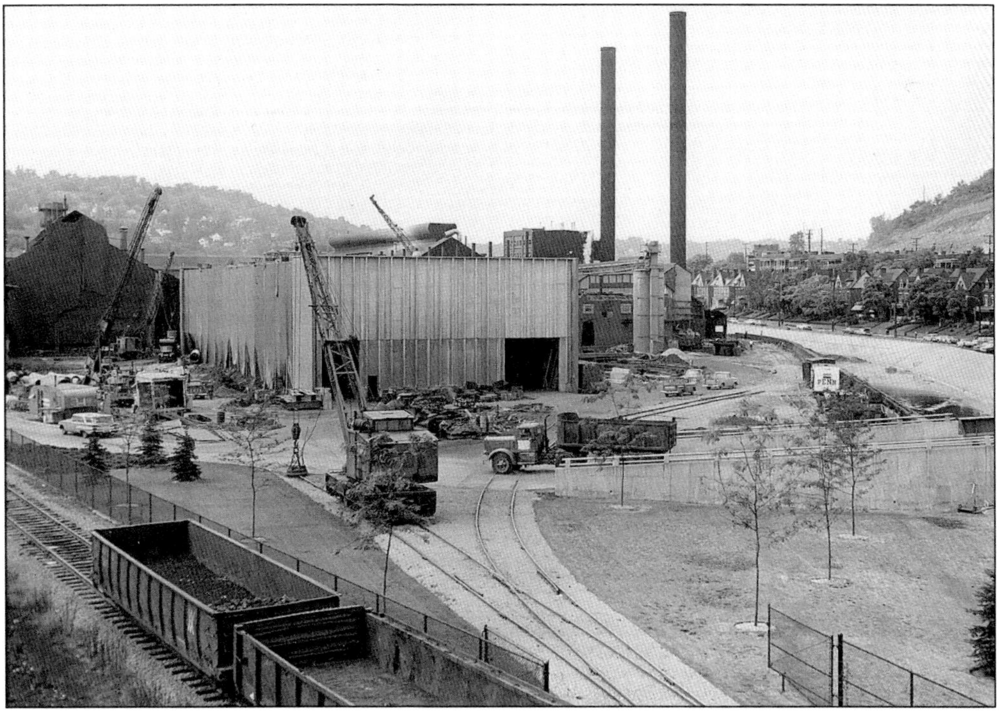

Here is a photograph that shows the construction of a new foundry building on the far east end of the Westinghouse Air Brake Company property in the mid-1960s. The railroad tracks entering the site are being used by a crane car. Trucks bringing construction materials must enter from an access road on the right.

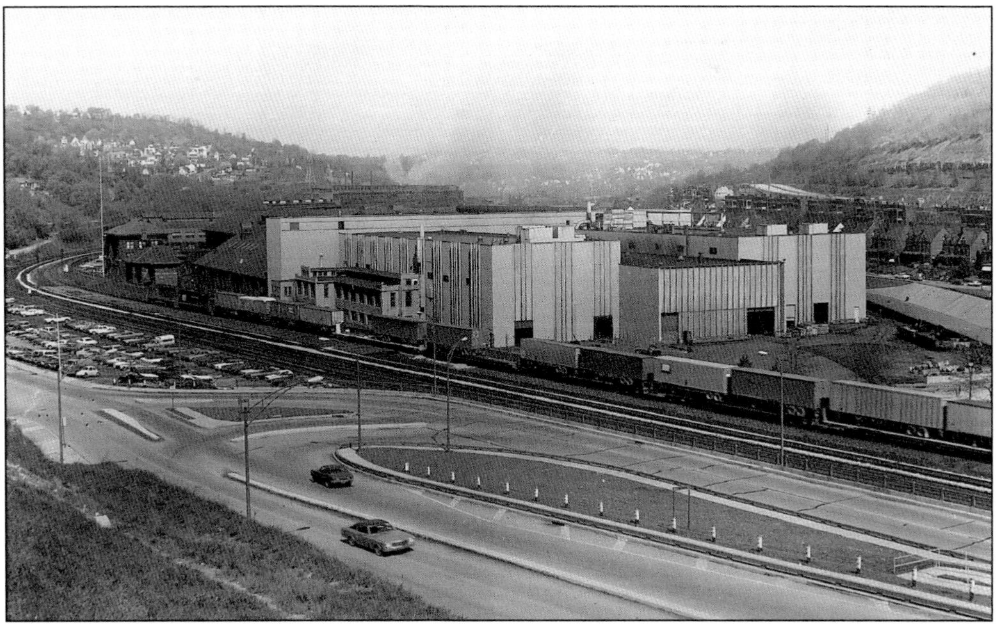

Taken in January 1965, this photograph shows the newly completed foundry building. Two 18-ton induction furnaces were installed; each had a maximum capacity of 5.6 tons per hour. A Penn Central diesel locomotive is seen pulling freight westward toward the city of Pittsburgh.

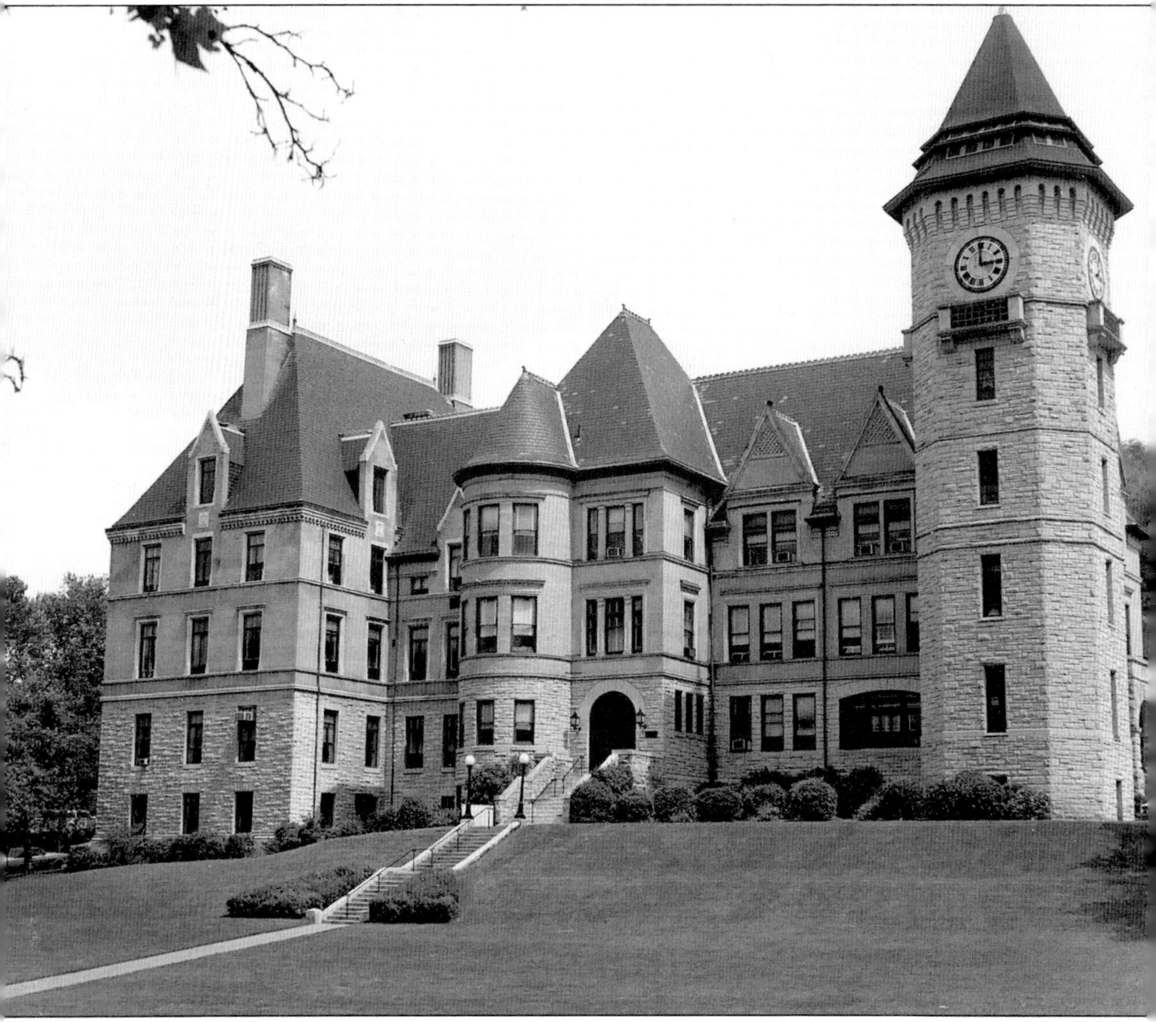

Perhaps the most beautiful view of the former Westinghouse Air Brake general office building is shown in this photograph. In the 1970s, many of the Westinghouse Air Brake plant buildings were cleaned, which enhanced their appearance. Today, the corner clock still chimes on the hour and on the half-hour. The grounds are immaculate. No one is permitted to use George Westinghouse's old office on the third floor, or the second floor if entering through the front. Although some of the space is rented to tenants, all those who work in the building respect its past and maintain its dignity. The building is home to the George Westinghouse Museum. The American Production Inventory Control Society now governs the property. George Westinghouse would be proud of how well they have maintained his legacy.

Four

HOMES

From the outset, George Westinghouse was concerned about the welfare of his employees. Housing was of prime importance, and to this end, employees were offered a variety of home locations, sizes, and styles. The first row of houses built in Wilmerding was on Caldwell and Westinghouse Avenues. Homes were five, six, and seven rooms and constructed in the Victorian and Tudor styles. The first tenant on Caldwell Avenue was William Moles, a machinist.

The upper management personnel mainly had homes on Welsh and Marguerite Avenues. T.W. Welsh, plant superintendent, lived in a home on Marguerite Avenue that would be considered a mansion by any standard. The exterior was brick and cement; the interior exhibited marble with two beautiful full staircases and a full complement of rooms. Stables were to the east of the house. The home would later become the YMCA.

Across town, on the north side, the company built the "flats"—mainly on Middle and Airbrake Avenues. They included three floors, front and back porches, each unit connecting together in a row. The area from Watkins Avenue to State Street was the ethnic element of the borough, housing a variety from every European country. Patton Street was chosen to hold the large influx of southern blacks who migrated to Wilmerding in search of work and better living conditions.

Since George Westinghouse had a strong affinity for his employees and their welfare, the townspeople benefited with good housing (owned or rented), paved streets with lighting and garbage collection, and street maintenance (the large number of trees in the park was even diminished to discourage any misconduct).

Due to quality construction and workmanship, a great number of those early homes remain intact today. Some, however, have been torn down due to the Model Cities Program in the 1960s.

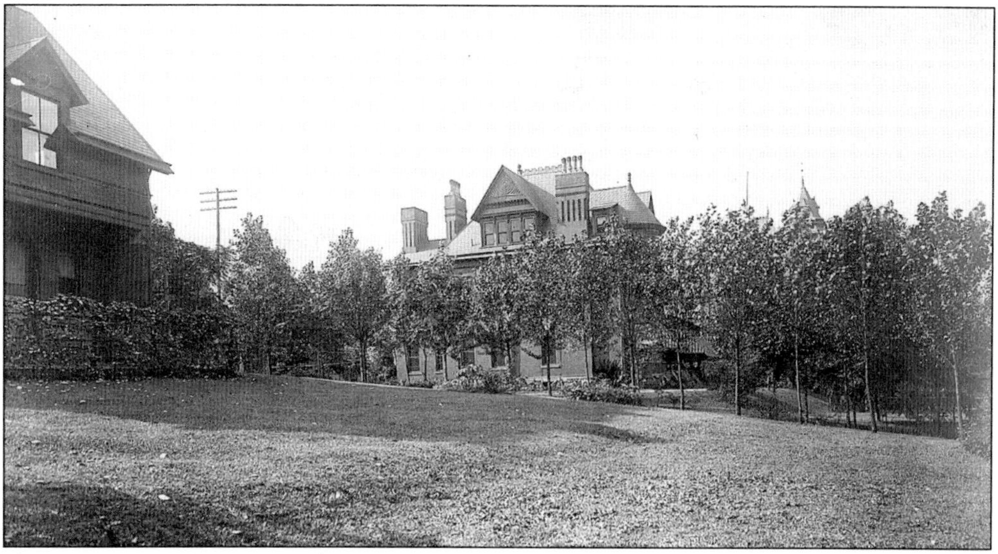

Shown *c.* 1902 is J.R. Brown's home on Marguerite Avenue. Brown was a plant superintendent for the Westinghouse Air Brake Company. This house was later vacated and remodeled to become the first welfare building. Still later, it became the home of the YMCA.

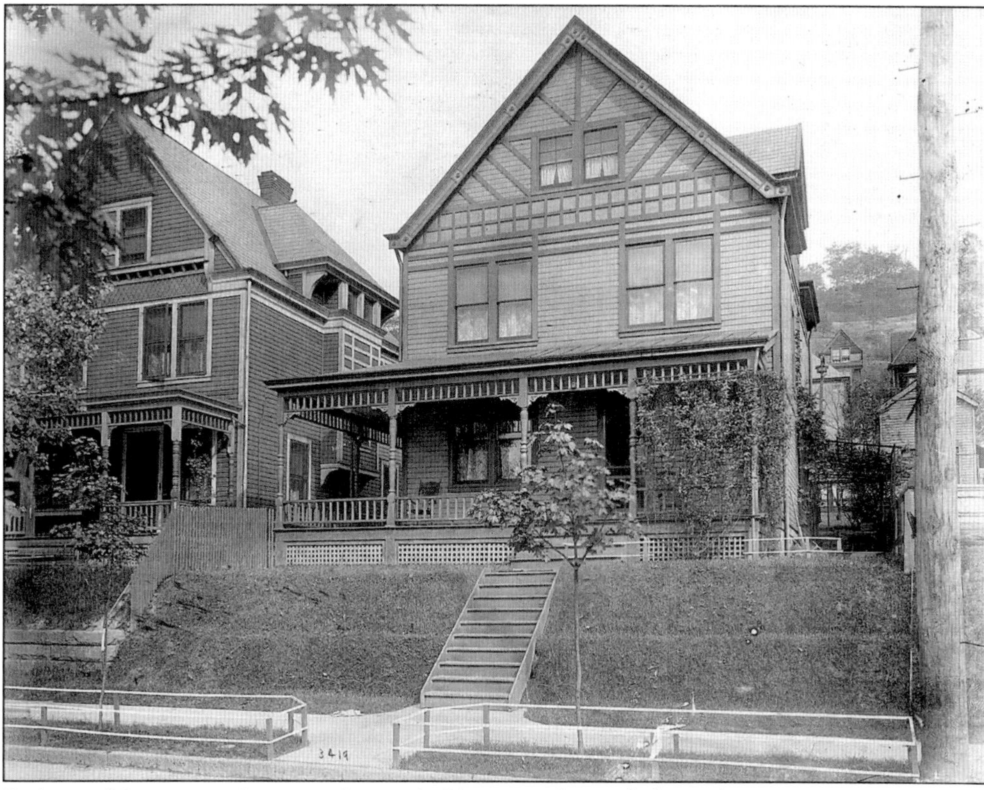

Built on Marguerite Avenue, this early-Victorian home belonged to A.B. Woods and is pictured *c.* 1902. Marguerite Avenue was named after the wife of George Westinghouse. It was believed that upper management resided on Marguerite Avenue. Notice the would-be fence surrounding the grassy areas on the sidewalk.

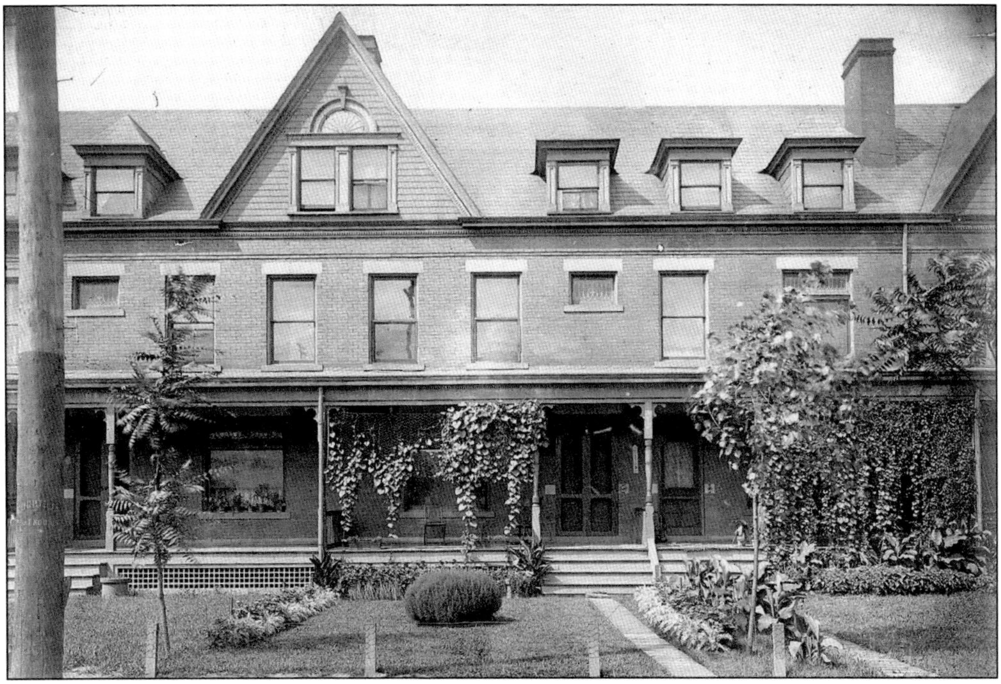

This six-family row house was located on Airbrake Avenue on the north side of Wilmerding. In 1902, the borough offered prizes for the beautification of residents' properties. This particular photograph represents the winner of a $5 prize: C.C. Cowell. Cowell, who lived in the center apartment house, won for his front lawn.

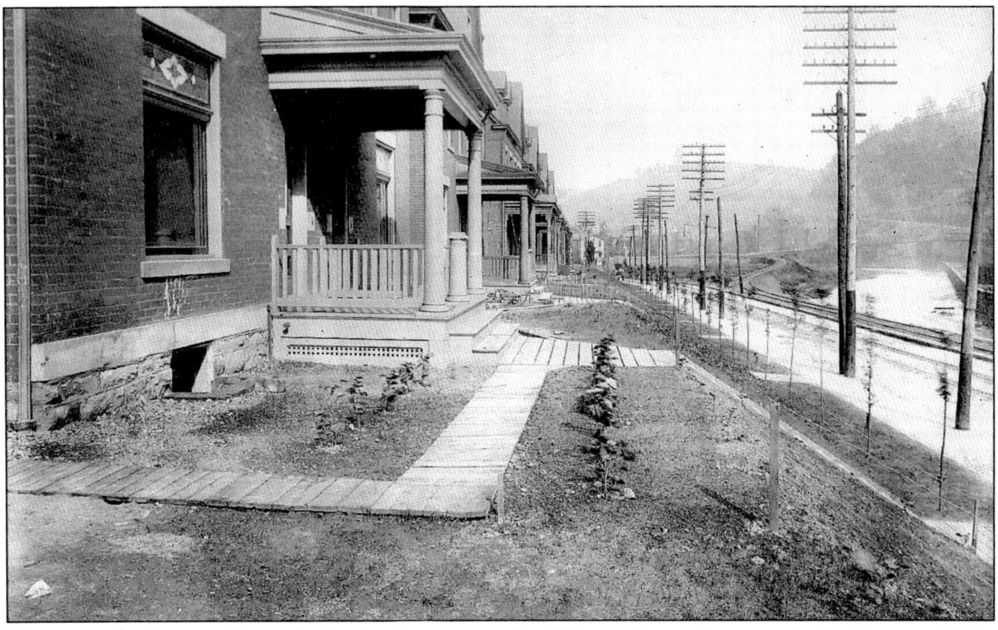

This view looks east down Airbrake Avenue at the Westinghouse Interworks Railway c. 1901. The railway system ran from the Westinghouse Electric & Manufacturing Company plant in East Pittsburgh, past the Westinghouse Air Brake plant and on to the Westinghouse Electric & Manufacturing Company plant in Trafford. The house at the left belonged to William Patton.

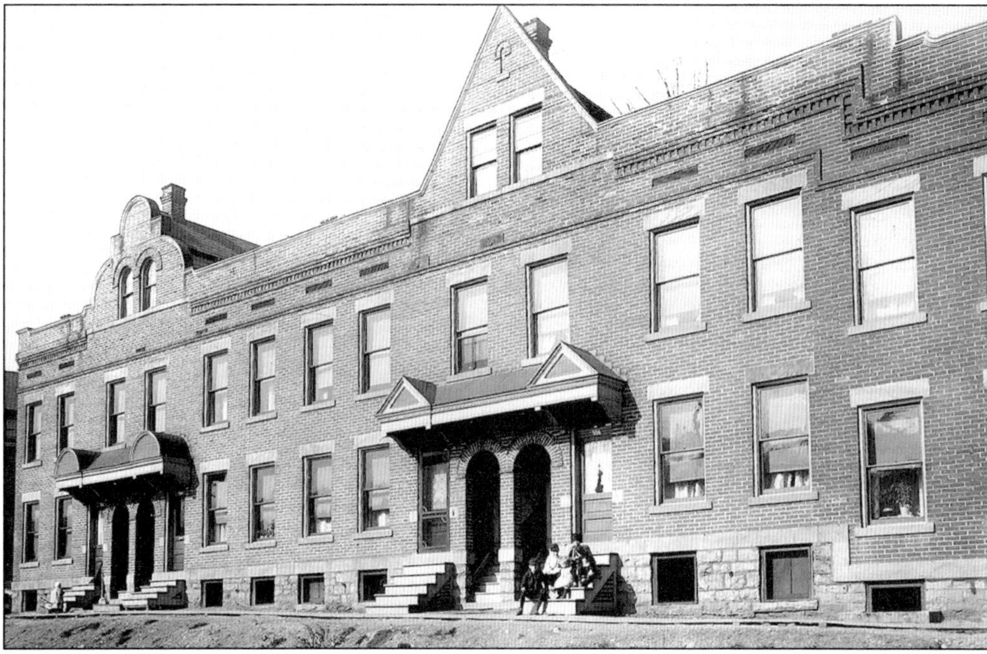

This photograph was taken in 1903 shortly after the company houses located on Middle Avenue, commonly called the "flats," were completed. Landscaping has not yet been done, but it appears that residents have already moved in. Three youngsters sit on the steps to one of four entrances shown in the center.

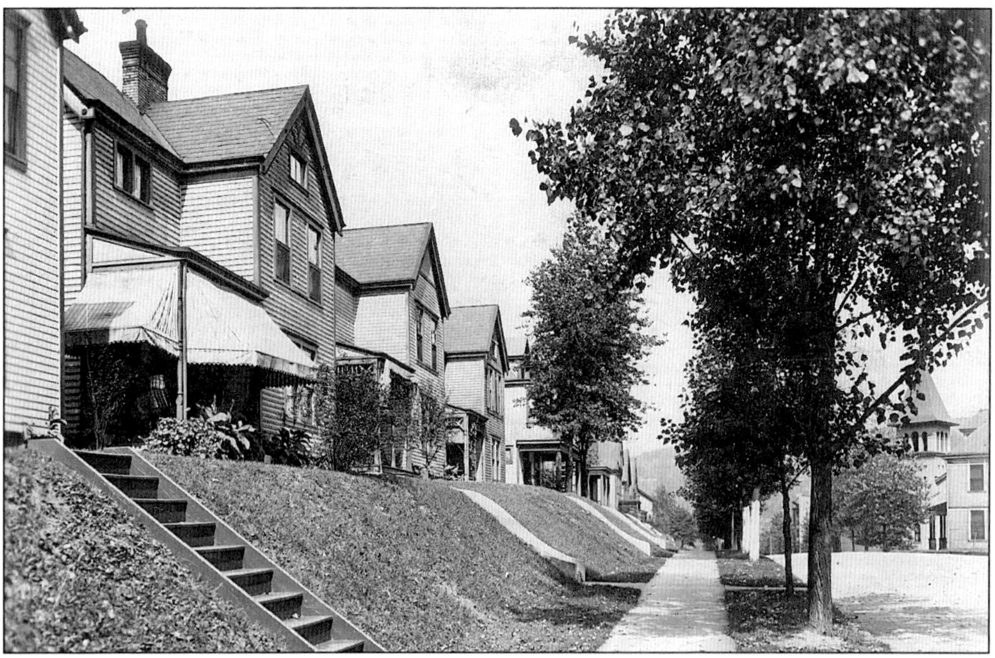

Shown in this photograph are some of the homes on Caldwell Avenue. On the right in the distance is the Christ Lutheran Church. The church, constructed in 1904, is located at the corner of Caldwell Avenue and Clara Street. This view, looking north, was taken in 1909.

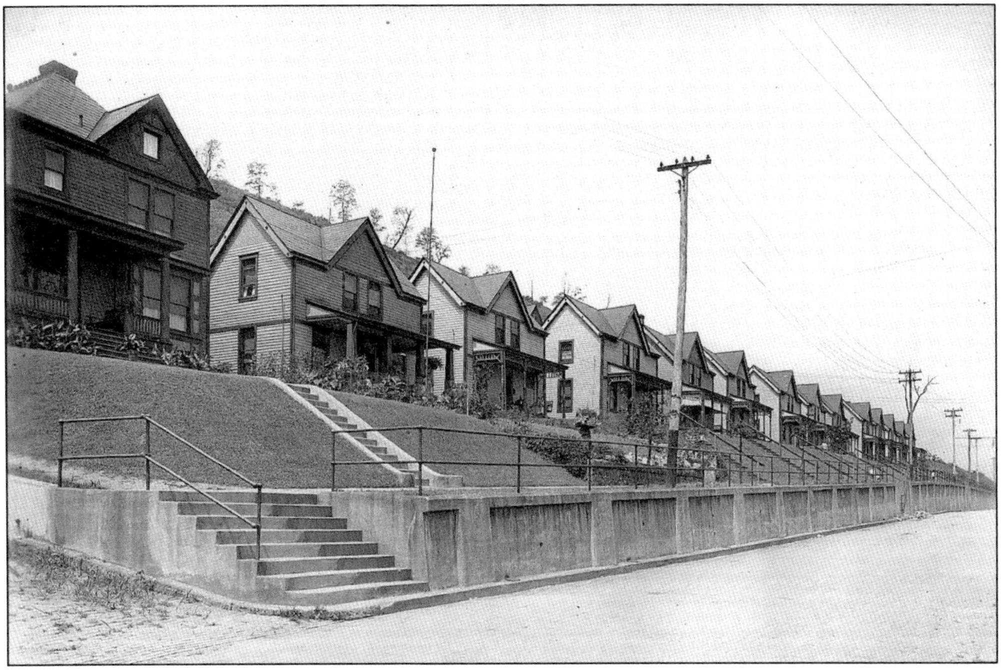

Sprague Street, shown c. 1914, is one of Wilmerding's original streets and first group of homes built. Notice the concrete retaining wall in front. With no convenient means of access from the rear, residents had to carry belongings up the front steps from the street.

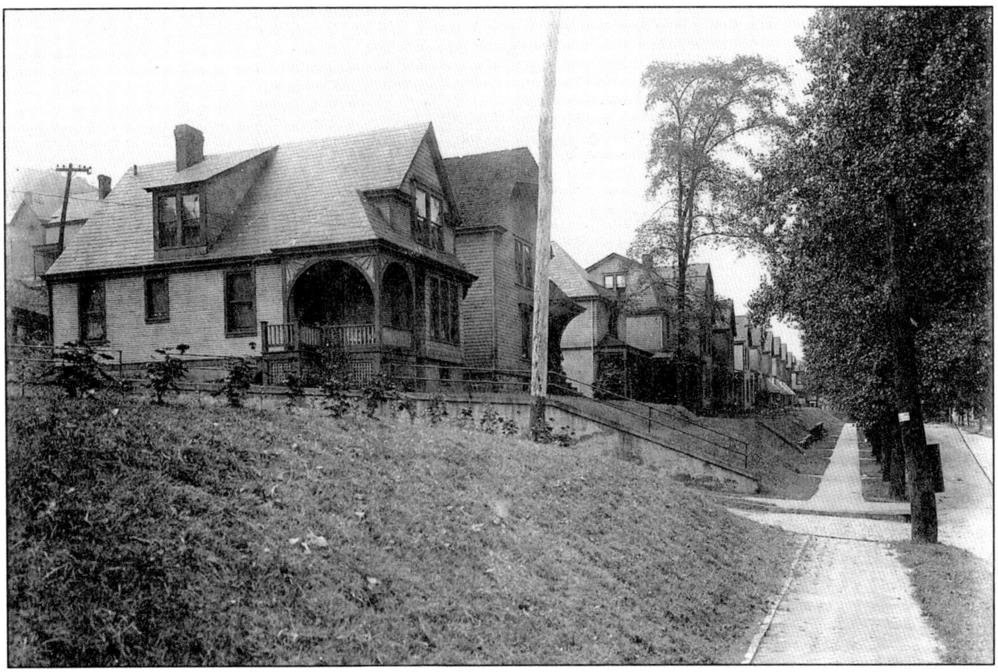

Shown c. 1912 are the company houses on Caldwell Avenue at the corner of Brown Street. Caldwell Avenue was generally tree-lined and beautiful in the summer. Another retaining wall can be seen below the first home shown. There is an alleyway behind this row of homes that serves as a rear entrance.

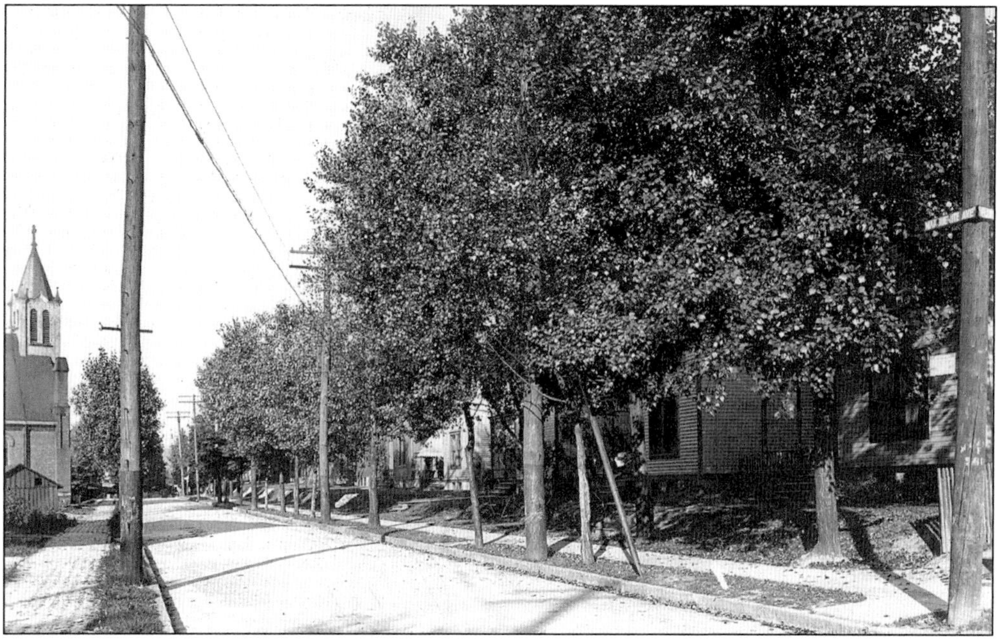

This 1912 view shows upper Marguerite Avenue at the corner of Florence Street. The old St. Aloysius Roman Catholic Church is on the left-hand side of the photograph. Some of the same men who had moved with George Westinghouse from his Pittsburgh plant formed the church in 1895. At the time, the congregation comprised 100 families.

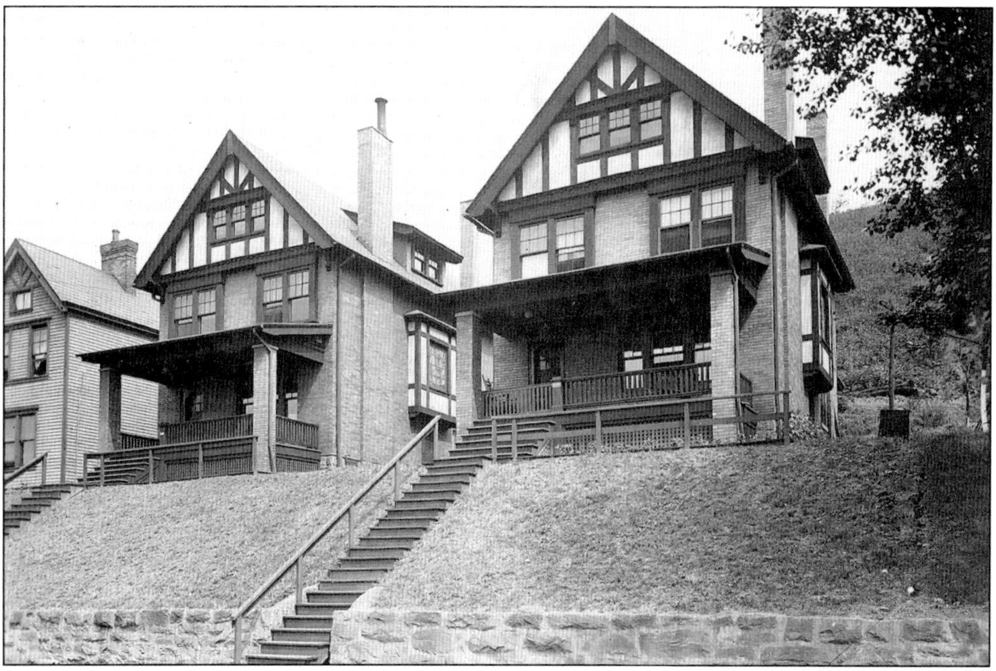

Taken in 1914, this photograph shows two brick Tudor-style homes situated on Welsh Avenue near the corner of Frank Street. An access alley out back made it easier for residents to enter the homes. Note, again, the stone retaining walls in the front of the property helping to hold back the hillside.

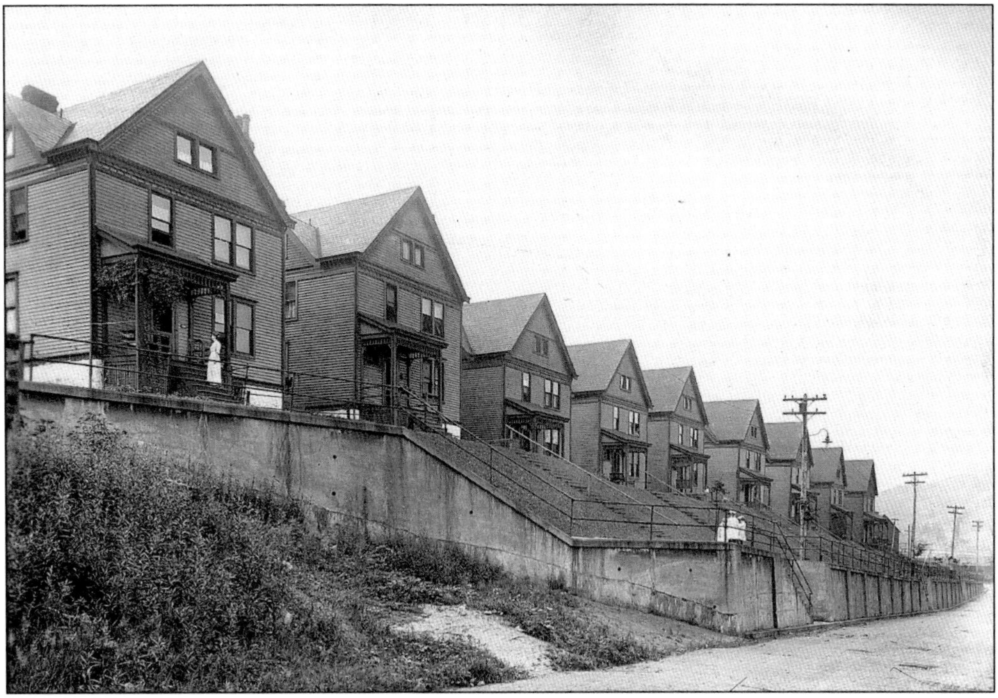

Card Avenue, pictured in 1914, was one of five streets where the first company homes in Wilmerding were built. The avenue was named after W.W. Card, the first man to permit George Westinghouse to equip a train with his new untested air brake system.

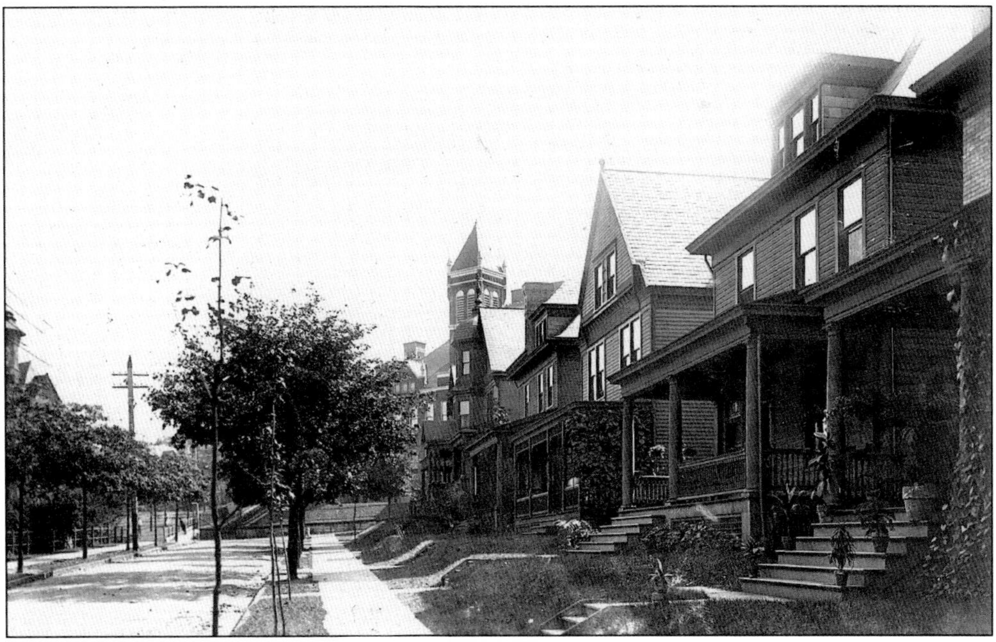

This view, from the post office's fifth location (the Patch Building) at the corner of Westinghouse Avenue and Annie Street, looks east toward the Horrocks School, showing homes along Annie Street. No buildings shown in this 1915 photograph exist today. Note the tree-lined sidewalks and relatively easy access to the front porches.

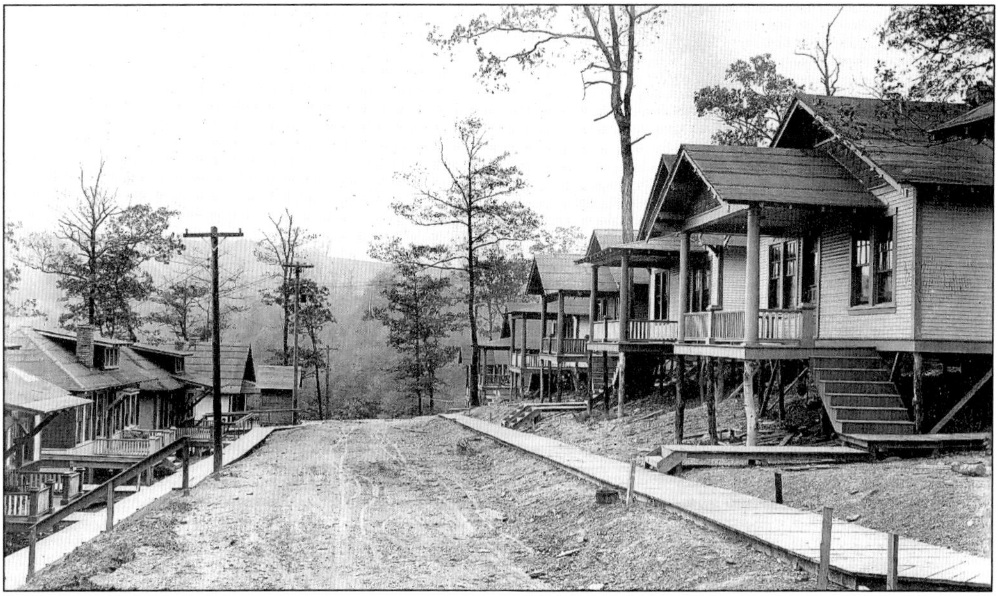

Boyd Hill was a section of Wilmerding inhabited by black residents. This photograph was taken shortly after construction was completed in 1918. The sidewalks are wood with no railings, and there are no foundations under the homes. Wood posts support each structure.

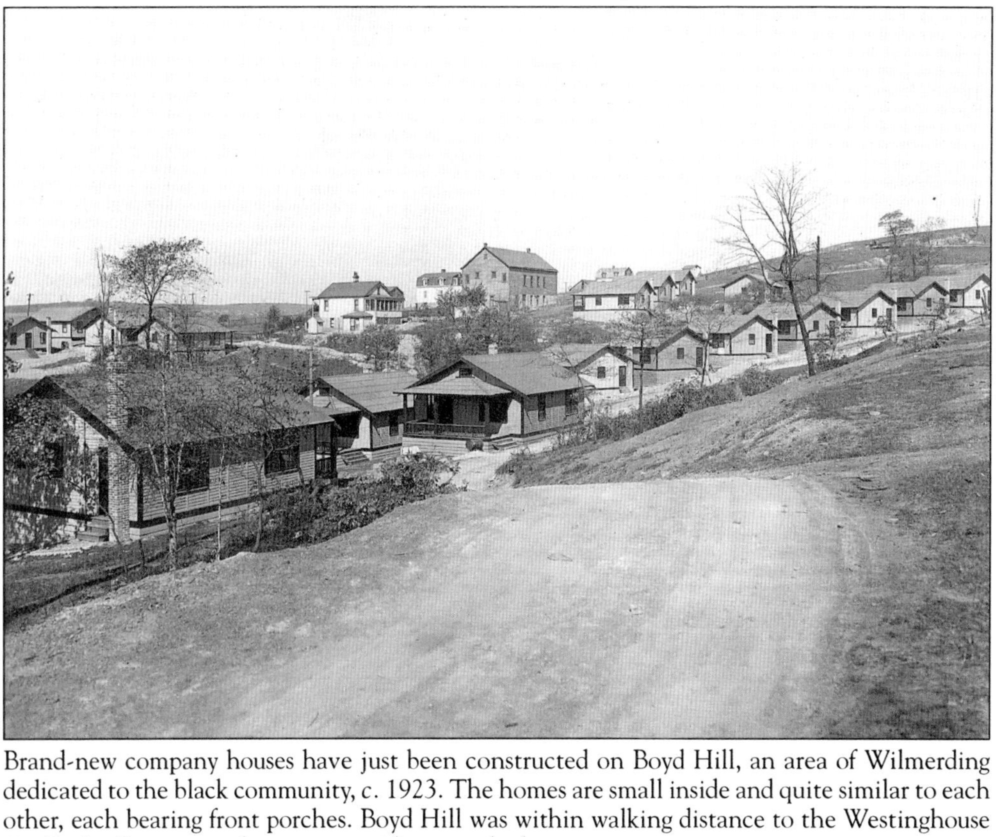

Brand-new company houses have just been constructed on Boyd Hill, an area of Wilmerding dedicated to the black community, *c.* 1923. The homes are small inside and quite similar to each other, each bearing front porches. Boyd Hill was within walking distance to the Westinghouse Air Brake Company, where most residents worked.

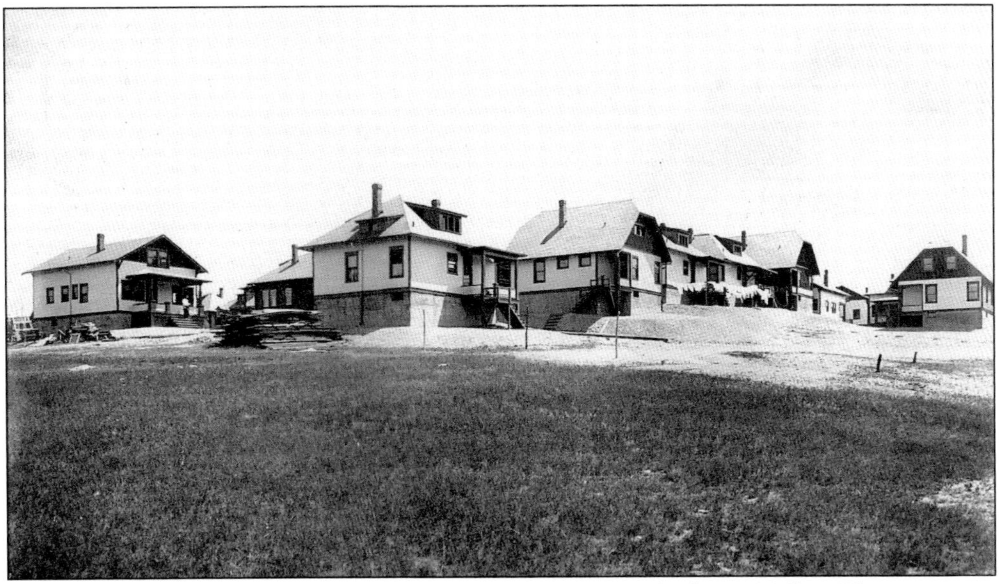

Looking north, this view shows a group of company houses built on Mellon Plan, a section of ground located just above the north side of Wilmerding. Landscaping is in place and most residents are settled. Notice at least three different rooflines. A man walks up the steps to his home on the left side of the photograph.

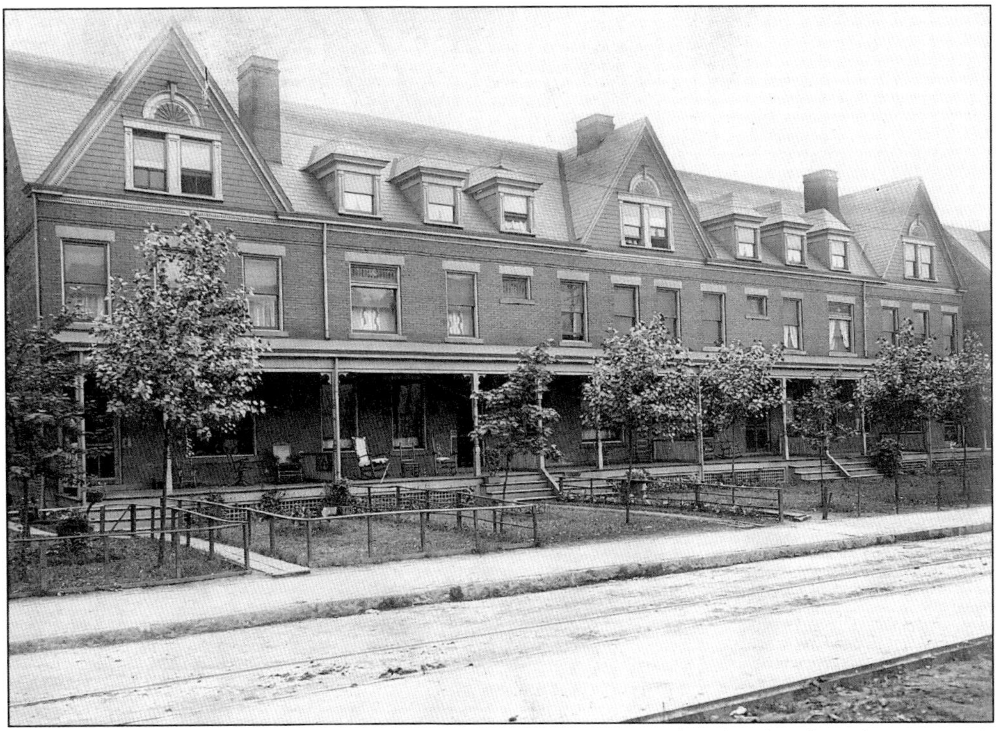

A six-family row house stands on Airbrake Avenue on the north side of Wilmerding in 1903. The homes face the Westinghouse Air Brake facility. Notice the young trees out front, a feature of many streets in the borough. Some of the lots have been fenced, but others have not. No one has yet placed a privacy partition between the porches.

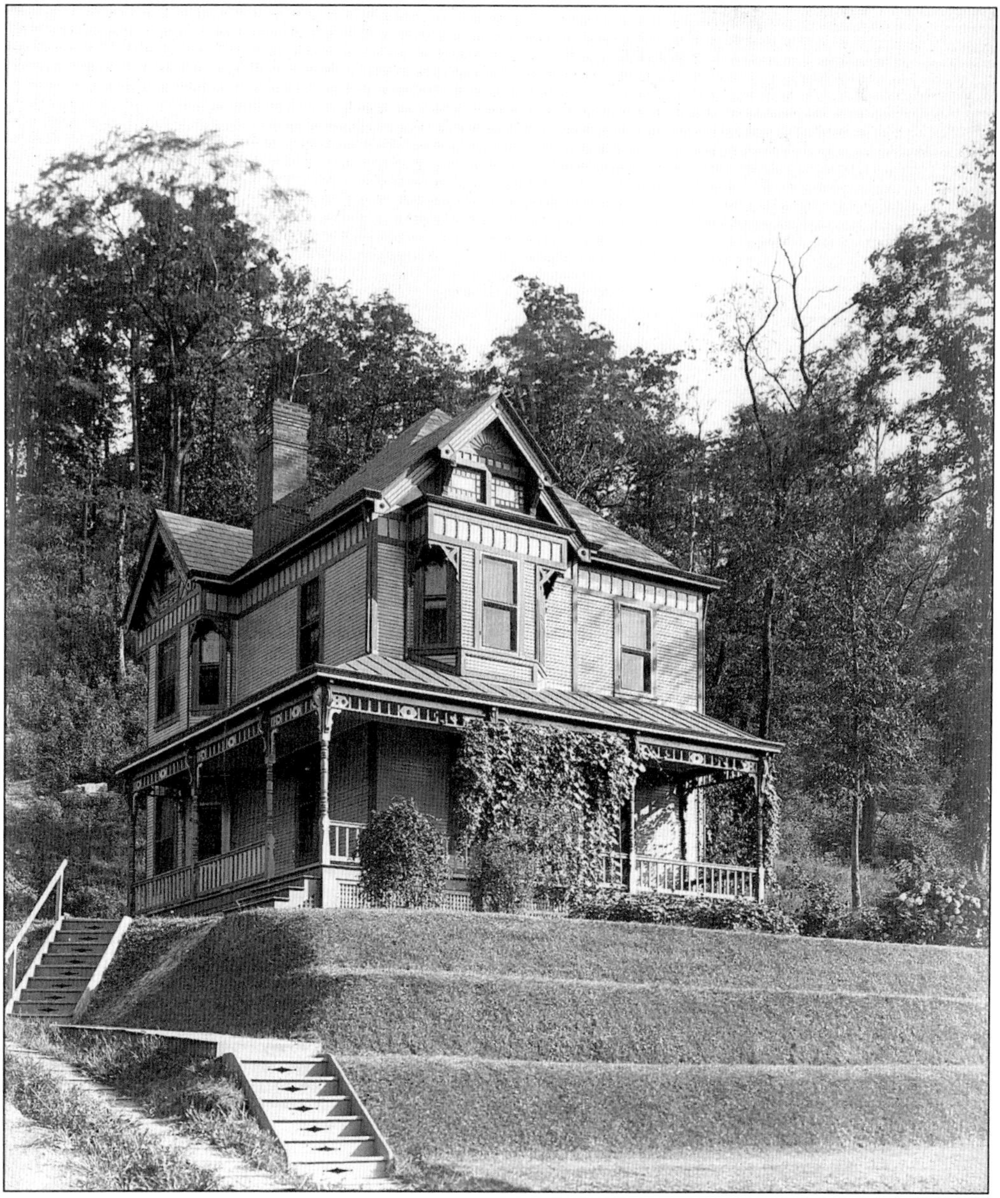

Mr. Sluthis owned this Victorian-style home at the time of this 1901 photograph. Notice the triple-terraced landscape as the front lawn gradually reaches the sidewalk. Since the steep hillsides of Wilmerding presented a physical challenge for property owners, lawn maintenance and easy home access were difficult. Ascending a long series of steps before reaching the front porch is a requirement of many homes in Wilmerding. Retaining walls help with the issue of lawn maintenance because slopes fall less quickly and ground shifts less easily if one is used. In this photograph, notice the wraparound front porch with spindled porch posts and wooden handrails. Located at the intersection of Welsh Avenue and Frank Street, this turn-of-the-century Victorian is perfectly placed. Welsh Avenue is named for T.W. Welsh, the first burgess of Wilmerding. Frank Street is named for the nephew of George Westinghouse Jr., Frank Moore, who was the son of George's older sister Catherine Westinghouse Moore.

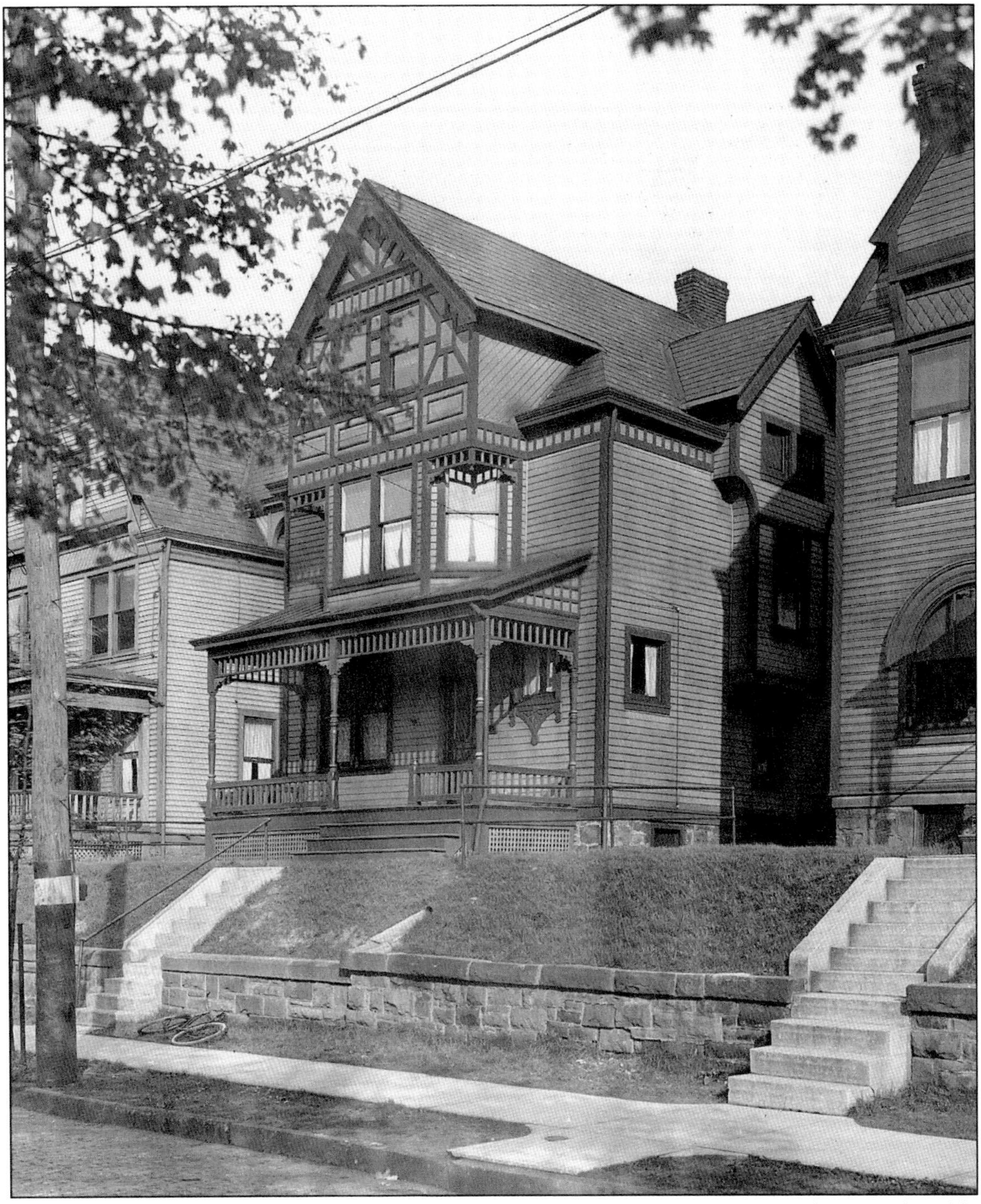

The Type A-5 company house located at 325 Marguerite Avenue was a more than comfortable residence for Westinghouse Air Brake Company employees. The first floor included the entry hall and parlor with fireplace, kitchen with pantry, and adjoining dining room with fireplace. All hearths were of polished flagstone and set with firebrick for safety. Four bedrooms were on the second floor, and each was adequately sized. A bathroom located at the end of the central hallway was furnished with a polished copper bathtub, washstand, and water closet with flushing cistern. The general appearance of the home was neat, and it was desirably located. The lot was 40 feet wide by 200 feet deep. P.W. Morgan, a close neighbor, at 321 Marguerite Avenue, acquired the first telephone in Wilmerding. The Horrocks School, on the opposite side of tree-lined Marguerite Avenue, provided a solid public school education for the children of the borough.

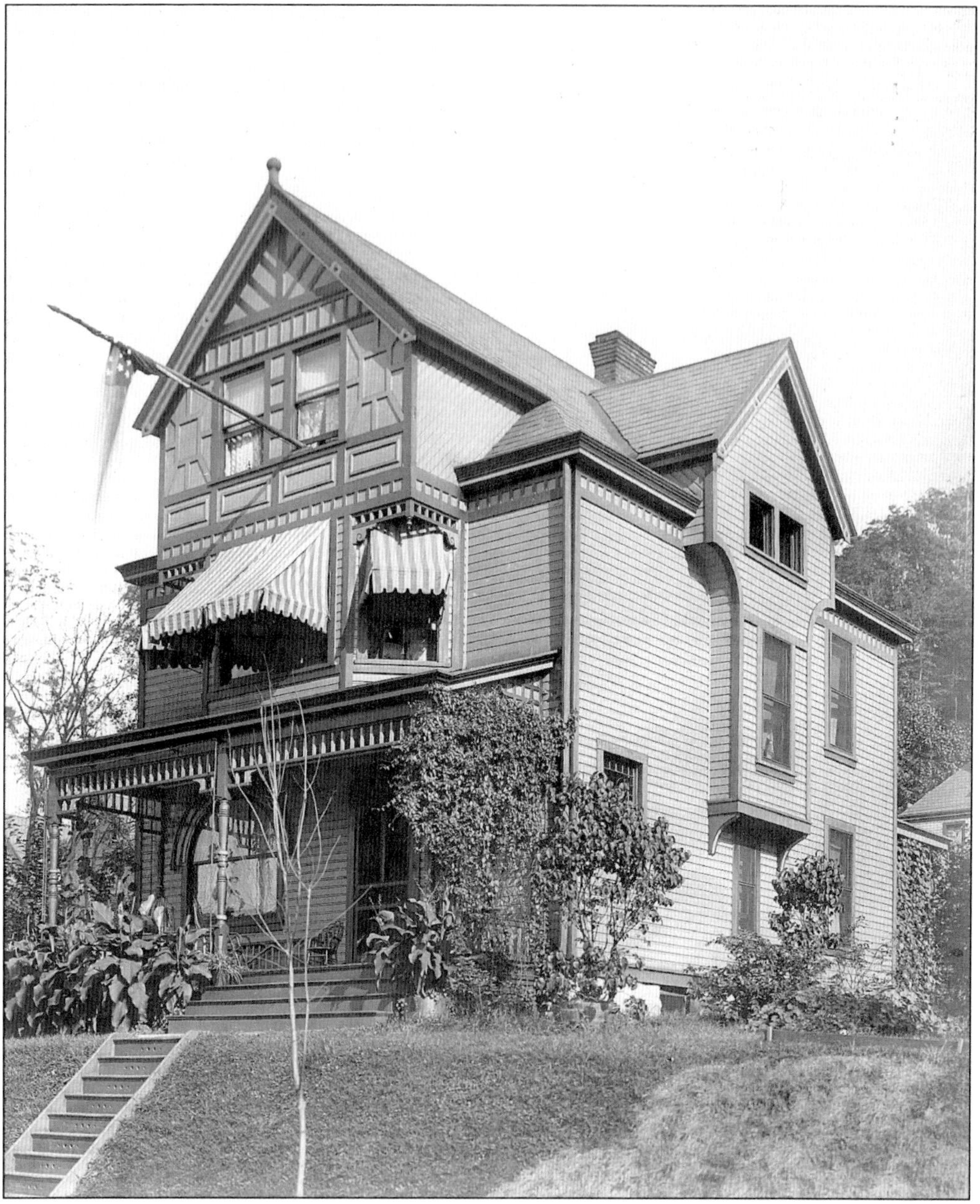

Homes on Marguerite Avenue were generally reserved for upper management of the Westinghouse Air Brake Company. H.H Welsh lived in this particular Type A-3 house located on Marguerite Avenue. H.H. Welsh was the burgess of Wilmerding from 1897 to 1899. At the time of this 1901 photograph, B.F. Welsh was the elected burgess. During the early years, Wilmerding elected a burgess and six council members to govern the small town. These seven members of council then appointed a secretary, treasurer, engineer, solicitor, and street commissioner. Town size had increased rapidly from a population of roughly 1,000 in 1890 to a population of 4,179 in 1900. Houses on Marguerite were occupied quickly. Marguerite is named after the wife of George Westinghouse Jr. Marguerite Erskine Walker Westinghouse never spent much time in Wilmerding, but the street that bears her name is quite charming.

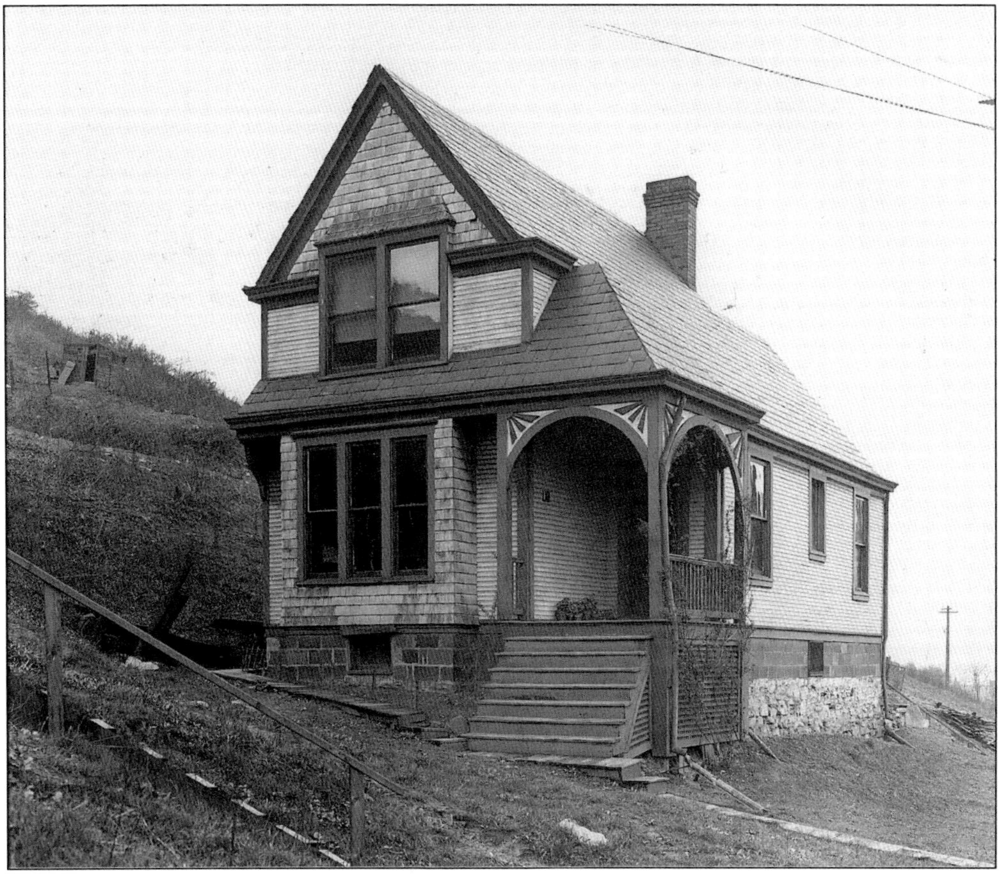

Unskilled laborers from the Westinghouse Air Brake Company may have lived in this Type J house. To the rear, a steep hill rises. On top of the hill sits a small shed. Amenities appear to be few. Notice the landscape, and the exterior paint is ragged. Perhaps a fix-up project looms near. Potted flowering plants are on the front porch ready for planting. Spring must be coming soon to this 704 George Street address. The 1900 U.S. Census boasts machinists, office clerks, boiler foreman, electricians, assistant superintendents, painters, foundry workers, shop laborers, brass finishers, core makers, carpenters, iron molders, and many others all lived in Wilmerding. A need to develop more property for housing definitely existed.

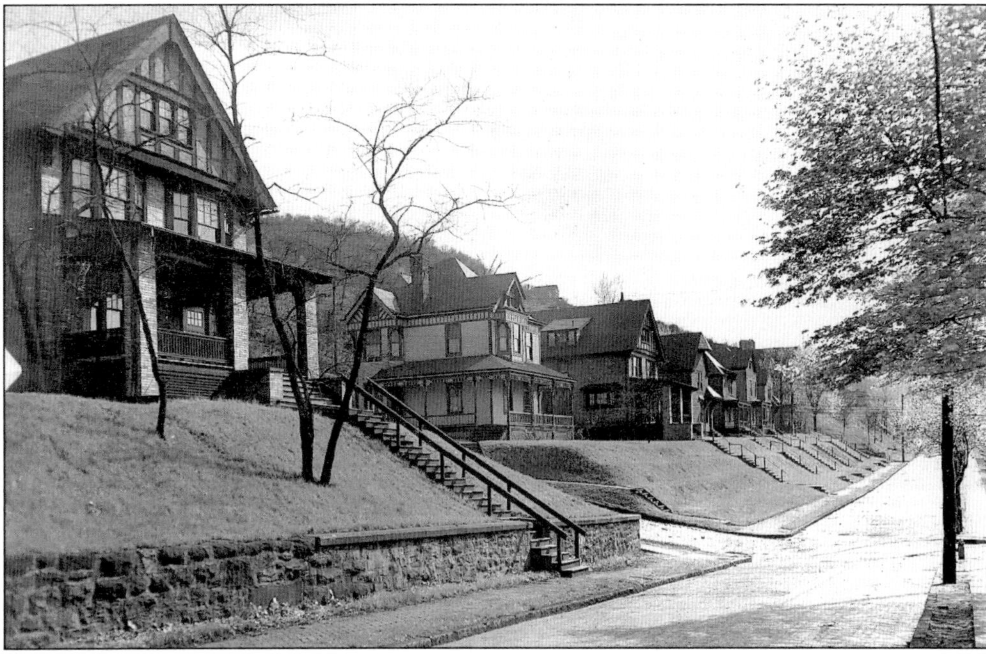

Shown is a view looking south on Welsh Avenue near the intersection of Frank Street. Turn right on Frank Street, and at the bottom of the hill is the Westinghouse Air Brake general office building. Turn left and go up to an alley, which accesses the homes from behind. There is parking on both sides of the street, but where are the cars?

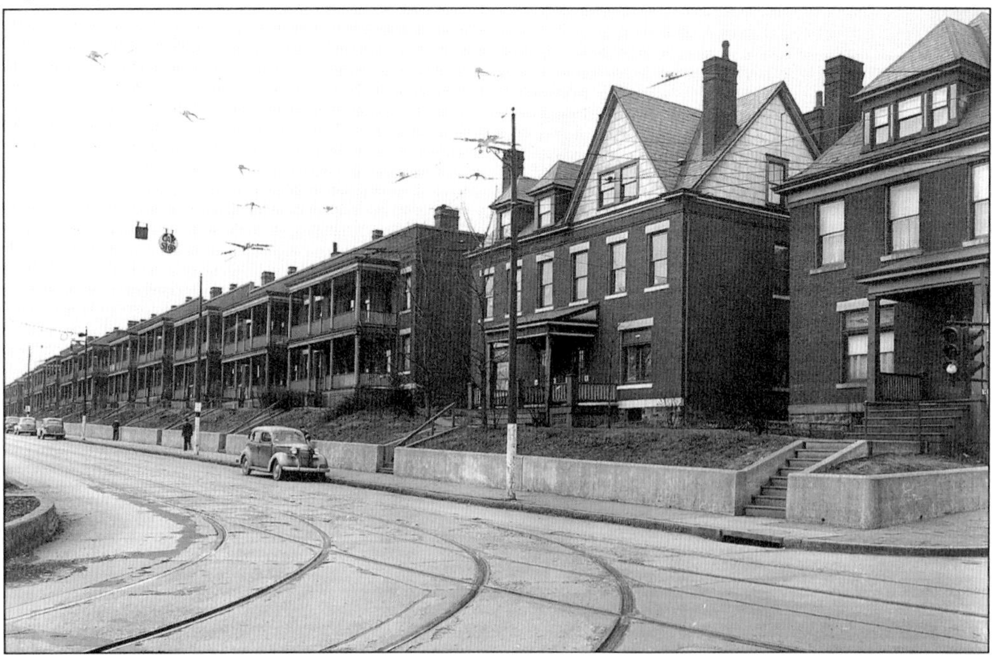

Here is another view of the "flats" on Middle Avenue, east of the viaduct, in 1940. This was the junction for the trolley line. The tracks to the right went to Pitcairn, and those to the lower left went over the viaduct and into downtown Wilmerding. Note the familiar retaining walls in front of the homes.

Five

GETTING AROUND

Transportation in and around Wilmerding posed no problem for the fledgling community. One of the reasons that George Westinghouse had chosen the location where he built his manufacturing plant was because the Pennsylvania Railroad ran its mainline directly through it. Since a good number of trains ran east and west at short intervals, a railroad station and a freight station were early priorities. The first railroad station was at the end of Herman Avenue; the second was at Bridge and Station Streets, where steps led from the station platform to and from the building. The third and last location was at Station Street and Westinghouse Avenue. To facilitate more local travel, the McKeesport and Wilmerding Railways Company had a streetcar line between McKeesport and Wilmerding; the Ardmore trolley (No. 87) ran from Pittsburgh to Wilmerding. In later years, the McKeesport Transit Company operated buses between Wilmerding and Wall every 30 minutes. The Pittsburgh Motor Coach Company operated buses between Wilmerding and McKeesport every 20 minutes.

Not long after George Westinghouse had formed the Westinghouse Electric & Manufacturing Company in 1886, he inaugurated the Westinghouse Interworks Railway. The railway operated from the Westinghouse Electric & Manufacturing plant up the valley through Wilmerding, Wall, and on into Trafford. The railway lasted into the 1960s.

However, the most prevalent source of transportation was by foot. Since most employees lived in the borough, they could easily walk to and from their jobs.

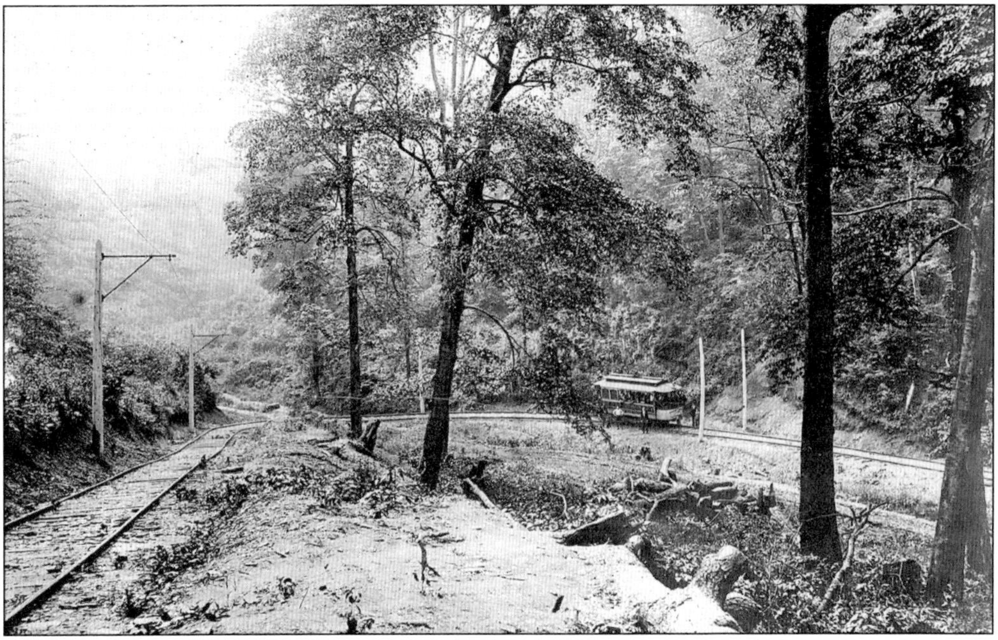

The first streetcar line in the borough was built by the McKeesport and Wilmerding Railways Company in 1893. The car line began at the intersection of Station Street and Marguerite Avenue and then ran across Station Street and south up Westinghouse Avenue to the Concourse in the area of the old Wilmerding Ball Field. From there, it turned left, winding up the hill to East McKeesport and ultimately on into McKeesport.

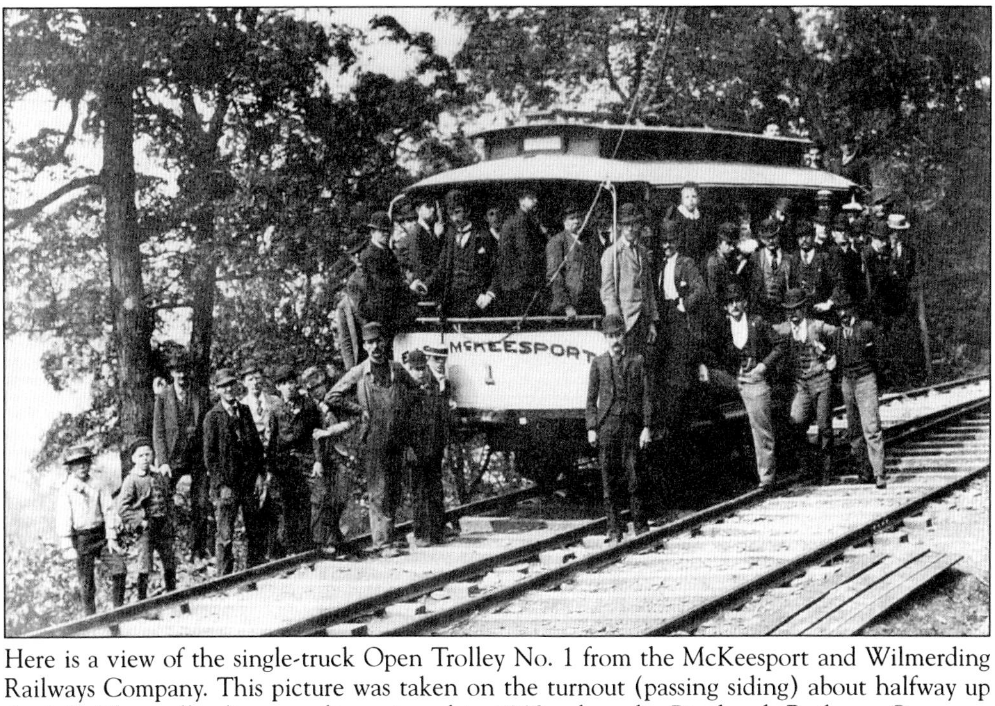

Here is a view of the single-truck Open Trolley No. 1 from the McKeesport and Wilmerding Railways Company. This picture was taken on the turnout (passing siding) about halfway up the hill. The trolley line was discontinued in 1903, when the Pittsburgh Railways Company entered Wilmerding over the completed viaduct.

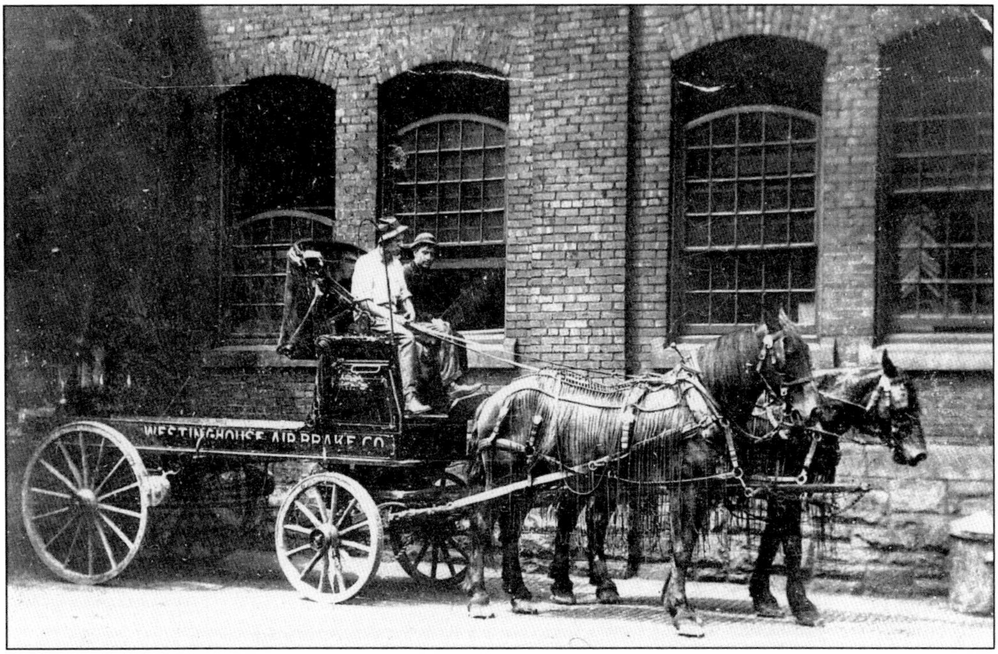

Driver Henry Linhart and his assistant move freight around the Westinghouse Air Brake plant c. 1908. "Westinghouse Air Brake Co." is seen clearly painted on the side of the wagon. Henry is in shirt sleeves, so it may be the summer of 1908. Henry later became the personal chauffeur to George Westinghouse Jr.

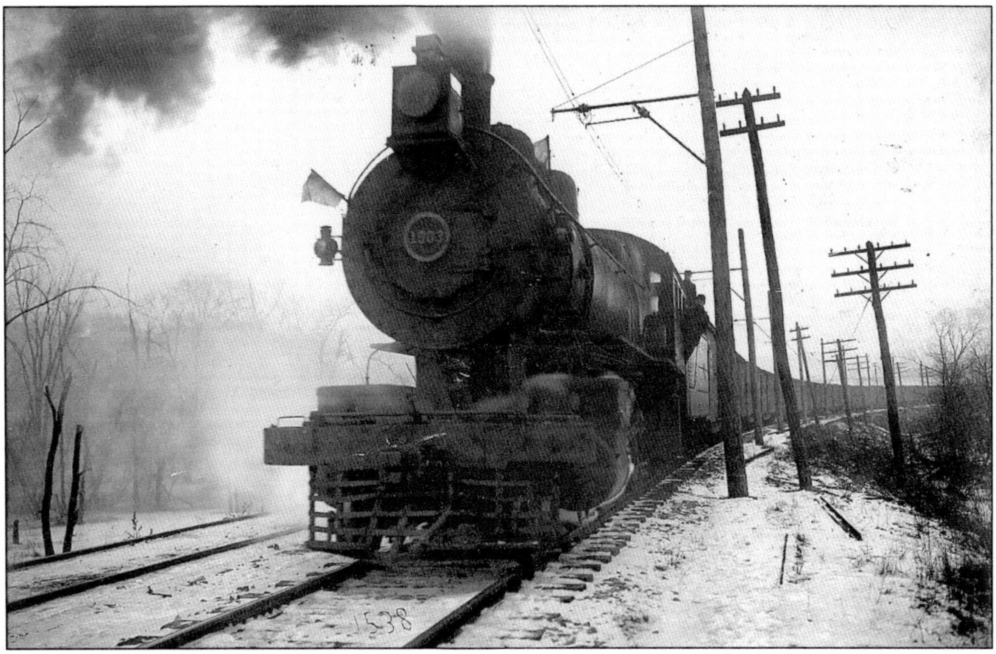

Here comes Pennsylvania Railroad Locomotive No. 1903 pulling a train of heavy freight cars on the Westinghouse Interworks Railway in February 1905. The exact location of this wintry scene is not known. Do you see the engineer leaning out of his cab and the brakeman standing on a car above him?

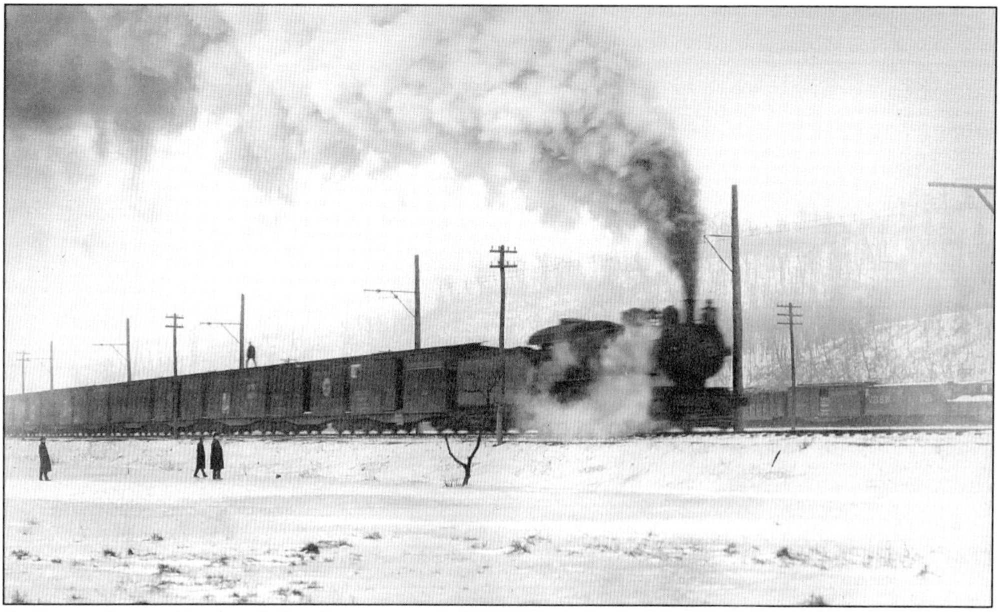

A Pennsylvania Railroad freight train on the Westinghouse Interworks Railway approaches Turtle Creek in February 1905. Note the catenary (overhead wires) used for testing Westinghouse Electric & Manufacturing Company electric locomotives. Also, look at the brakemen riding astride on the top of a freight car. Several onlookers stand to the side.

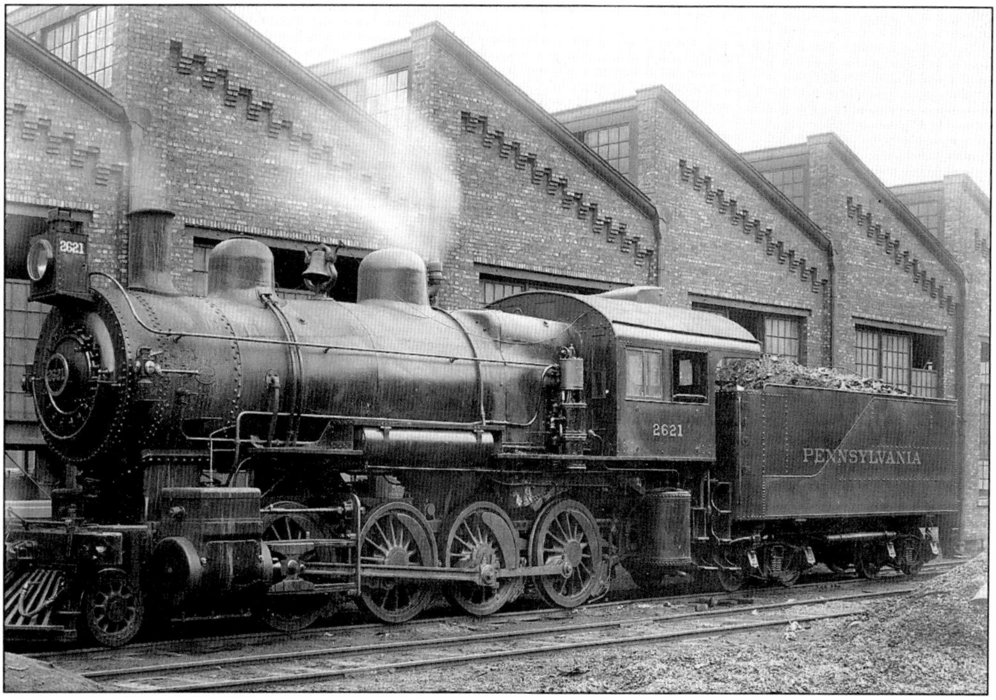

Pennsylvania Railroad Locomotive No. 2621 sits idle in the Westinghouse Air Brake plant yard. This photograph was taken in 1905 while the engine was stopped next to the Sawtooth Building, one of the first Westinghouse Air Brake buildings erected west of the viaduct. Coal brims over in the tender.

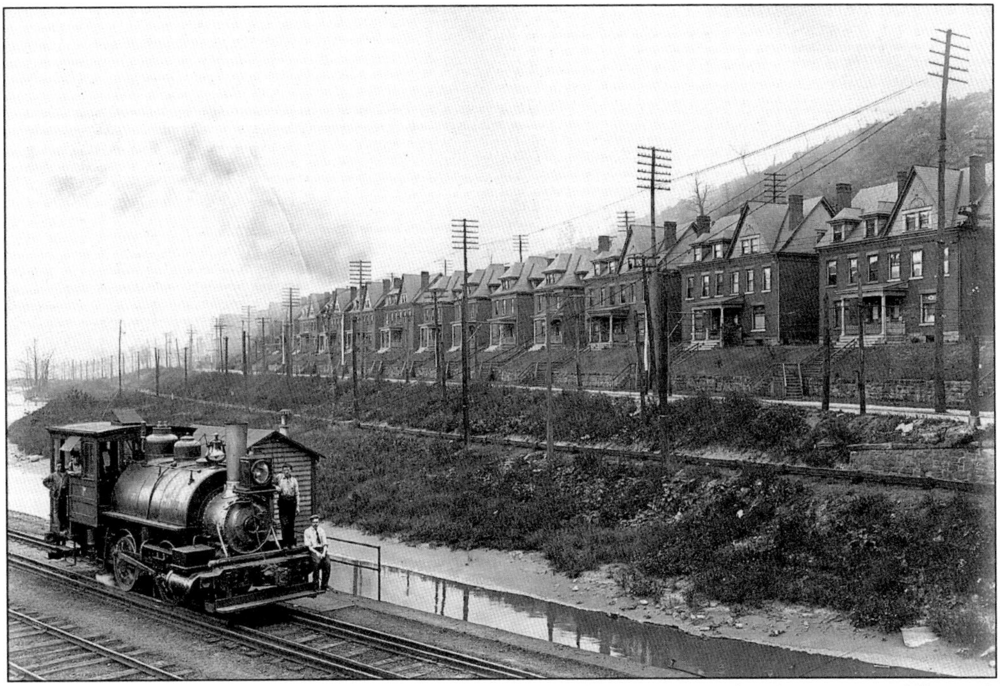

This 1909 view, looking west, shows an early Westinghouse Air Brake Company saddle tank locomotive nearing the weighing scales located along Turtle Creek. The company houses in this photograph were, and still are, located on Airbrake Avenue. The Interworks Railway can be seen just below Airbrake Avenue. Who is the man wearing the tie?

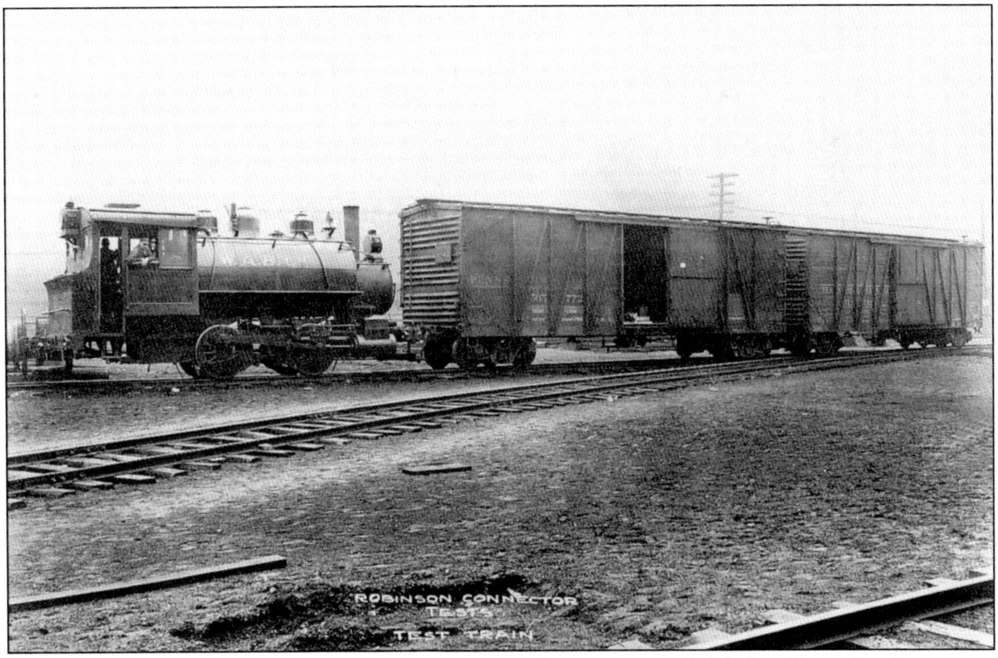

Westinghouse Air Brake Company's Locomotive No. 1 sits coupled behind two freight cars at the far west end of the plant. Locomotive No. 1 was used to move freight around the plant and yard. The engineer and fireman seem to be in no particular hurry on this day in 1930.

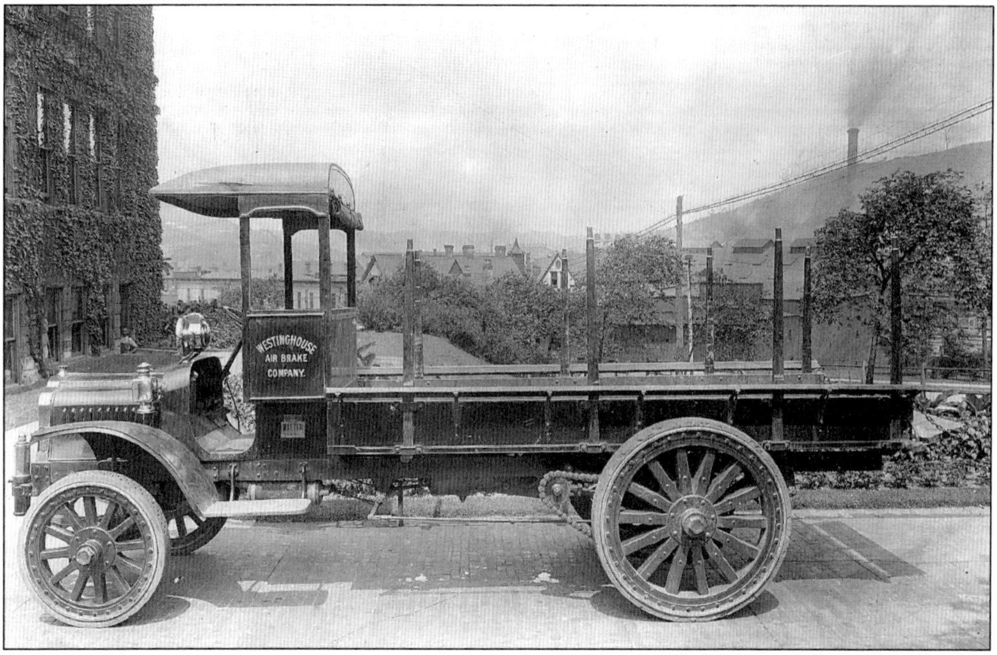

Westinghouse Air Brake Company's Walter Truck sits silently on a brick street near the general office building *c.* 1912. The Walter Truck was one of the first motorized trucks used by the Air Brake Company. Smoke pours from a smokestack seen in the upper right-hand corner.

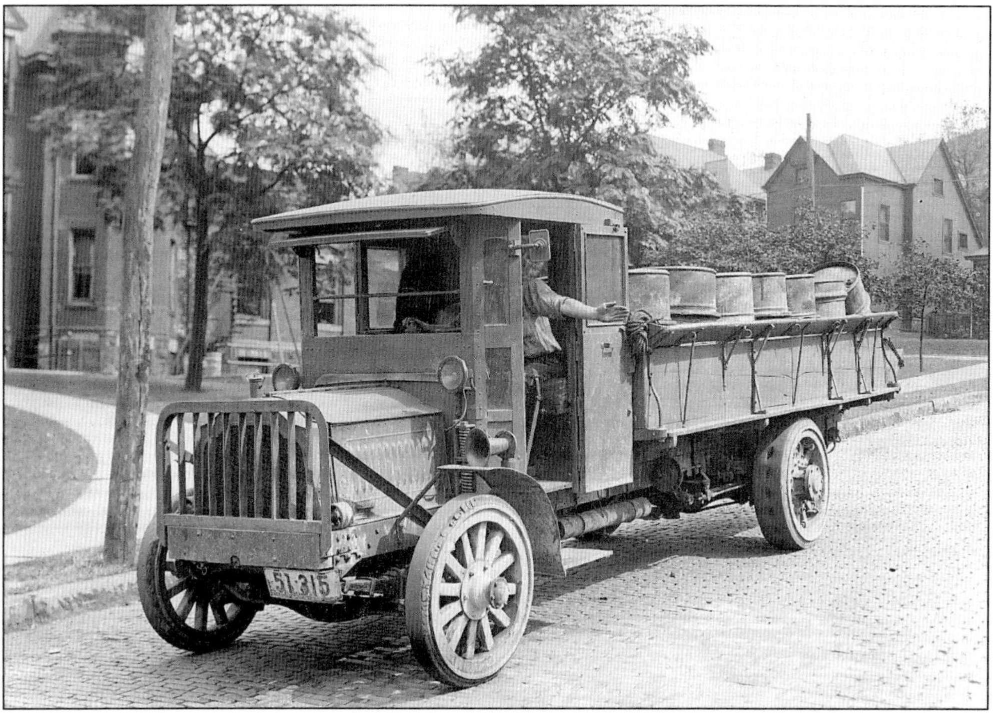

Heading nowhere, an early Westinghouse Air Brake Company truck, a Packard, rolls along Bluff Street near the Wilmerding YMCA. The driver of the truck is attempting to signal others of his intention to either turn or stop. Notice the steel drums in the back of the truck.

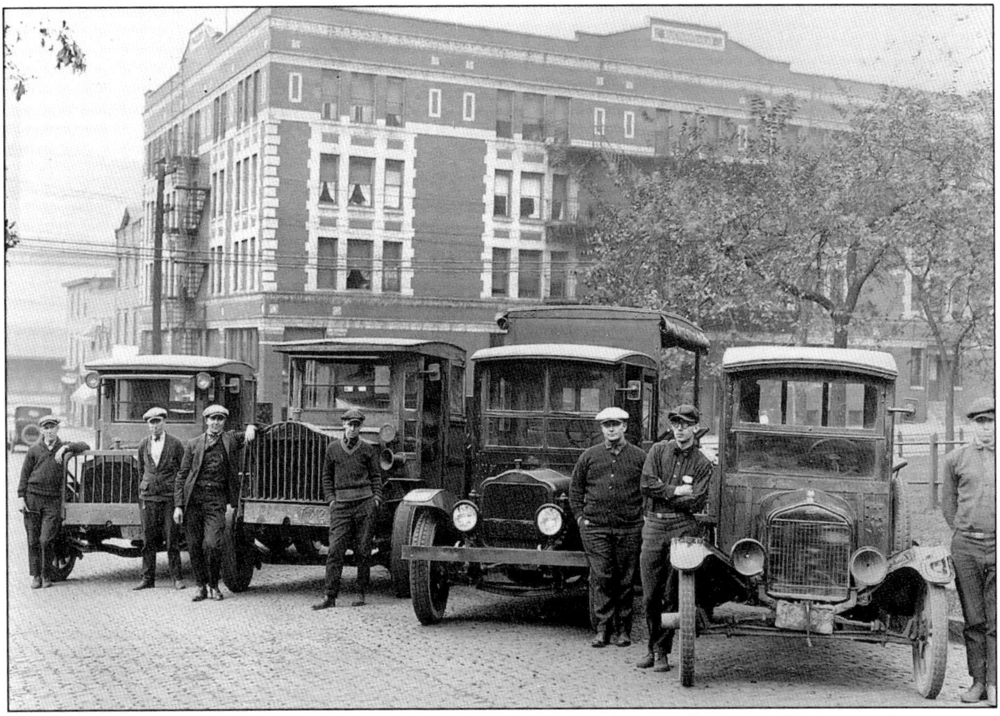

A fleet of Westinghouse Air Brake Company trucks has parked on Herman Avenue in Wilmerding. The men in the photograph are, from left to right, Ray Stewart, Henry Linhart, Steve Kazusky, Sam H. Smith, Richard Wise, Frank Hunter, and Moffet Maxwell. The building in the background is the Faller Building.

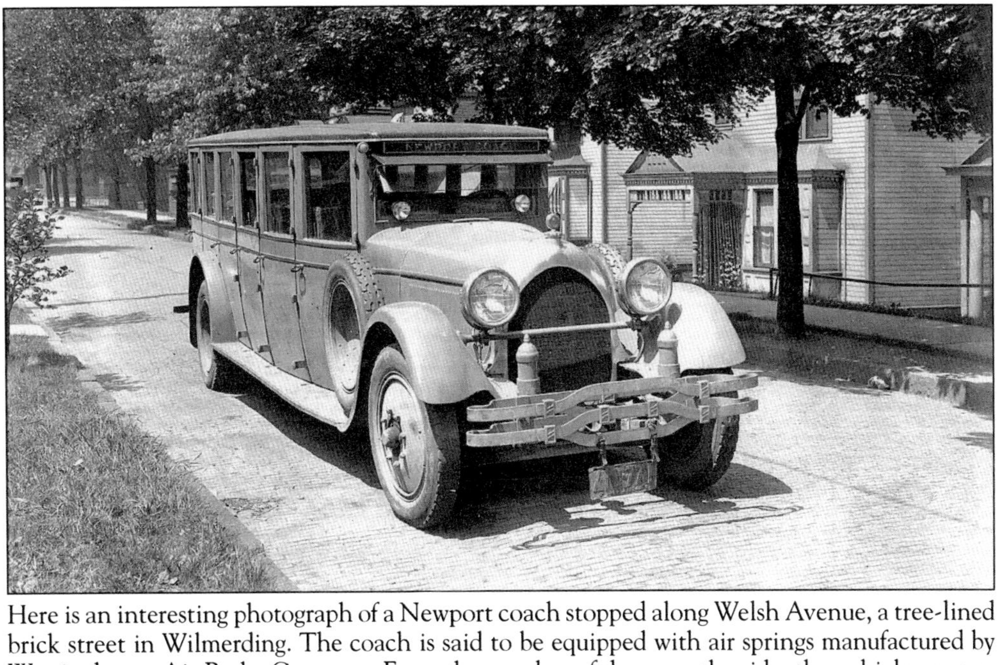

Here is an interesting photograph of a Newport coach stopped along Welsh Avenue, a tree-lined brick street in Wilmerding. The coach is said to be equipped with air springs manufactured by Westinghouse Air Brake Company. From the number of doors on the side, the vehicle appears to have served as an early bus.

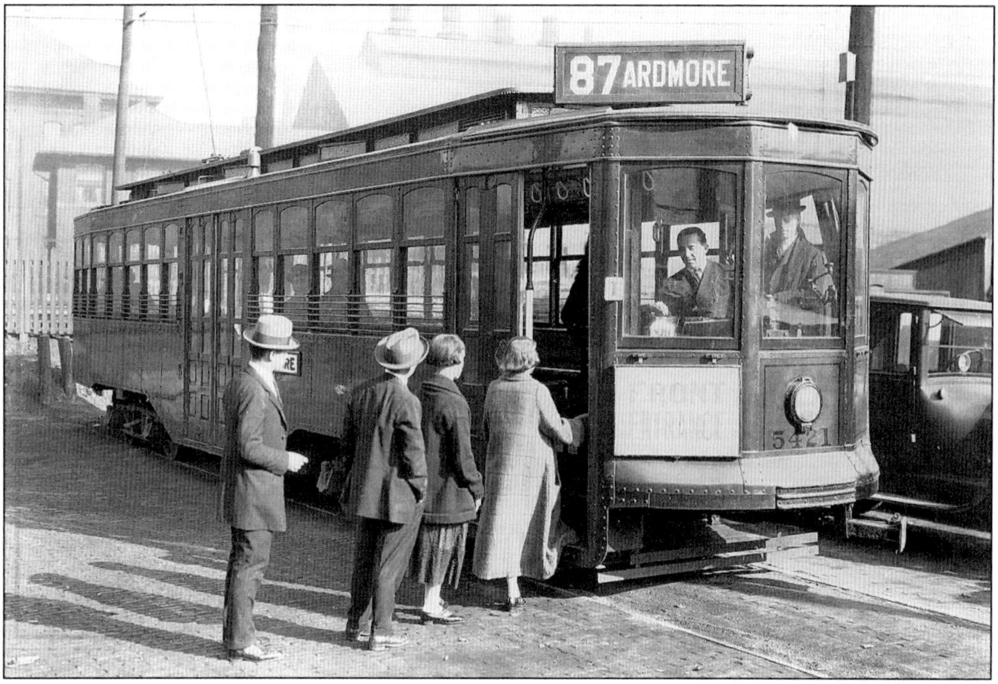

On a clear day sometime in 1924, passengers board Pittsburgh Railways Trolley No. 5421 at the front entrance to the Westinghouse Air Brake plant in Wilmerding. The trolley line to Wilmerding was known as 87 Ardmore. If you wanted to go to Pittsburgh, this was the trolley to take.

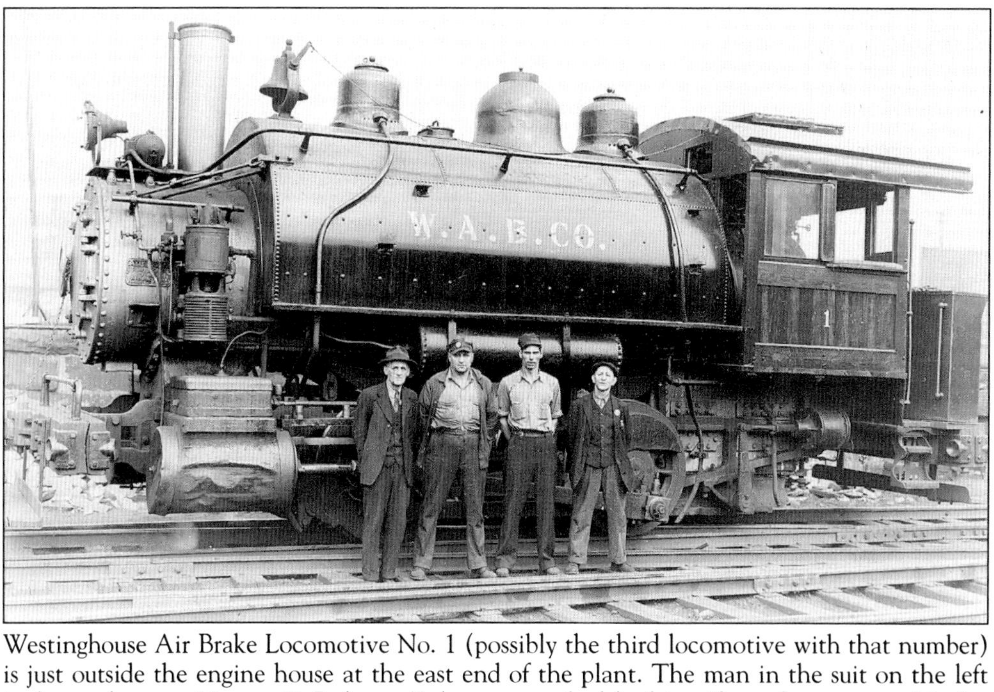

Westinghouse Air Brake Locomotive No. 1 (possibly the third locomotive with that number) is just outside the engine house at the east end of the plant. The man in the suit on the left is the yardmaster, Homer C. Roberts. Roberts was asked by his wife to dress up on this day for the picture.

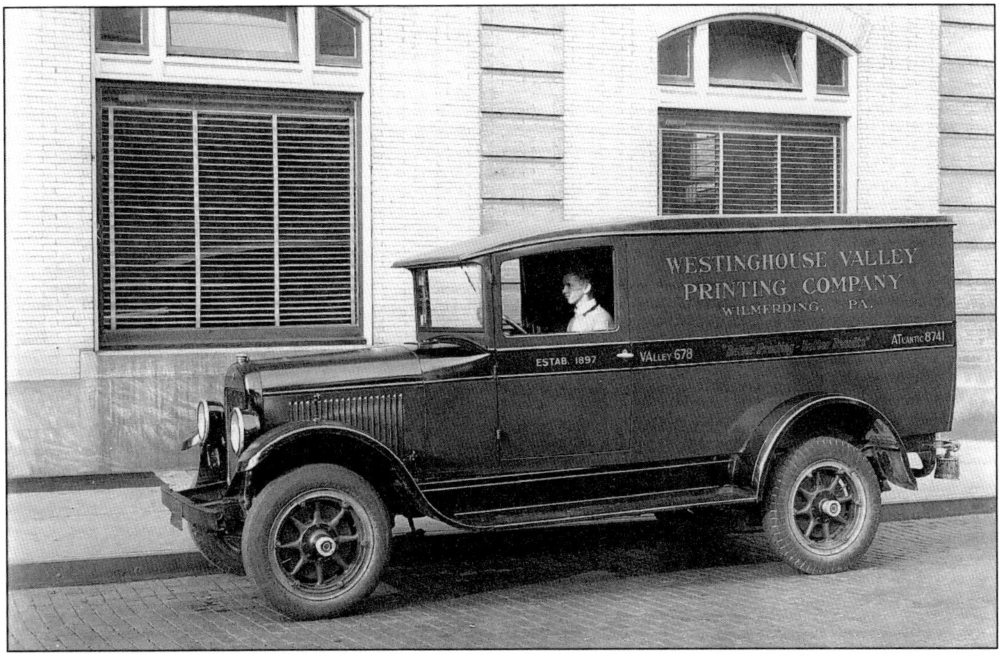

Parked in front of the General Office Annex on Commerce Street is a delivery truck for the Westinghouse Valley Printing Company. Details on the side of the truck tell that the printing company was founded in 1897. The local phone number is also given. The street, sidewalk, and building look exceptionally clean.

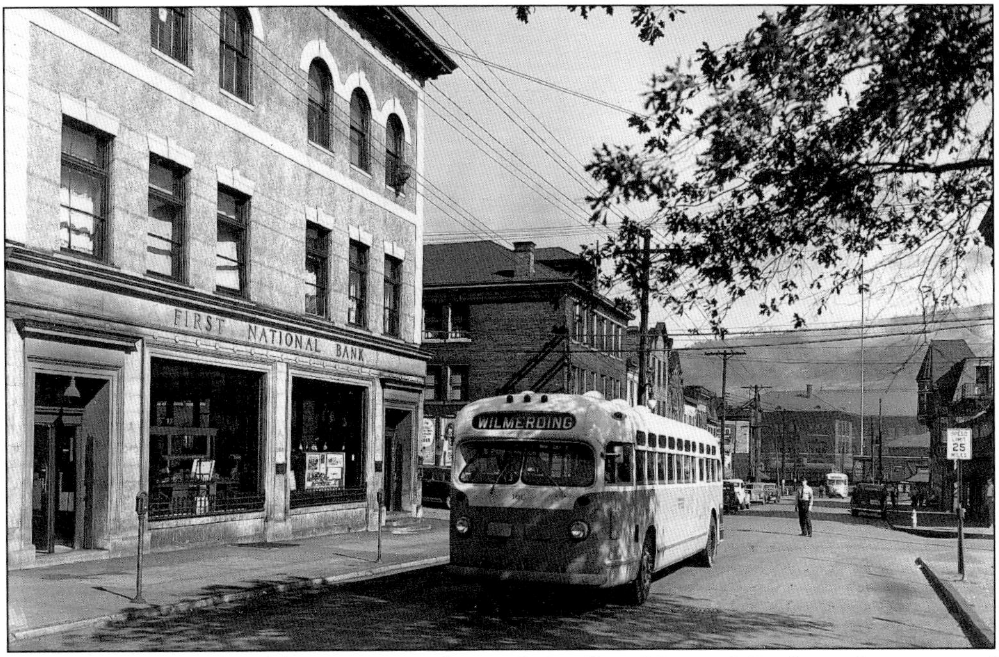

Traveling south, a local bus passes in front of the First National Bank at the corner of Commerce Street and Westinghouse Avenue in Wilmerding. A Pittsburgh Railways Company trolley can be seen in the distance at the entrance to the Westinghouse Air Brake plant. The photograph was taken in the late 1940s.

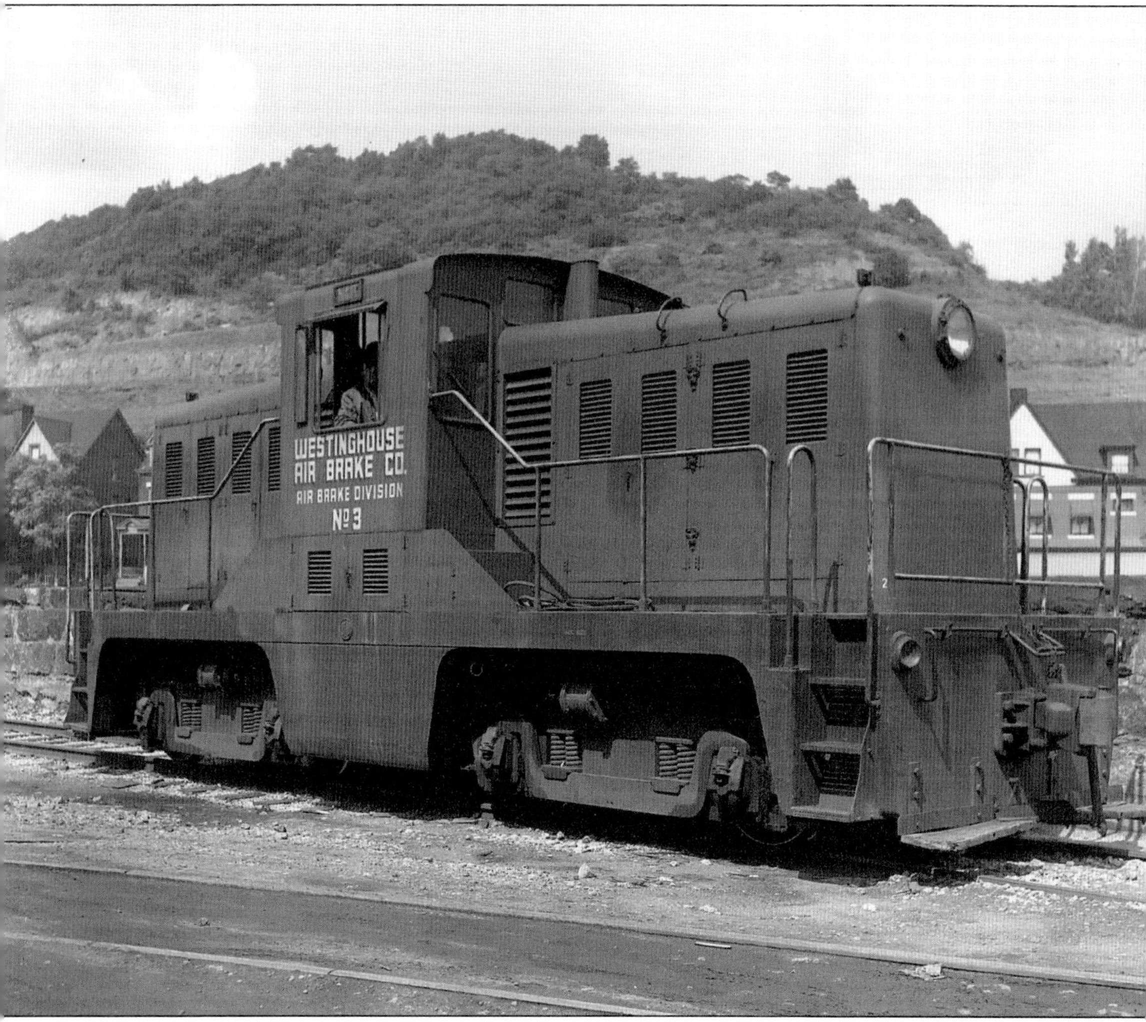

The engineer of Diesel No. 3 stops to have his picture taken on one of the plant's inside tracks. This diesel locomotive was one of two operated by the Westinghouse Air Brake Company in the 1960s. The diesel locomotive replaced the steam engine in plant operations. Behind the locomotive, notice the retaining walls, so common in Wilmerding. Those unfamiliar with the borough can surely gain insight into its terrain by observing the steep hills seen directly above the engine. Imagine building homes on these hills. When George Westinghouse came to this area, he saw the same thing but was not daunted. Many Wilmerding homes are built into the hillside. No one seems to mind because when diesel locomotives pass through the valley, the wonderful sounds of the railroad echo.

Six

Social Activities and Recreation

The expression "All work and no play makes Jack a dull boy" left an impression on the Westinghouse Air Brake Company and Wilmerding's planners. The two YMCAs (Marguerite Avenue and Airbrake Avenue) provided ample opportunity for sports and recreation. Baseball, track, tennis and basketball were the most popular sports. When the borough's baseball team disbanded in 1915, the Westinghouse Air Brake Company took it over. They proved to be champions, winning the Western Pennsylvania League pennant in 1918. YMCA basketball teams prevailed from 1902 until the late 1930s. The YMCA teams easily garnered one championship after another. Track meets were held at the Wilmerding Field (the concourse) at the bottom of Ice Plant Hill. In the early 1900s, tennis was also a YMCA favorite. The tennis court was located at the corner of Westinghouse Avenue and Florence Street.

Summertime brought increased bicycle use along with bus excursions to picnic areas and amusement parks. Children especially liked to visit such parks as Idlewild in faraway Ligonier. The young ladies of the YMCA's Industrial Girls Club ventured on one occasion to Washington, D.C.

Entertainment was not overlooked. In 1906, the first movie theater opened on Station Street. John Abrams owned it. The Wilmer Theater came later. Wilmerding was also the home of a famous group known as the Fowler Sextet. The Westinghouse Air Brake Company's brass band, under the direction of Joseph D. Nirella, became well known throughout the entire country. They played concerts in the park and in auditoriums and had the distinction to be the first band to broadcast over the radio on Westinghouse's premier station, KDKA. Another recognized form of entertainment was the minstrel show. The Westinghouse Air Brake Company produced an ample supply of talent to perform in the YMCA auditorium. No dull times were to be had in Wilmerding!

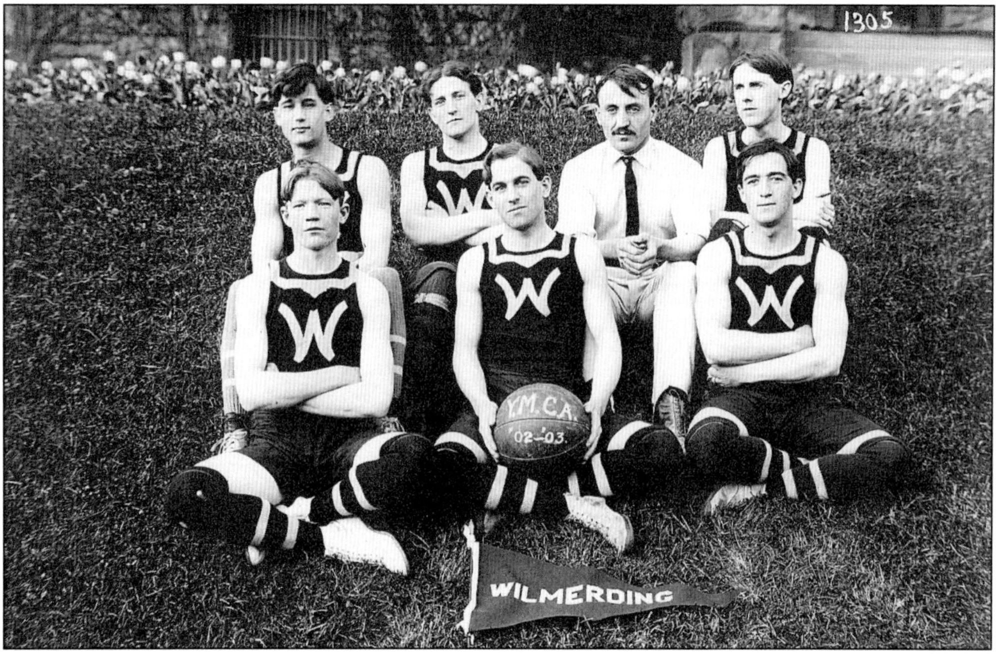

This photograph shows the Wilmerding YMCA's 1902–1903 basketball team. Basketball was probably played more extensively in Wilmerding than any other sport. Up until the late 1930s, the only basketball floor space available was the YMCA court, and, on these floors, both youngsters as well as adults played thousands of games.

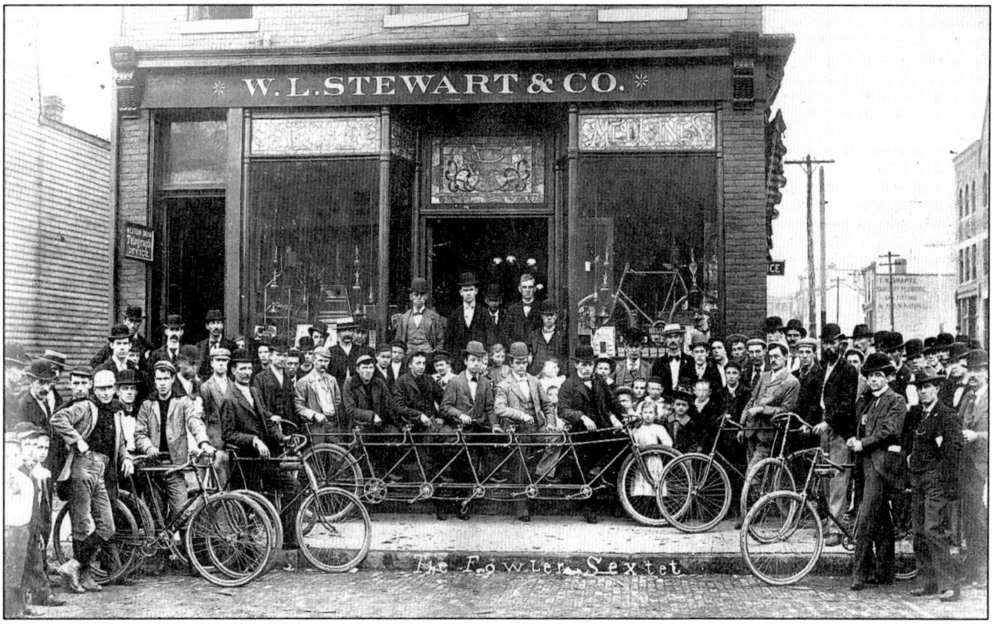

This early-1890s photograph of the famous Fowler Sextet was taken in front of the W.L. Stewart drugstore on Station Street at the corner of Westinghouse Avenue. It is interesting to note that the drugstore might have sold bicycles in addition to other sundries, judging from the cycle in the window. In the early days of the borough, up until 1897, bicycle races were quite popular in Wilmerding.

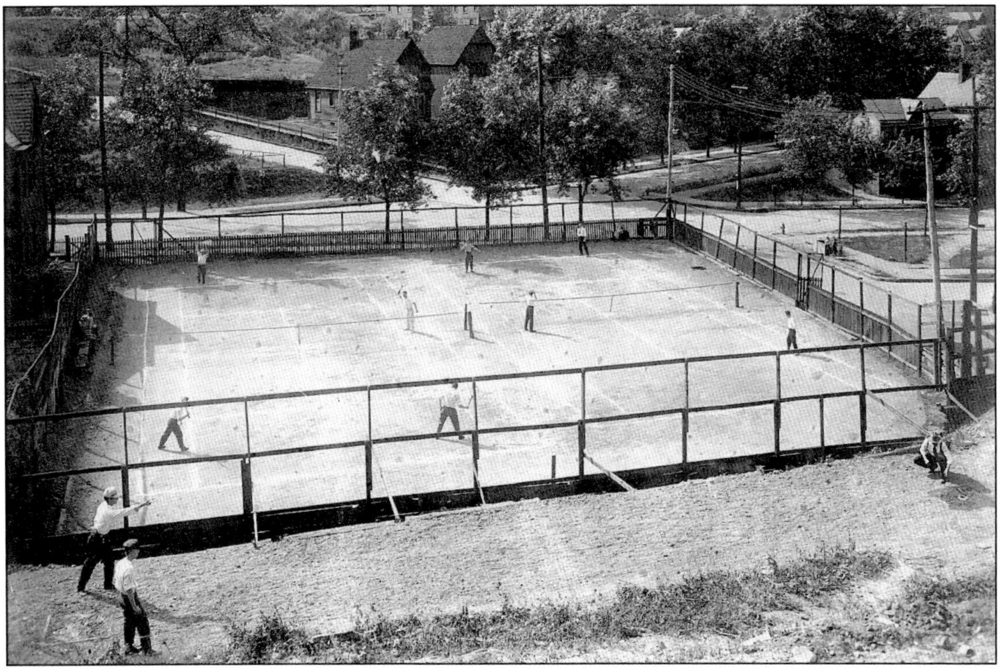

Those who enjoyed tennis played the game at the YMCA tennis court, located at the corner of Westinghouse Avenue and Florence Street at the end of Marguerite Avenue. The photograph shown here was taken in 1914. In later years, Carl and Russ's Atlantic Gas Station opened on this same site.

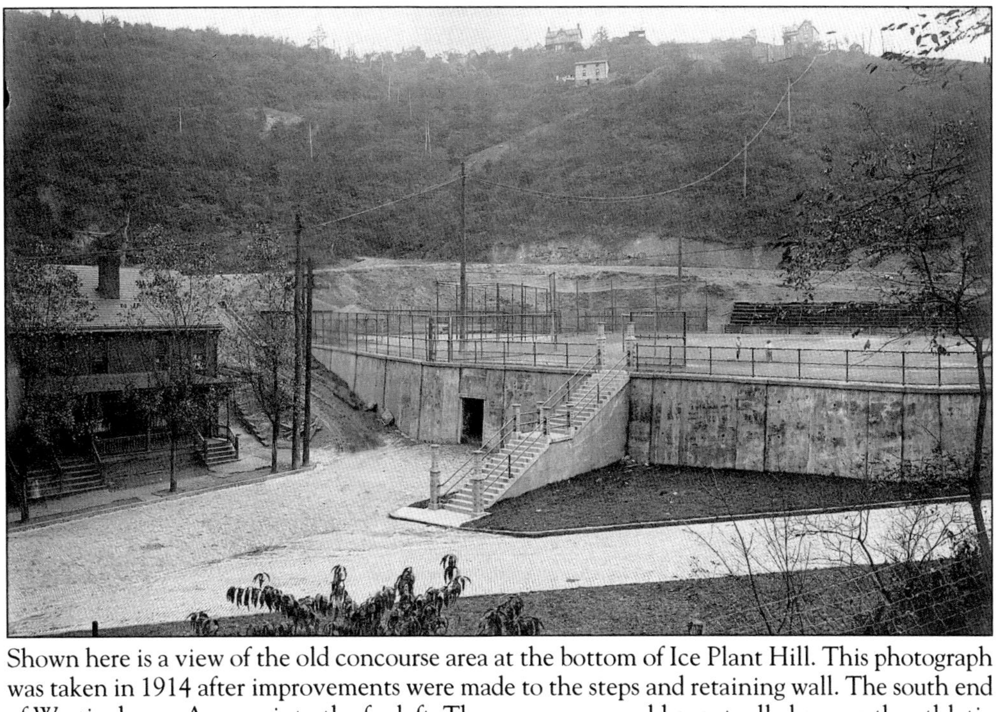

Shown here is a view of the old concourse area at the bottom of Ice Plant Hill. This photograph was taken in 1914 after improvements were made to the steps and retaining wall. The south end of Westinghouse Avenue is to the far left. The concourse would eventually become the athletic field for Westinghouse Memorial High School.

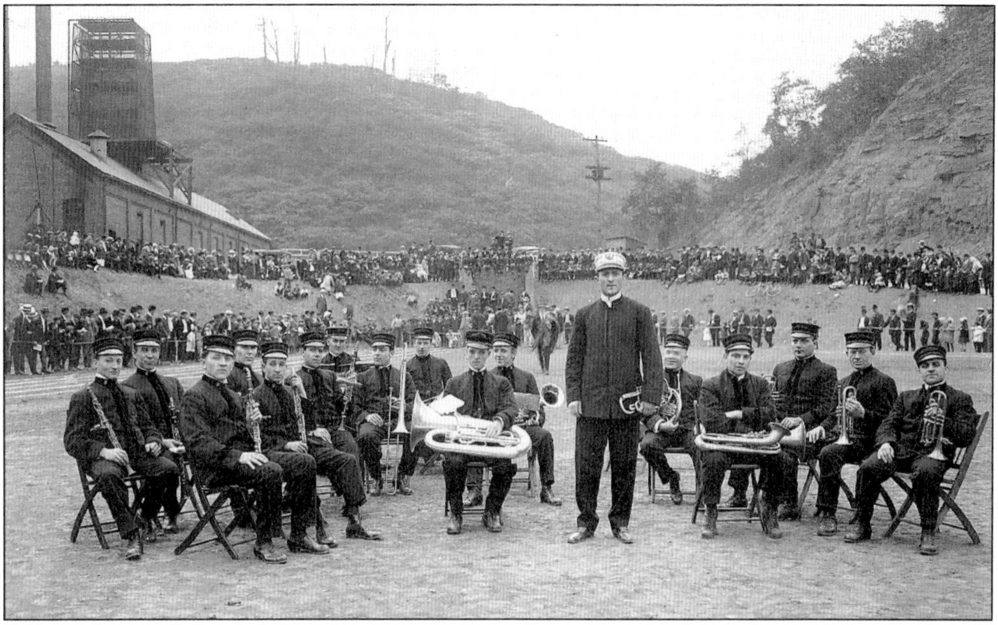

The Westinghouse Band of Wilmerding is shown here performing at a track meet held at the Wilmerding field in September 1914. The field was located at the bottom of Ice Plant Hill, a road that led to East McKeesport. The ice plant appears on the left in this particular view.

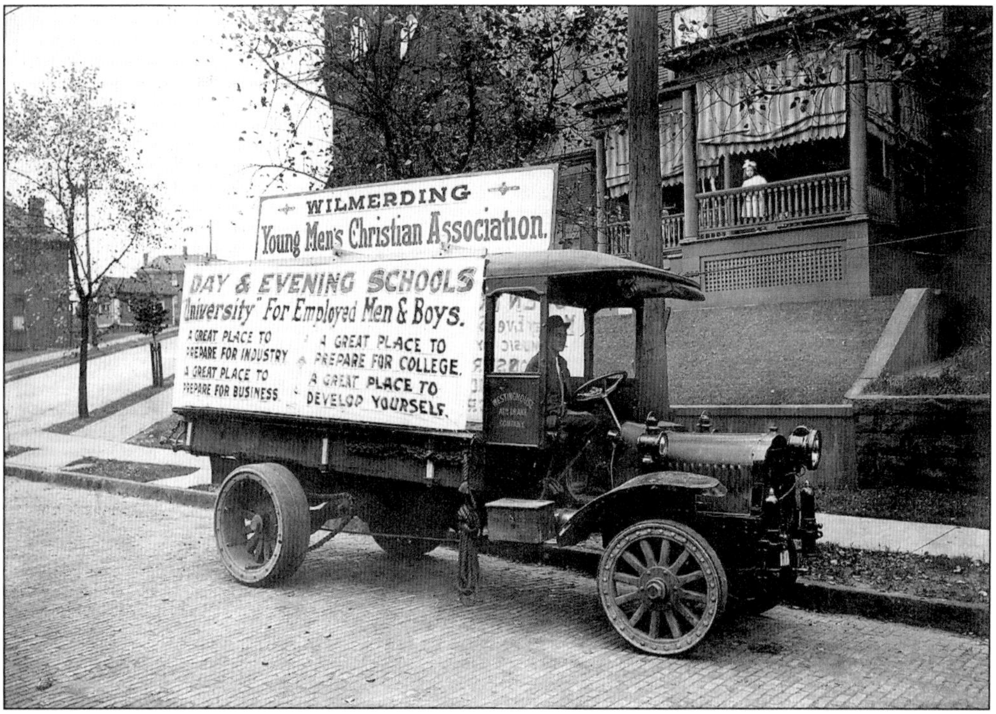

To promote the opening of the YMCA's educational department in 1915, one of the Westinghouse Air Brake Company's trucks was decorated to advertise the event. This Walter Truck was parked on Marguerite Avenue just below Wall Street. Notice the bold yet naïve advertising copy on the side of the truck.

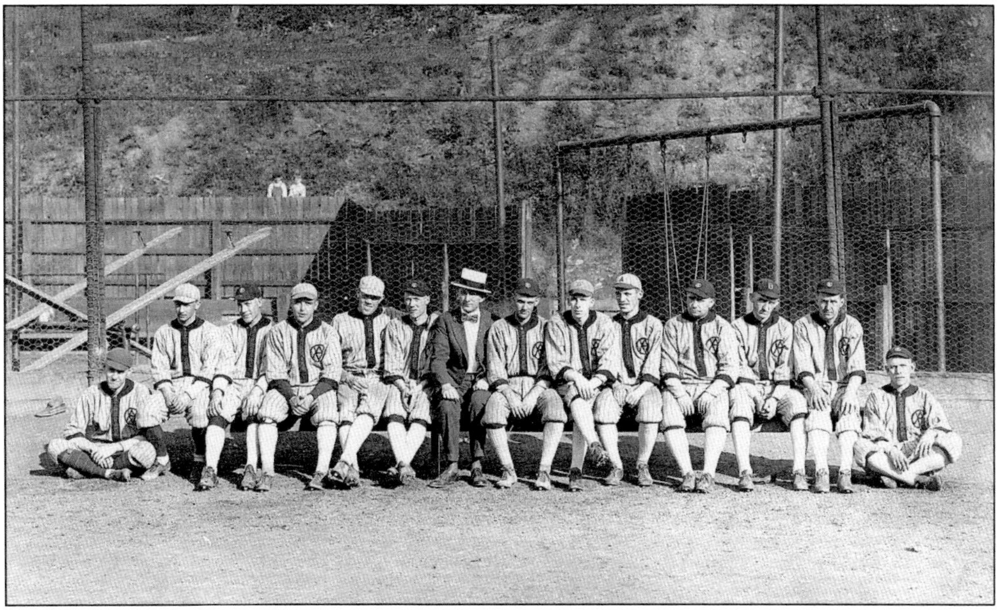

Baseball was the sport of choice in early 1891 Wilmerding. By 1915, interest in the sport waned. However, in 1915, when local businessmen backed a strong team under the management of Jimmy Ferguson, baseball returned. The 1915 team included Joe Matson, Dr. William Barrett, Frank McEvoy, Walt Kimmick, John Burgan, Dave Creed, "Fat" Now, James Beswick, Eddie Artman, A.H. Wardwell, and Shively and John Shenefelt. This 1916 view was taken on the Concourse grounds.

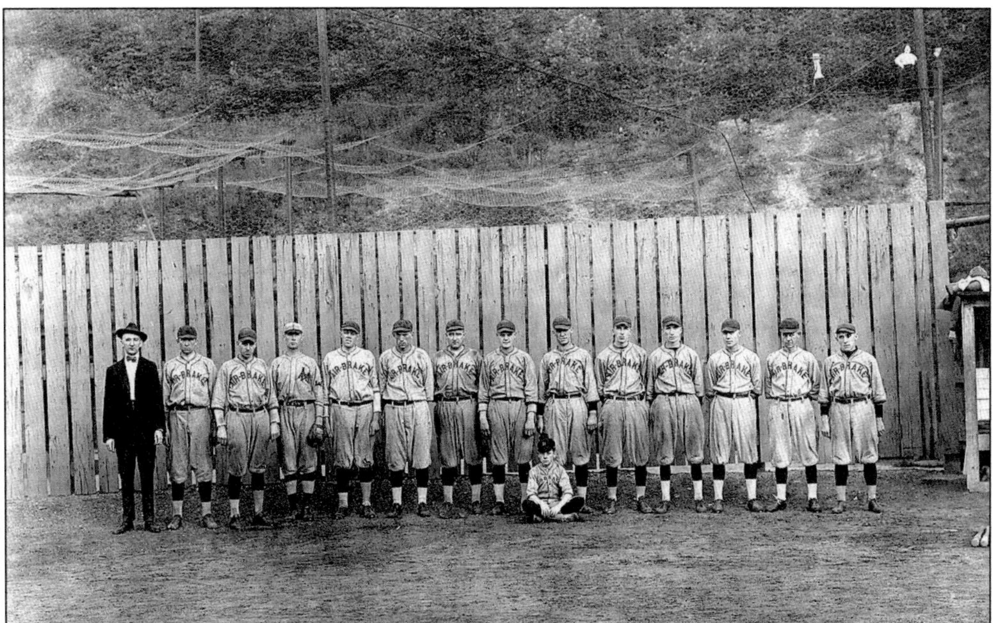

Baseball was big in Wilmerding. Here is a photograph of the Westinghouse Air Brake Company's baseball team, who were pennant winners in the West Penn League in 1918. With only 13 players in uniform, there must have been little substitution. Back then, the team members had to play the entire game and the next and the next.

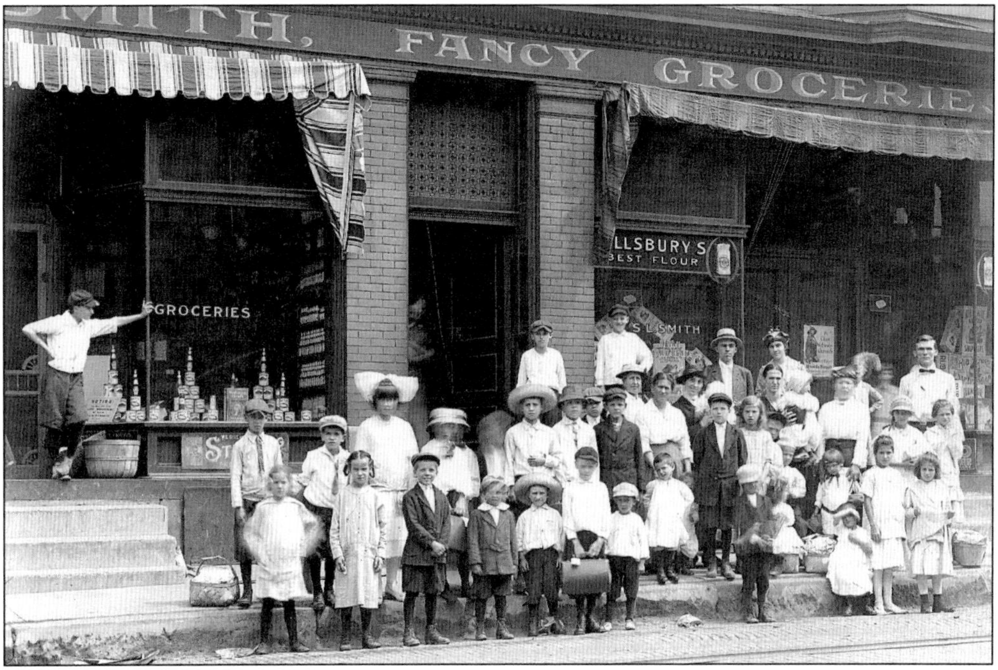

A group of anxious children stands ready to board a trolley car for a YMCA basket picnic. This 1916 photograph was taken on Middle Avenue on the north side of Wilmerding. Even though the weather must have been rather warm, notice that many of the boys are wearing jackets. Just about everyone is sporting a hat or cap.

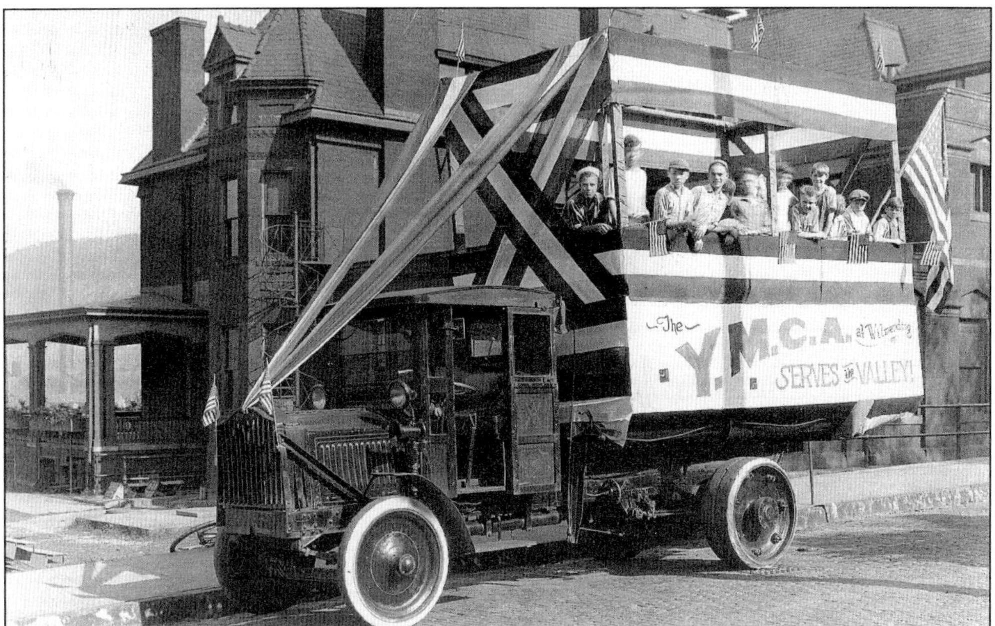

Westinghouse Air Brake Company's Packard is used as a float in the Wilmerding-Trafford road opening parade in 1925. This photograph was taken on Marguerite Avenue behind the YMCA. What is peculiar about this float's construction is how high off the truck's bed the children's platform is.

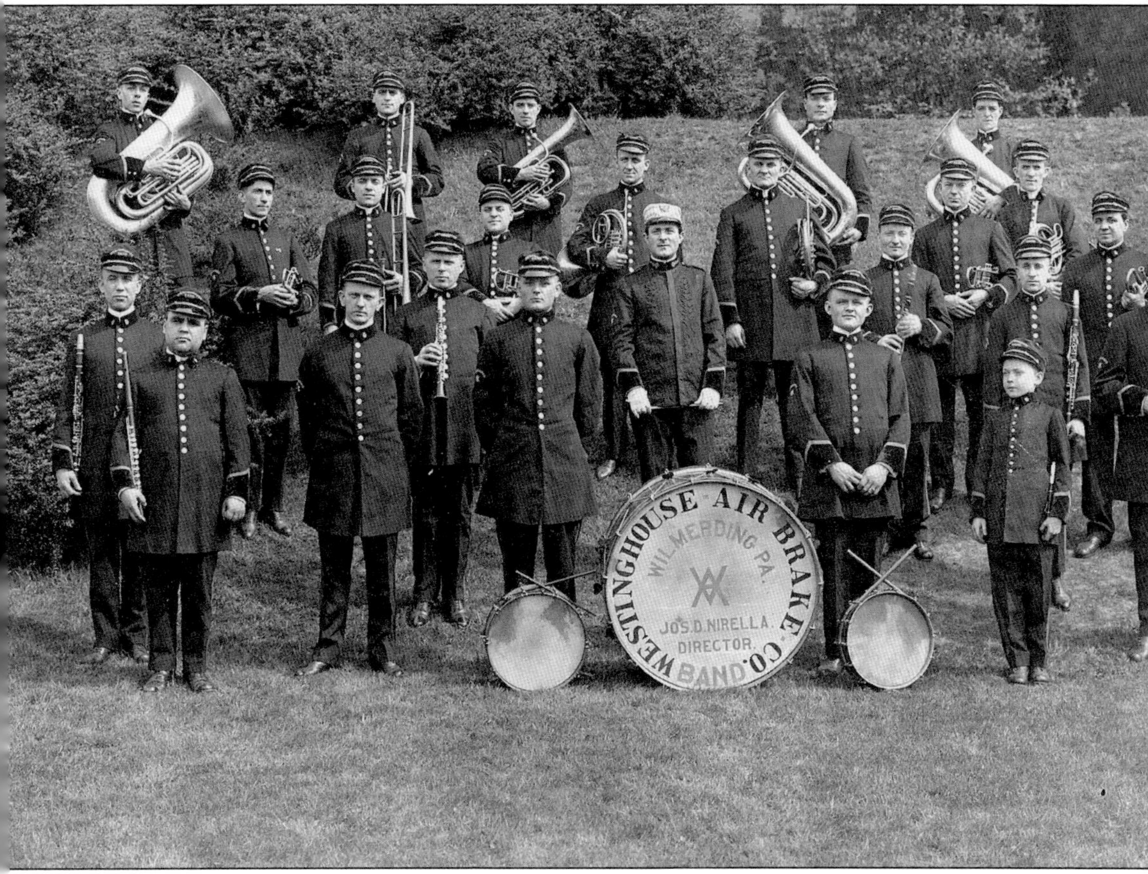

Standing on the lawn of the Westinghouse Air Brake Company, the company band stops practice to pose for the photographer. The band's director, Joseph D. Nirella, stands behind the big drum in the center of the picture. The band was organized in 1911 under the name Star of Liberty Band. Two years later, the name was changed to the Westinghouse Band of Wilmerding. In 1915, the band was taken over by the Westinghouse Air Brake Company and placed under the leadership of Nirella. Notice the young lad standing at attention to the right. Only two members of the band chose to face away from the camera; one is the young lad. Behind the band is the Castle.

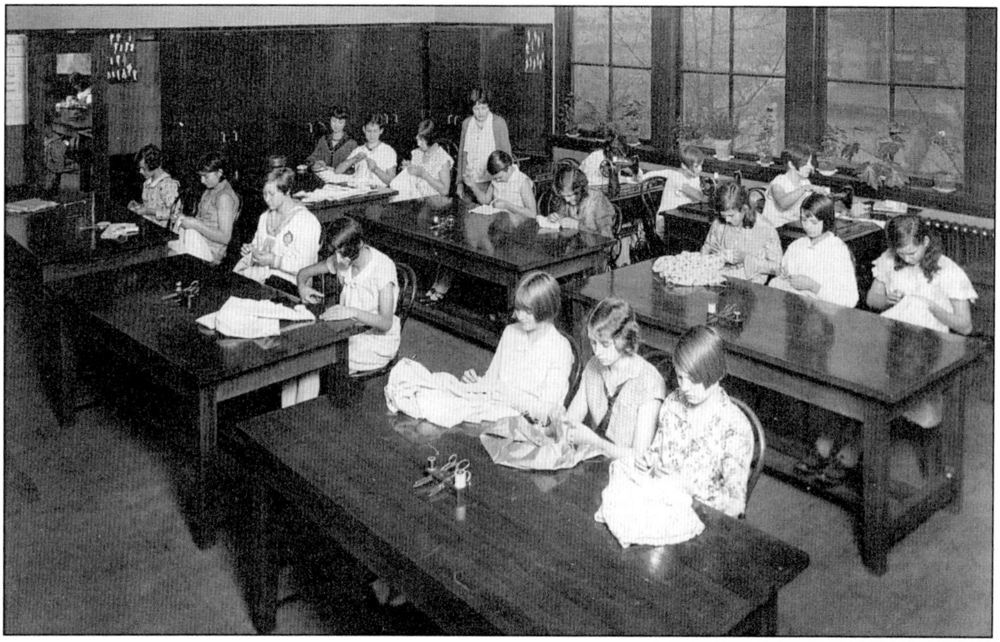

A 1929 Wilmerding Public School sewing class is shown here. All the young ladies are working despite the presence of a camera. Some of the hairstyles are not so much different from those of today. Three sewing machines are in use at the back of the classroom under the windows.

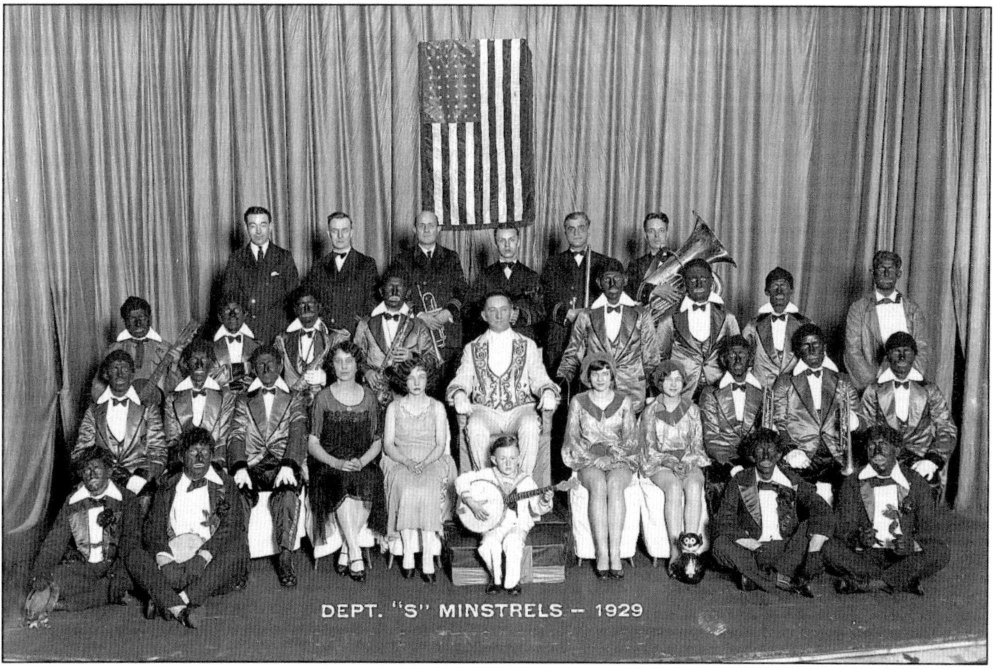

Various departments within the Westinghouse Air Brake Company held minstrel shows at the YMCA auditorium. This photograph shows the group from Department S of the Traction Brake Division. In addition to minstrels, the Westinghouse Air Brake Company formed the male chorus in October 1936 under the direction of P.R. Weight. On March 11 and 23, 1940, the chorus broadcasted shows from the Pittsburgh radio stations WWSW and WCAE, respectively.

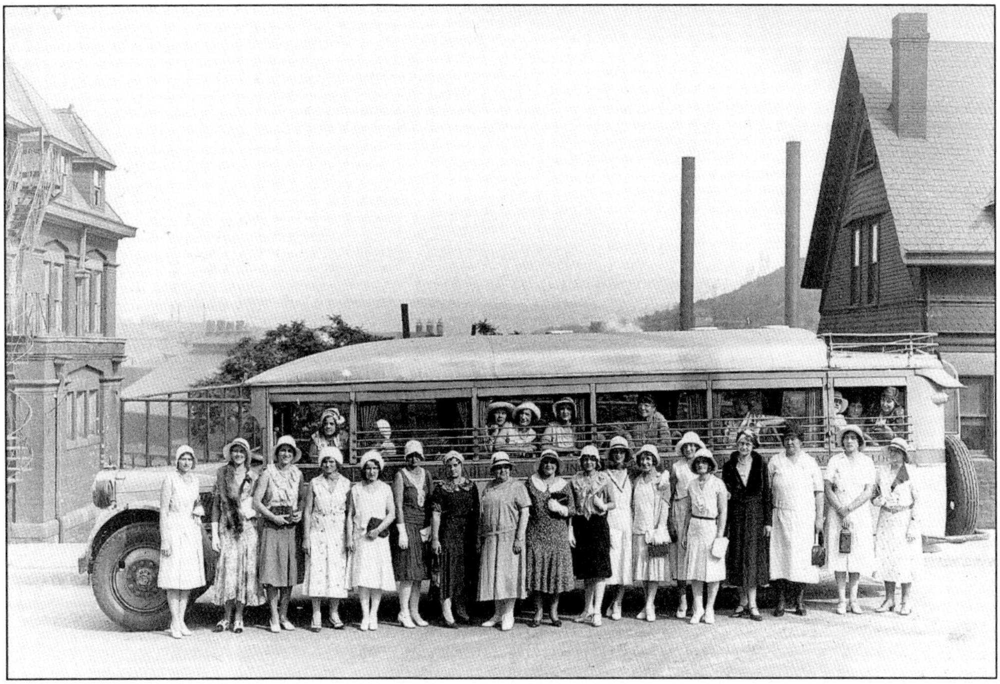

This YWCA Industrial Girls Club photograph was taken prior to a bus trip to Washington, D.C. The bus is parked on Marguerite Avenue, with the YMCA building on the left and the YWCA building on the right. No one is without a hat, a dress, or a purse.

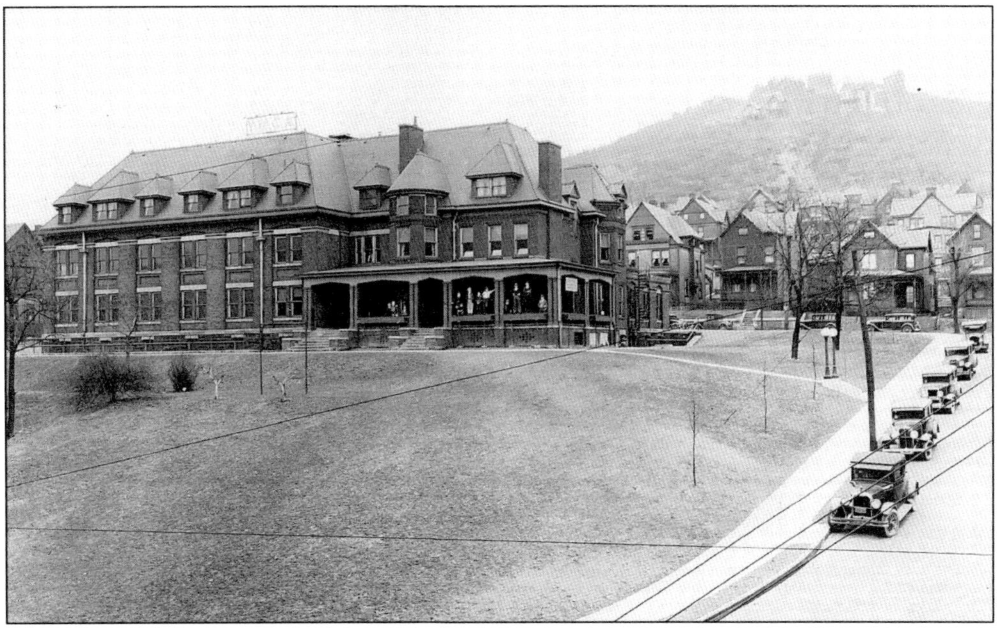

Here is an exterior view of the YMCA building, located at the corner of Bluff Street and Marguerite Avenue. The building was completed in 1906 after extensive renovation to one of the finest brick homes in Wilmerding. The Wilmerding YMCA was one of the largest in the state of Pennsylvania, second only to the Pittsburgh YMCA. The building was destroyed by fire in January 1976.

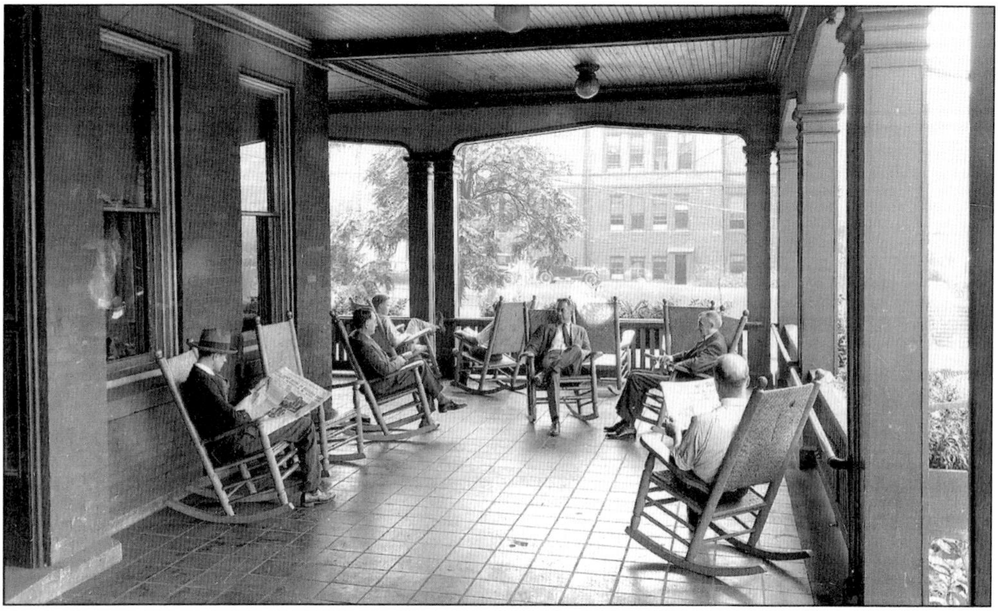

Several members of the YMCA are seen here relaxing on the porch in 1925. Everyone is sitting on a rocking chair. Some are reading, and others are talking. Most are dressed up. The Westinghouse Air Brake Company's general office building can be seen in the background. The downtown section of Wilmerding is to the right.

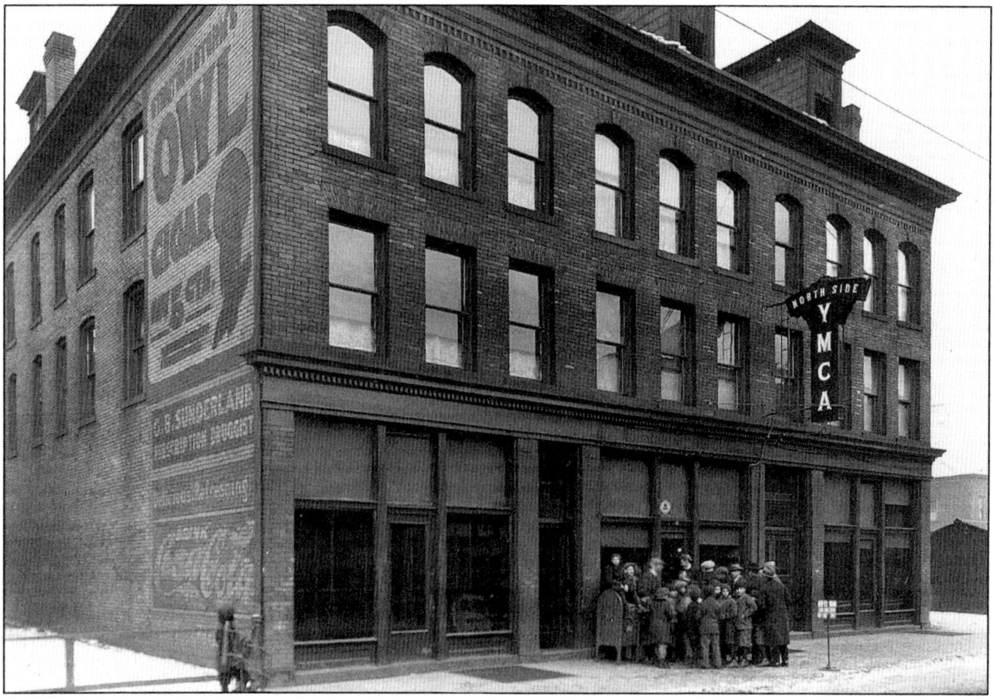

The Wilmerding YMCA has always been a popular place. This *c.* 1924 photograph shows the Wilmerding North Side YMCA, located on Airbrake Avenue. The building is still in existence, but, unfortunately, the unique sign on the side of the building has been painted over. Those standing at the front are waiting for the doors to open.

Seven

Important Events and Celebrations

No town is complete without some mishaps, and Wilmerding had its share. Most devastating were the floods. A combination of heavy rains and Turtle Creek's rising waters resulted in many serious floods. They came to an end, however, when a concerted effort engineered flood control in the 1960s.

On a lighter note, Wilmerding was always decked out in all its finery for top-notch celebrations. To celebrate its Silver Jubilee in 1915, all major buildings, houses, and streets were decorated with bunting and flags. A grand parade was held. Pageants, dances, speeches, and sporting events occurred day and night. Wilmerding glowed.

The first 25 years had shown much progress and development. There was an ever-increasing population, which caused more stores, churches, clubs, organizations, and schools to be established. Wilmerding was indeed a gem in the Turtle Creek Valley, and the people were proud to celebrate its progress.

Ironically, it was noted that George Westinghouse Jr., Wilmerding's illustrious founder, passed away in 1914. During the 25th anniversary celebration, his remains, along with his wife, Marguerite's, were taken to Arlington National Cemetery.

The year 1937 saw the celebration and dedication of the newly constructed high school on Herman Avenue opposite the park. Appropriately enough, it was named Westinghouse Memorial High School in honor of George Westinghouse Jr.

If the 25th anniversary of Wilmerding was grand, the 50th was spectacular. Five grand theme parades with floats were held on four different days. Pageants, concerts, speeches, and poems were presented, all capped by the crowning of the queen of Wilmerding, Mary P. Gilmartin. The Air Brake Company lent assistance to the committees, planners, and businesses, both monetarily and otherwise, as it had done throughout the first 25 years. Wilmerding was now modern, but the old-time values remained.

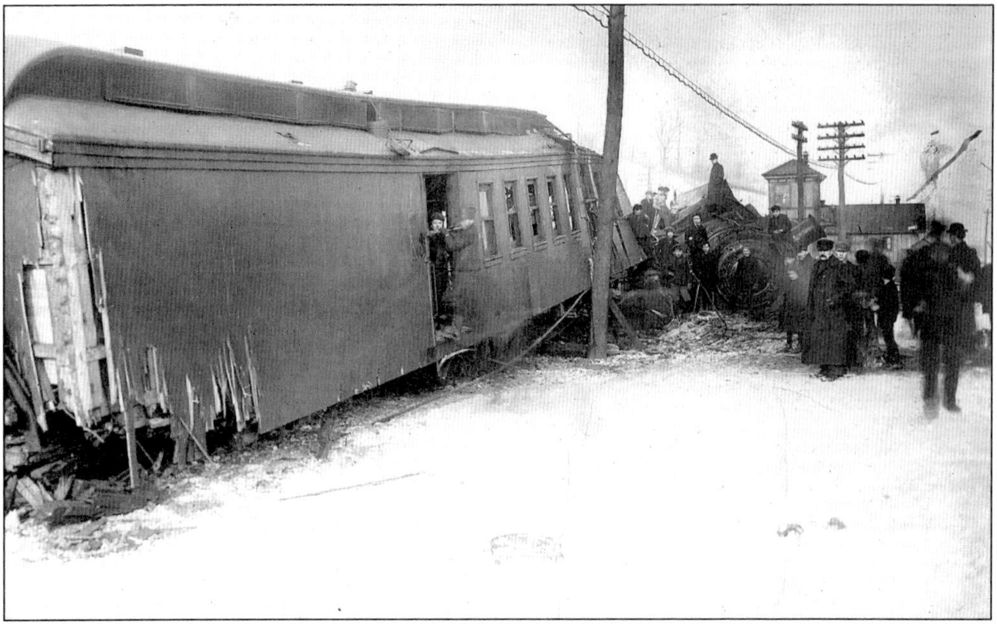

Here is a mighty train wreck that occurred west of Wilmerding Station. The Pennsylvania Railroad's fast mail train crashed, its engine overturned, and the car nearest the camera splintered beyond repair. The wreck happened at the far end of the Westinghouse Air Brake plant sometime in 1907. It is a wonder that the pole next to the car still stands.

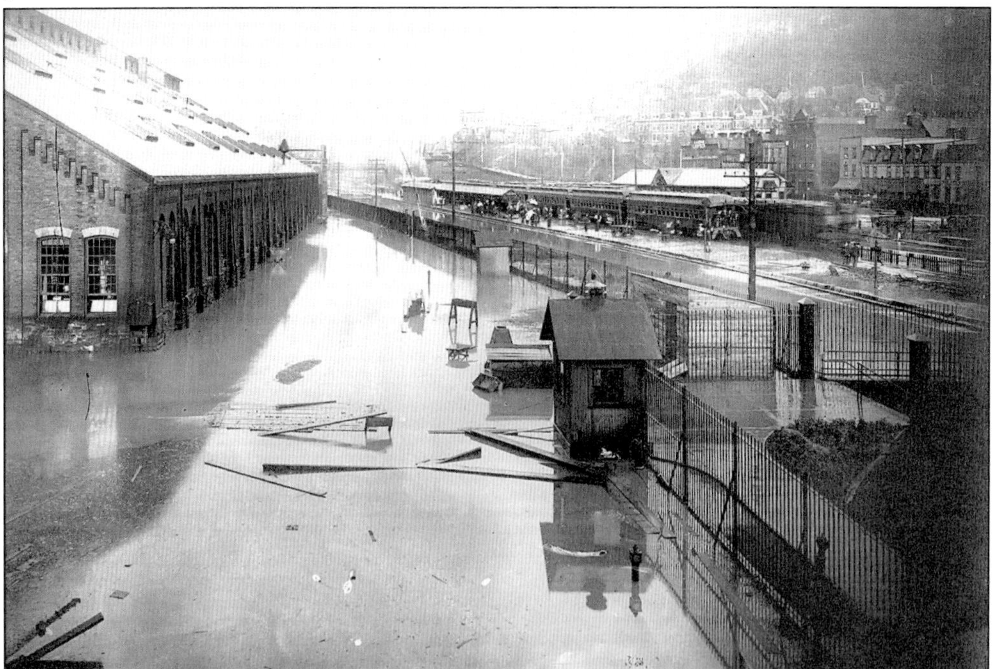

Wilmerding experienced many serious floods over the years. In the early 1900s, they occurred with much frequency. This picture is a view of the high water in 1907. The view is looking east down the Pennsylvania Railroad with the Westinghouse Air Brake foundry to the left and the flooded pedestrian tunnel entrance to the right.

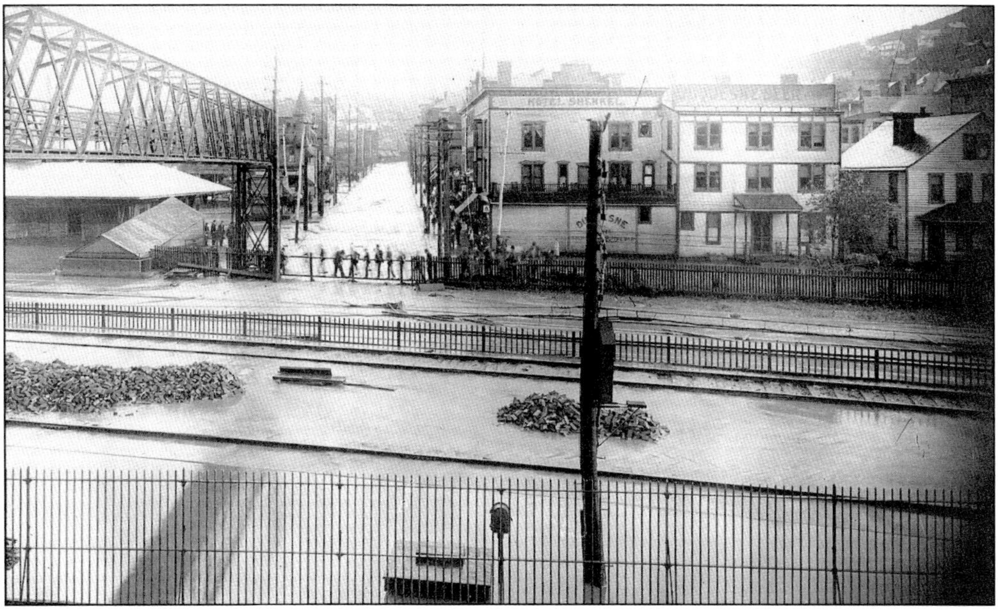

From the superintendent's building, located inside the yard of the Westinghouse Air Brake Company, another view shows the 1907 flood, looking south toward downtown Wilmerding. The new Pennsylvania Railroad station, just completed, can be seen under the pedestrian overpass, which was no longer in use. A newer tunnel entrance opened in 1903.

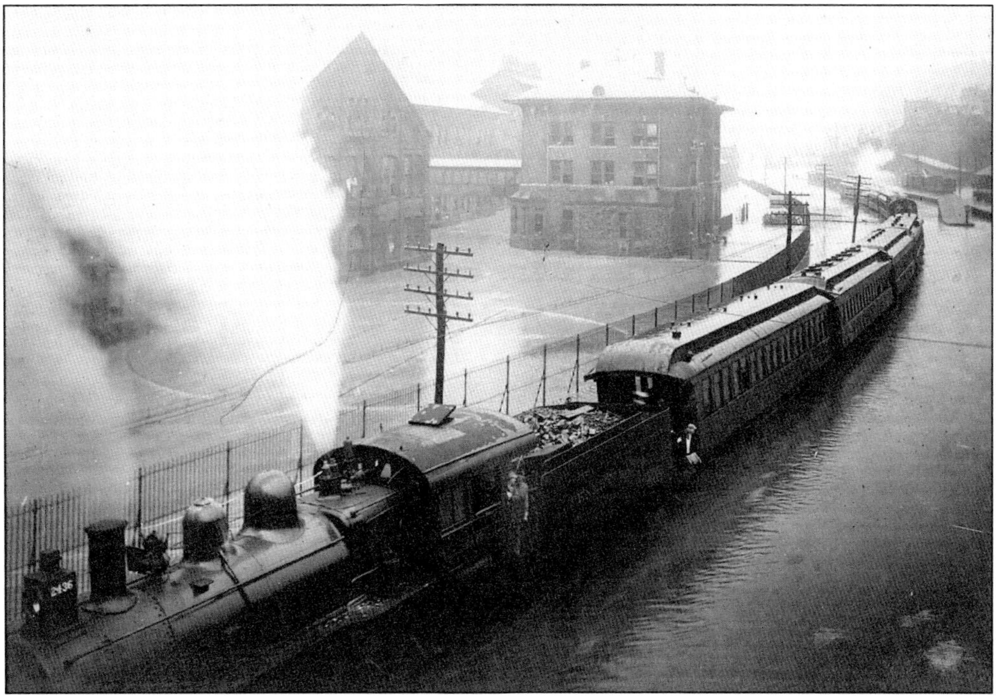

Another flood occurred in Wilmerding in September 1911. This photograph shows a Pennsylvania Railroad passenger train leaving the station. The photographer, looking east, took this shot from the trolley viaduct. The conductor, in his haste to be in the picture, stands dangerously close to the edge of the water.

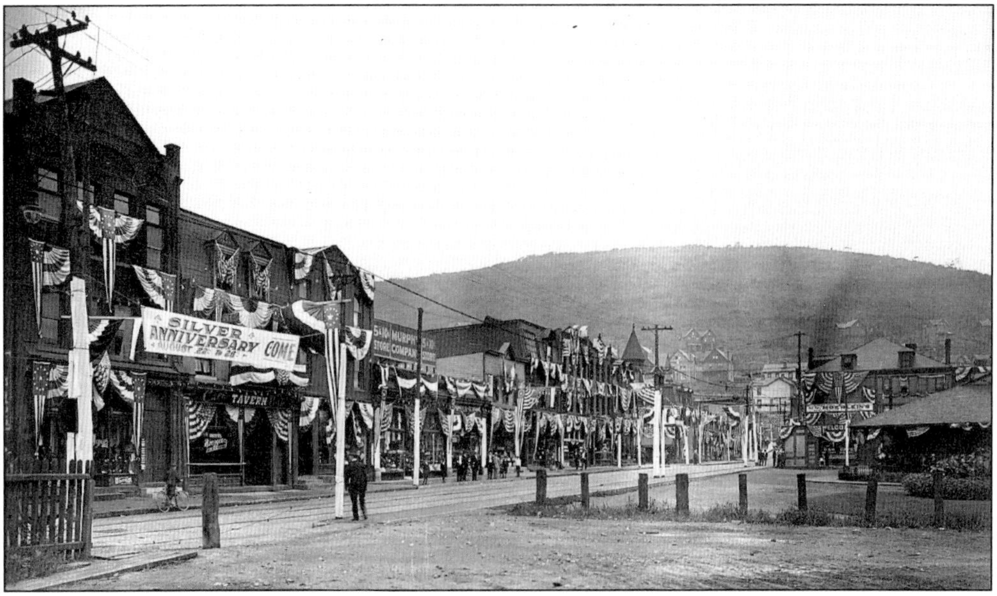

Wilmerding celebrated its 25th anniversary from August 21 to 28, 1915. This photograph of the decked-out town was taken on Station Street just west of Herman Avenue. The Pennsylvania station is to the far right. Several homes built into the hillside can be seen in the distance.

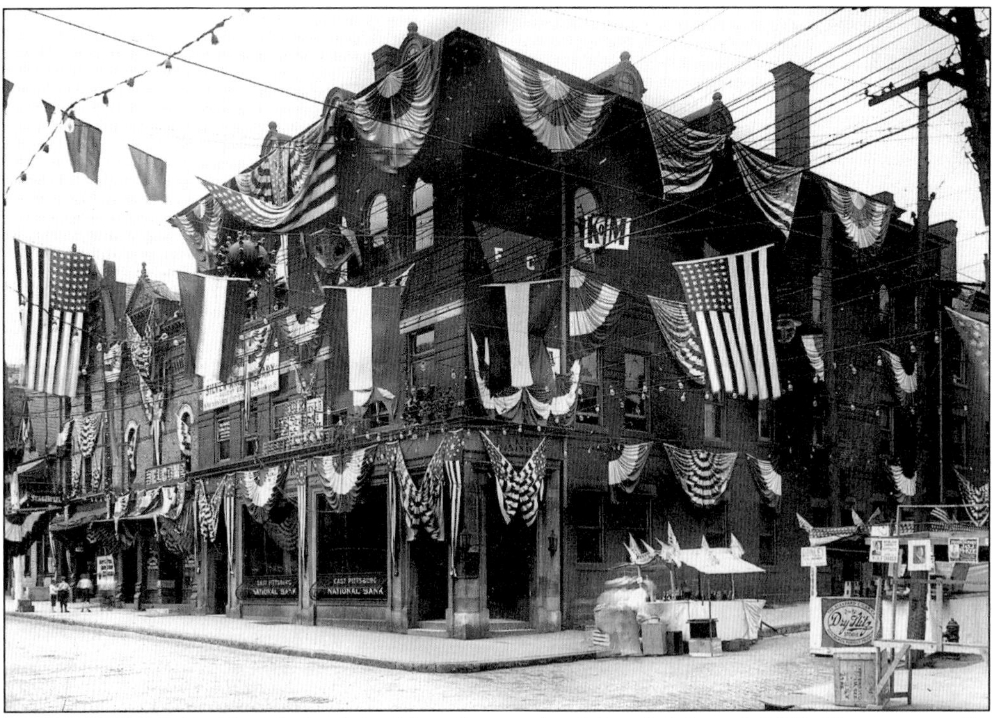

Look at the East Pittsburgh Bank building during the Silver Jubilee of 1915. Flags practically cover the facade. This photograph was taken at the corner of Westinghouse Avenue and Commerce Street. The bank would later merge with the Wilmerding National Bank and become the First National Bank of Wilmerding.

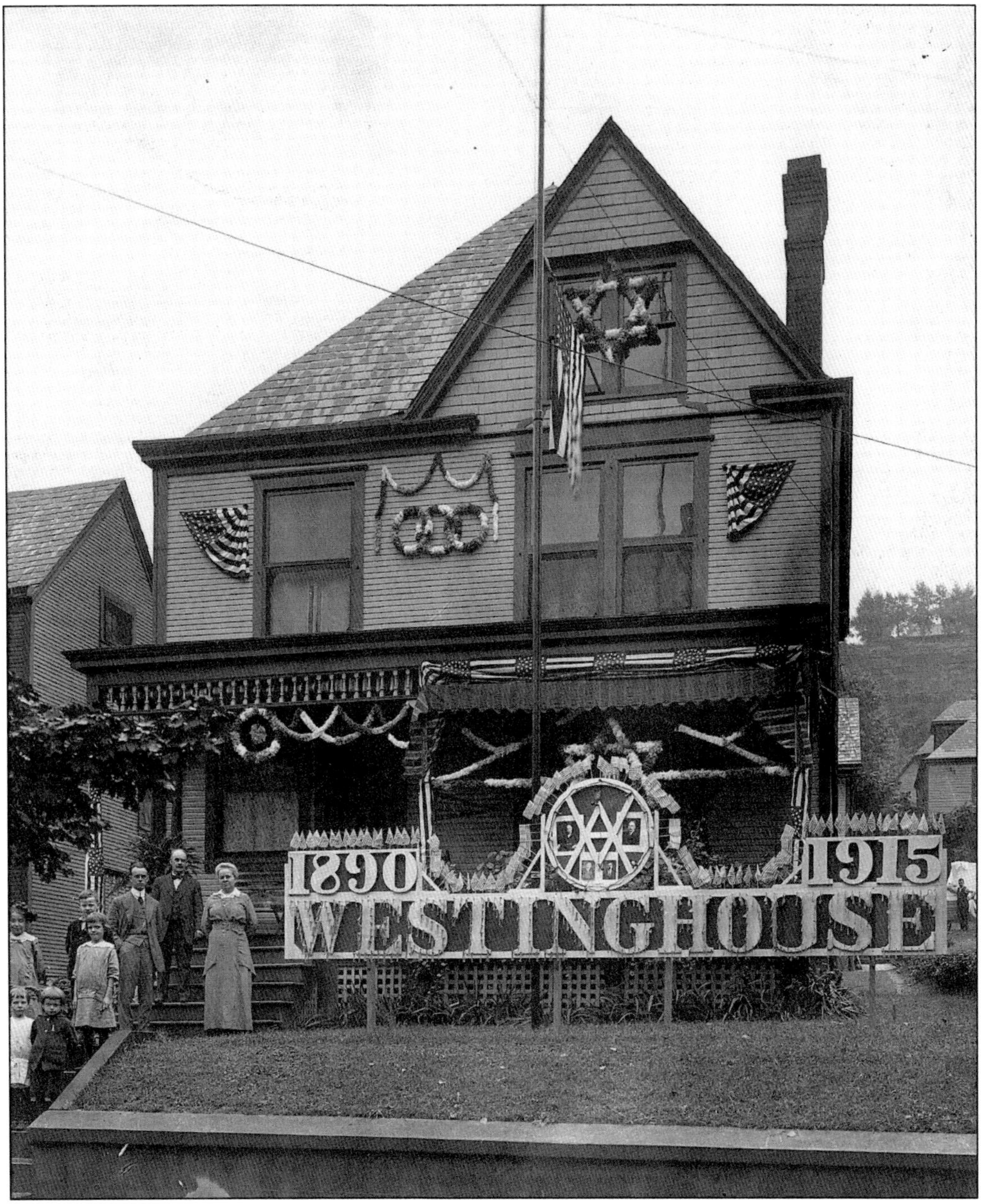

House decorations in celebration of the Silver Jubilee could not be more elaborate than those seen on the T.H. Abercrombie House. Notice the Westinghouse name is in lights with pictures of both George and Herman Westinghouse inside the company logo. Herman was the new president of the company after George's death in 1914. The location of this 1915 Abercrombie photograph is Caldwell Avenue. Indicative of the Abercrombies' religious preference is the Star of David hanging in two front windows. One can see the extremely formal attire of 1915—long dress, long sleeves. Caldwell Avenue was named for the treasurer of the Westinghouse Air Brake Company in the late 1880s.

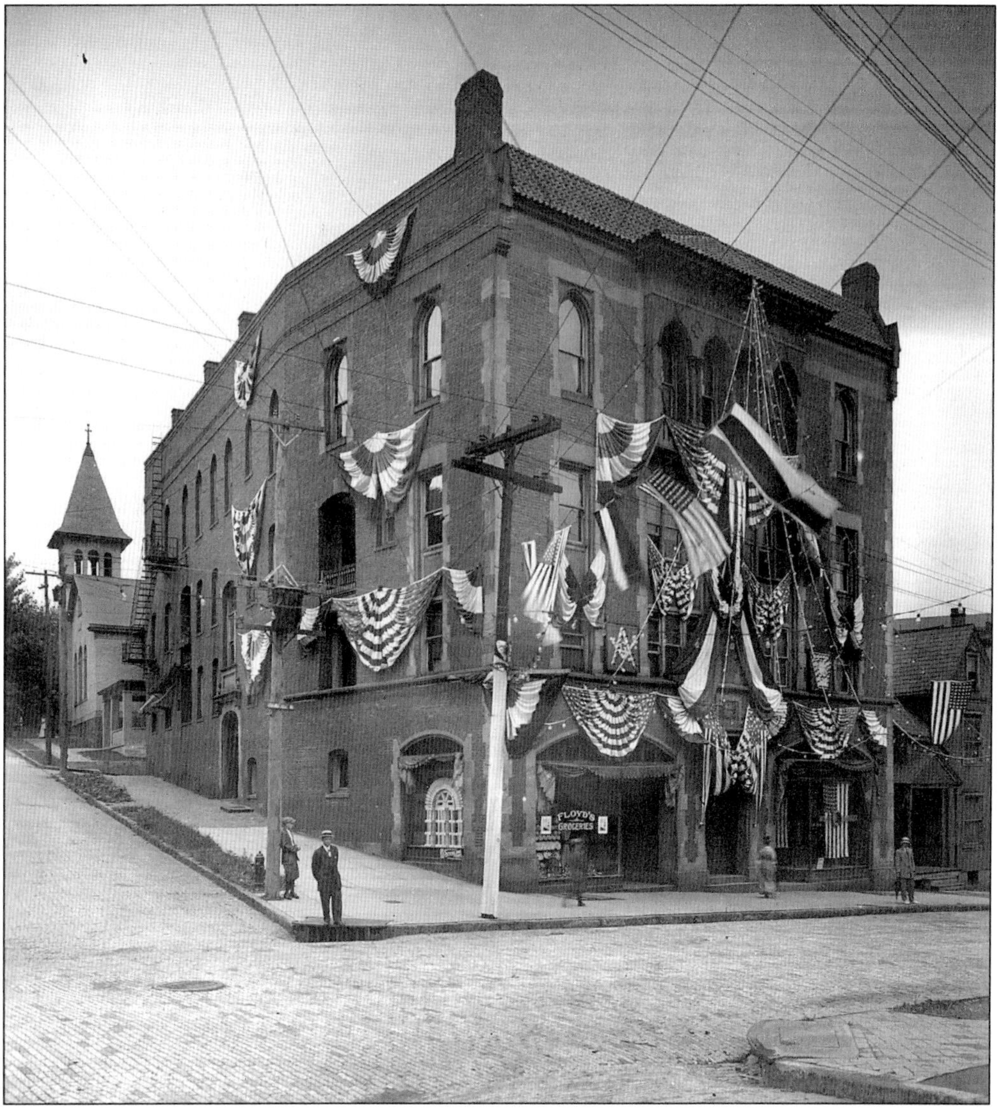

Shown here is the Masonic temple as it appeared during the Silver Jubilee in 1915. The building was located at the corner of Westinghouse Avenue and Clara Street. Floyd's Groceries was located in the corner storefront. At least seven strings of lights have been strung from the porch to the roof. Look up the street to the left of the Masonic temple and see the Lutheran church. Below the church is the parsonage. An alley separates the parsonage from the Masonic temple. Although not seen in this photograph, to the left and on the opposite corner stands the Methodist church, the first church to open in Wilmerding. A maze of electric wires is seen in the sky over the temple. The Masonic temple was razed during the Model Cities Program and replaced with apartment buildings.

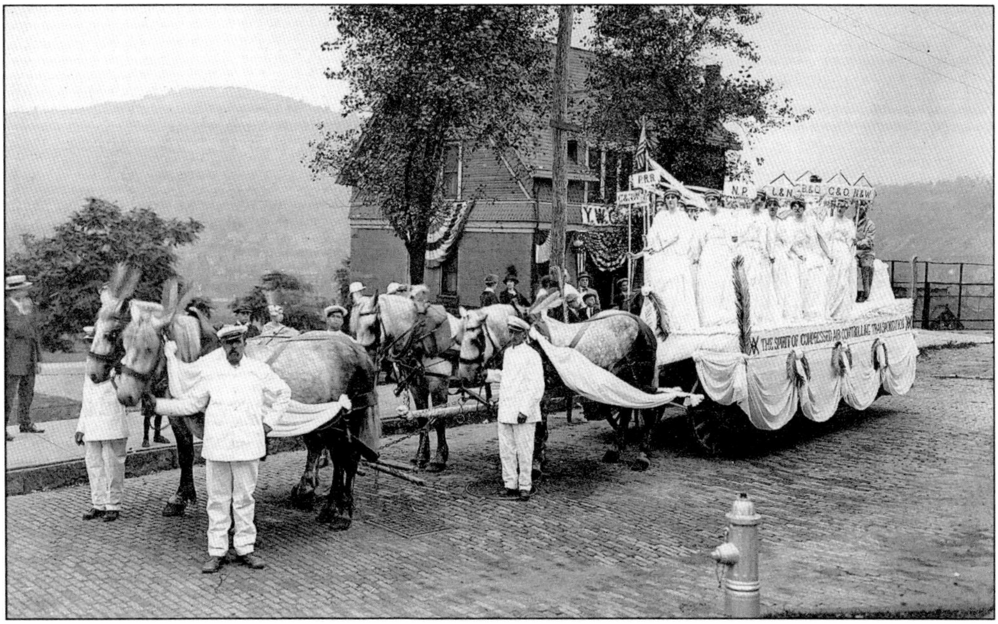

A Westinghouse Air Brake Company Silver Jubilee float stops on Marguerite Avenue in front of the YWCA. The young ladies on the float hold pennants naming the major railroads of the time. The float's banner reads, "The Spirit of Compressed Air Controlling Transportation." In the foreground is an early fire hydrant.

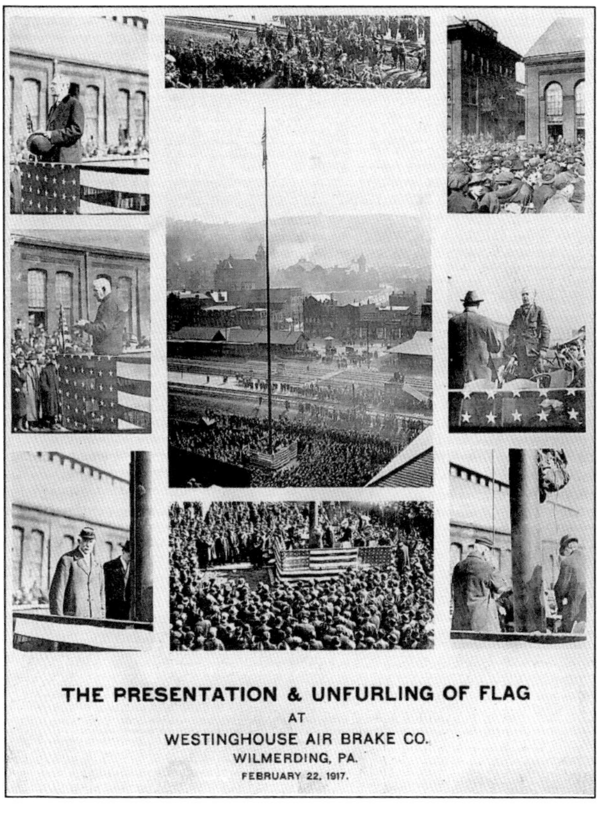

Shown here is the presentation of the flag at the Westinghouse Air Brake Company plant on February 22, 1917. America was then engaged in what was to be the war to end all wars, World War I. Naturally, the plant contributed considerably to the war effort by manufacturing goods. The flagpole was later moved west to its current location.

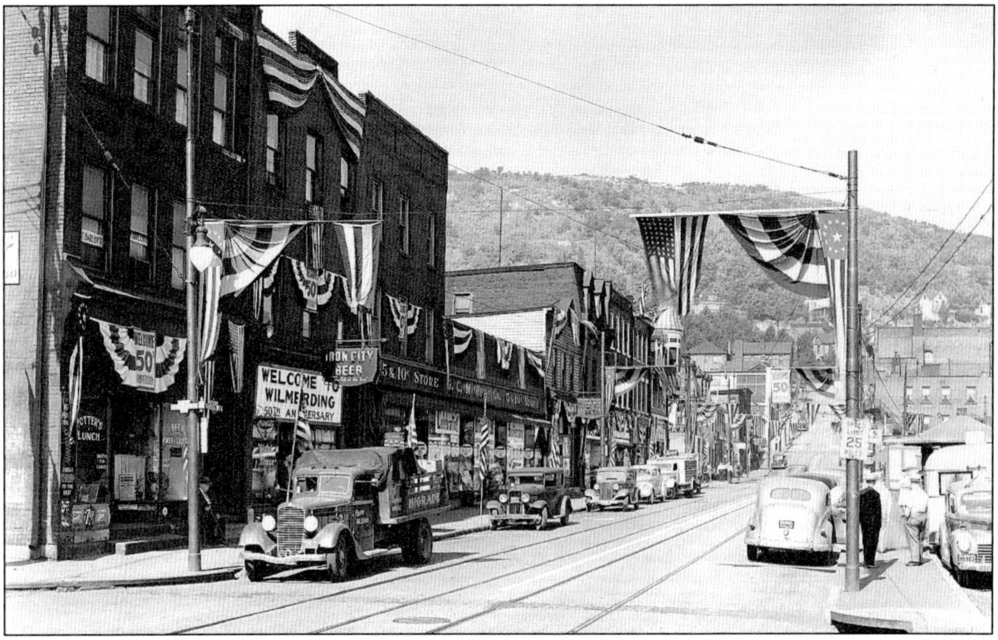

Wilmerding celebrated its 50th anniversary from June 30 to July 7, 1940. This view, looking west from Herman Avenue, shows Station Street. The celebration included a grand parade (one of five), which lasted five hours. The white line on the street indicates the direction of the parade route.

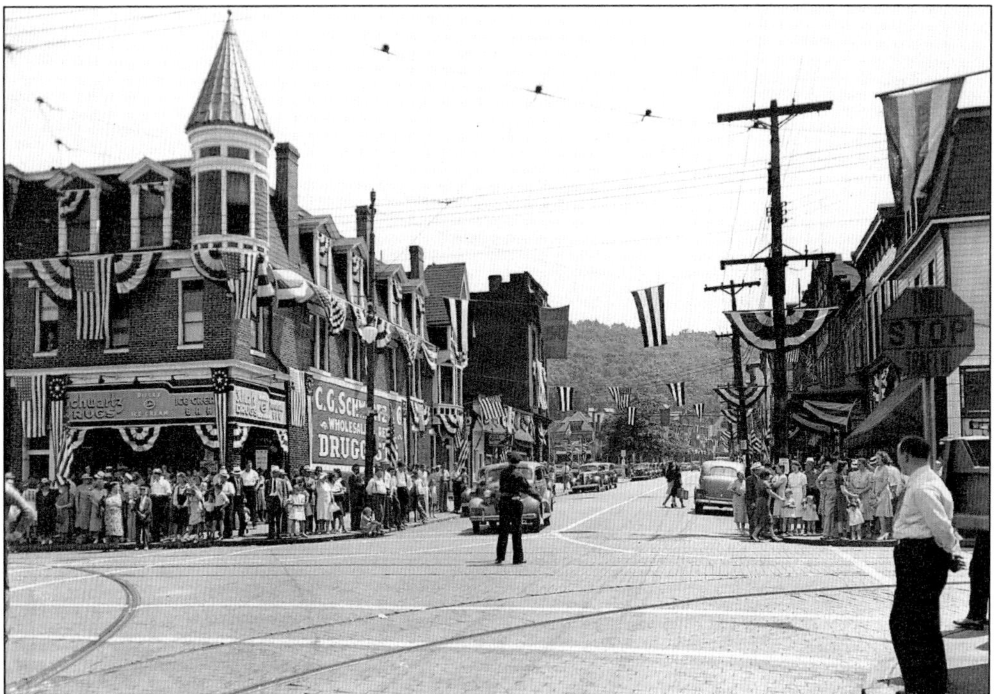

This July 1940 view of Wilmerding at the corner of Station Street and Westinghouse Avenue looks south on Westinghouse Avenue. A crowd is assembling to view a 50th anniversary parade.

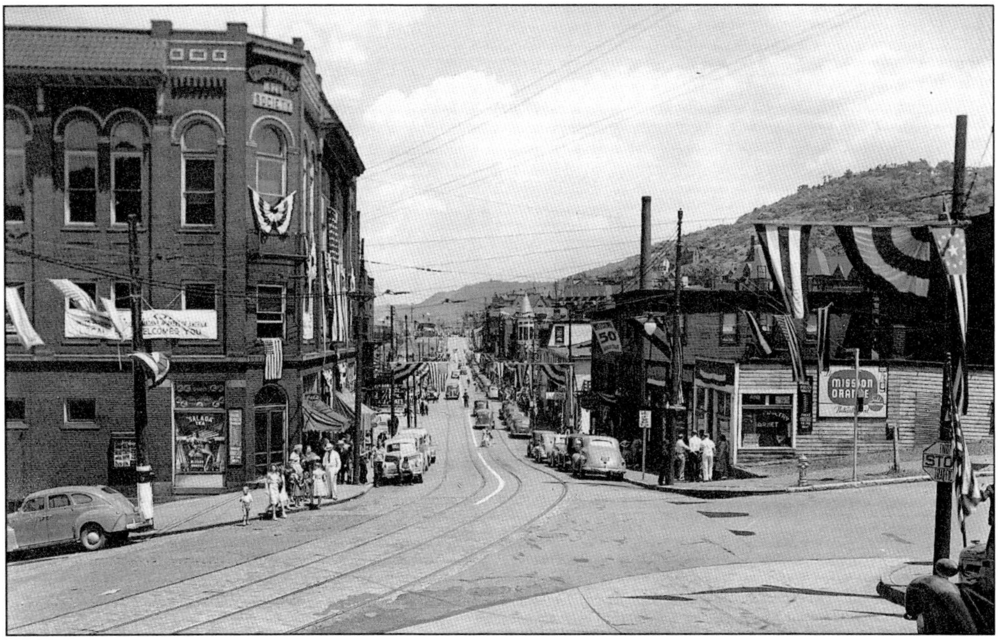

Parade watchers had a good seat here. This view looks down Station Street from Caldwell Avenue. Wilmerding's Golden Anniversary Celebration is in full swing, and a parade is about to come this way. The Philaretic Society building (later razed) is on the left. Today, on the same location, stands the Caldwell-Station Apartments. Townhouses are now directly across the street on the right.

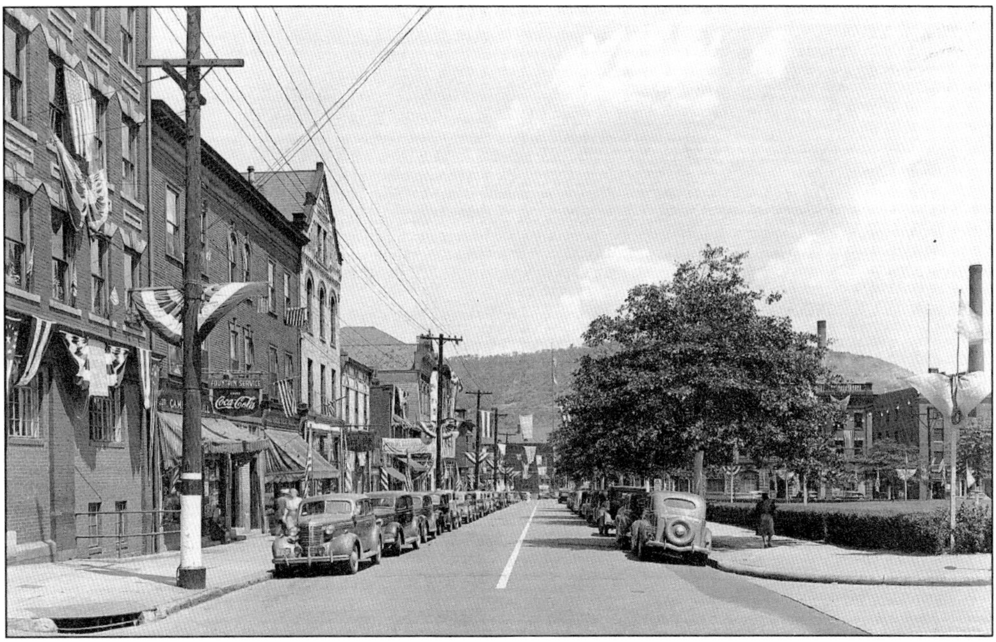

In this photograph of Westinghouse Avenue, taken at Annie Street looking north, the Westinghouse Air Brake Company can be seen in the distance. Westinghouse Park is on the right, surrounded by high shrubs. Most of the buildings in this picture have been demolished due to borough remodeling.

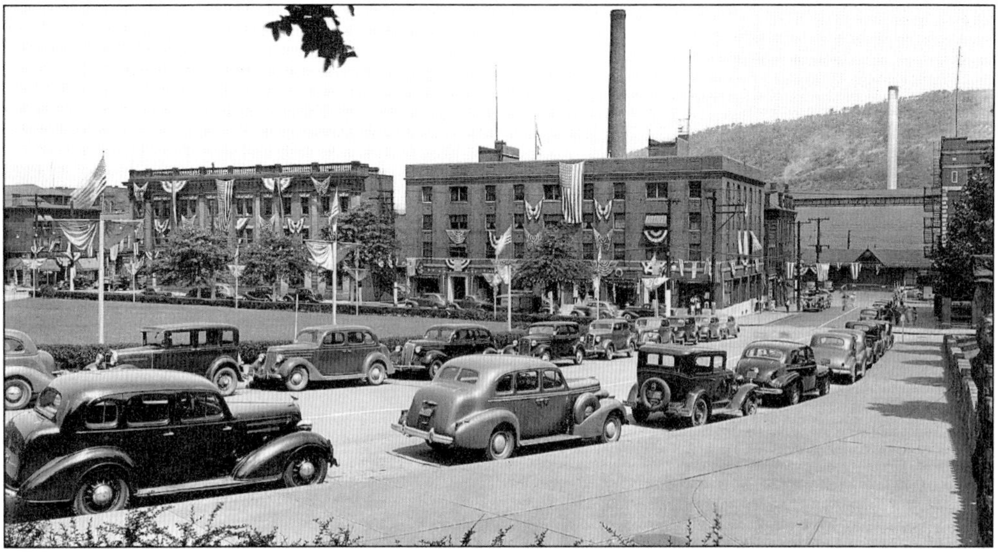

This view was taken in front of the new high school (Westinghouse Memorial), looking across the park toward the apartment house and Westinghouse Air Brake Company's general office annex building. The profusion of flags, banners, and lights was a scene repeated throughout the town for the Golden Anniversary Celebration in 1940.

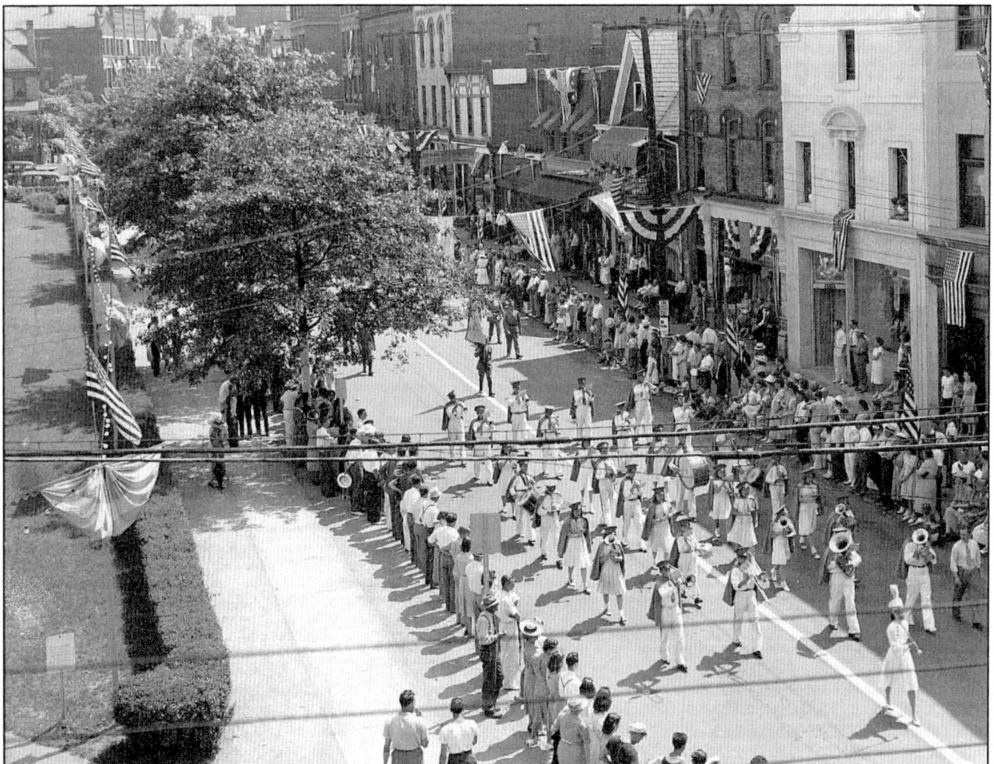

Here comes one of the 50th anniversary parades on Saturday, July 6, 1940. One of five parades, this particular one was the mammoth All-Nations-Day Parade traveling down Westinghouse Avenue in front of the park. From the look of the crowd gathered to watch, no one stayed home this day.

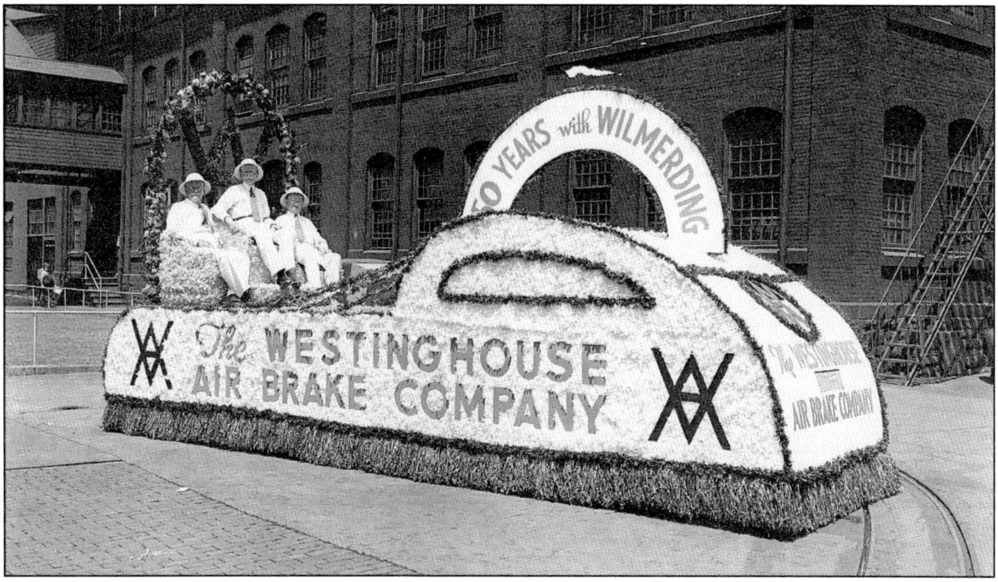

The Westinghouse Air Brake Company placed a float in the Wilmerding Golden Anniversary Celebration. The celebration took place from June 30 to July 7, 1940. This photograph was taken in front of the company's warehouse and engineering building. The three men riding the float are unidentified.

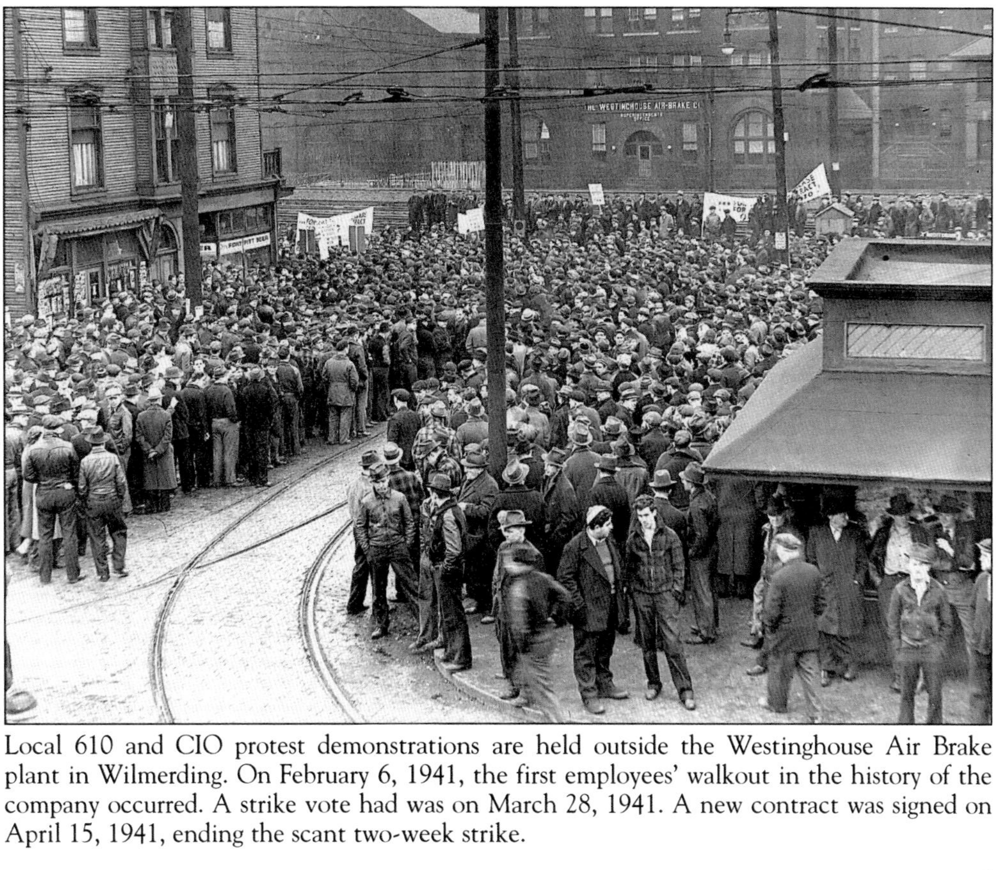

Local 610 and CIO protest demonstrations are held outside the Westinghouse Air Brake plant in Wilmerding. On February 6, 1941, the first employees' walkout in the history of the company occurred. A strike vote had was on March 28, 1941. A new contract was signed on April 15, 1941, ending the scant two-week strike.

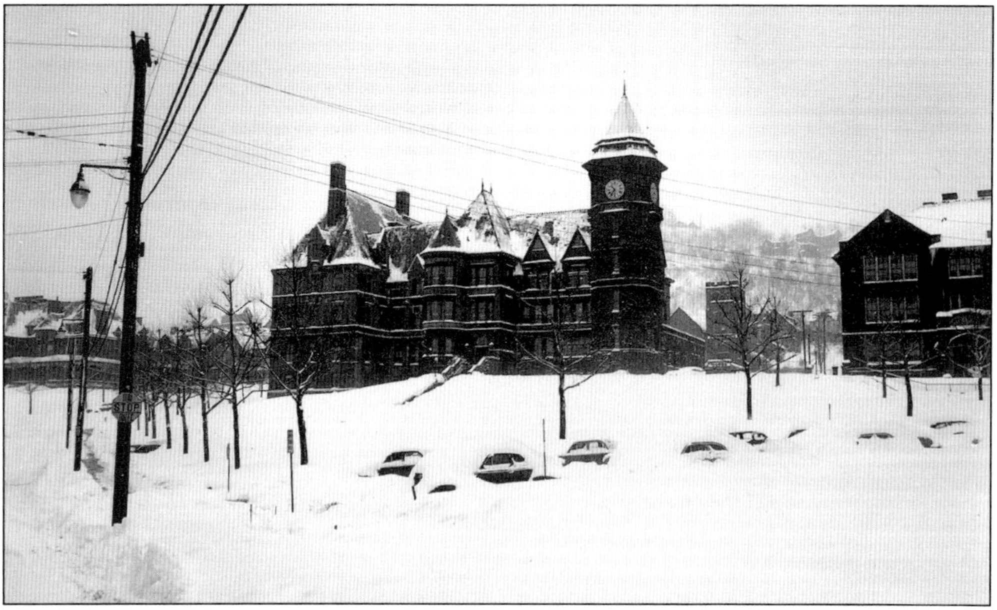

Another view of the November 1950 blizzard is seen here. The parked cars are barely visible under the heavy blanket of snow. The Castle in the background is reminiscent of a perfect Christmas card. The elementary school is to the right. The YMCA is seen to the left.

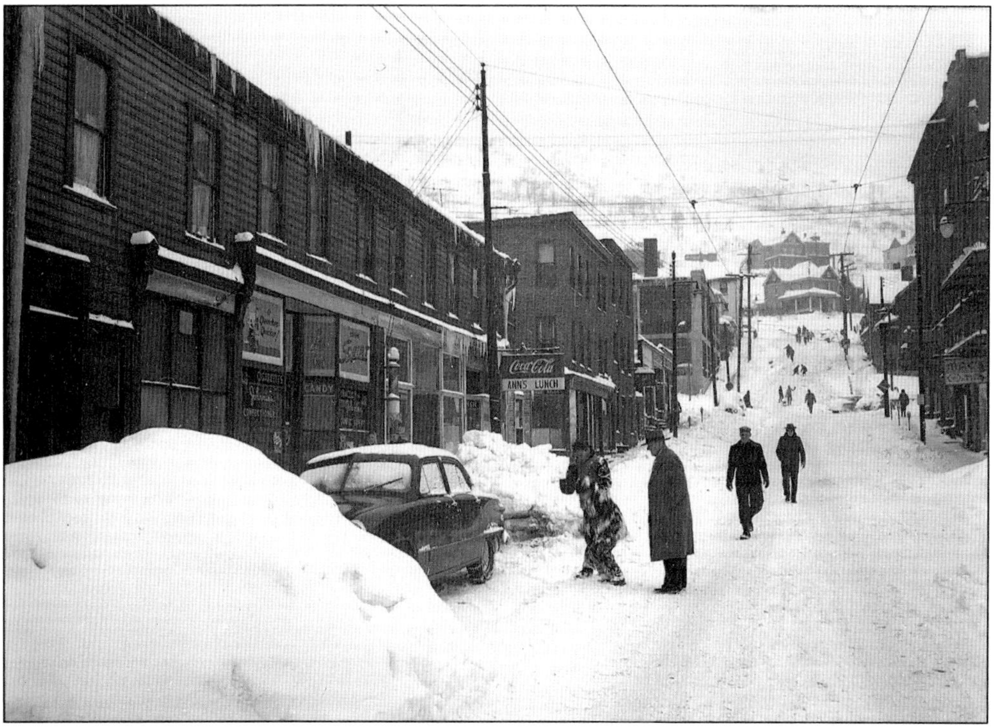

The blizzard that arrived on the day after Thanksgiving 1950 would not soon be forgotten by Wilmerding residents. The record snowfall blanketed the town, bringing it to a standstill. As evidenced by this photograph taken on Station Street, in some areas the accumulation was as high as the automobiles parked in the street. Children in the distance can be seen sledding.

Eight

Service to Town and Country

Directly after the inception of Wilmerding, Wilmerding Hose Company No. 1 was born. Company No. 1 dedicated itself to the safety and service of the brand-new community. In later years, the name was changed to the Wilmerding Fire Department. Fires were put out by hand-drawn equipment. In 1921, Wilmerding purchased its first fire truck, a White Chassis.

Service by Wilmerding to its country was demonstrated in 1917 during World War I. Many residents helped raise funds to purchase Liberty Bonds, for example, the War Song Singers Ladies Quartet from the Westinghouse Air Brake Company. The company itself produced war material in World War I and again in World War II. The young women of Department U assembled bomb fuses for World War II. The company kept a war bonds display in the front yard (by the foundry). A blood bank was set up inside Westinghouse Memorial High School. The school students helped with the wastepaper drive and the tin drive.

At the end of both wars, magnificent homecoming celebrations took place. Streets, buildings, and stores wore bunting, flags, and decorations. There was dancing in the streets as the young men and women who had defended America returned home to Wilmerding. A memorial was placed in the center of the park to honor those in World War I. Another memorial was placed in front of the high school for those who served in World War II. Lights blazed in tribute to fallen heroes, and plaques were erected, such as the World War I Honor Roll on the First National Bank building, at the corner of Westinghouse Avenue and Commerce Street, and the World War II Honor Roll, in front of Westinghouse Memorial High School. Patriotism shone supreme at all times.

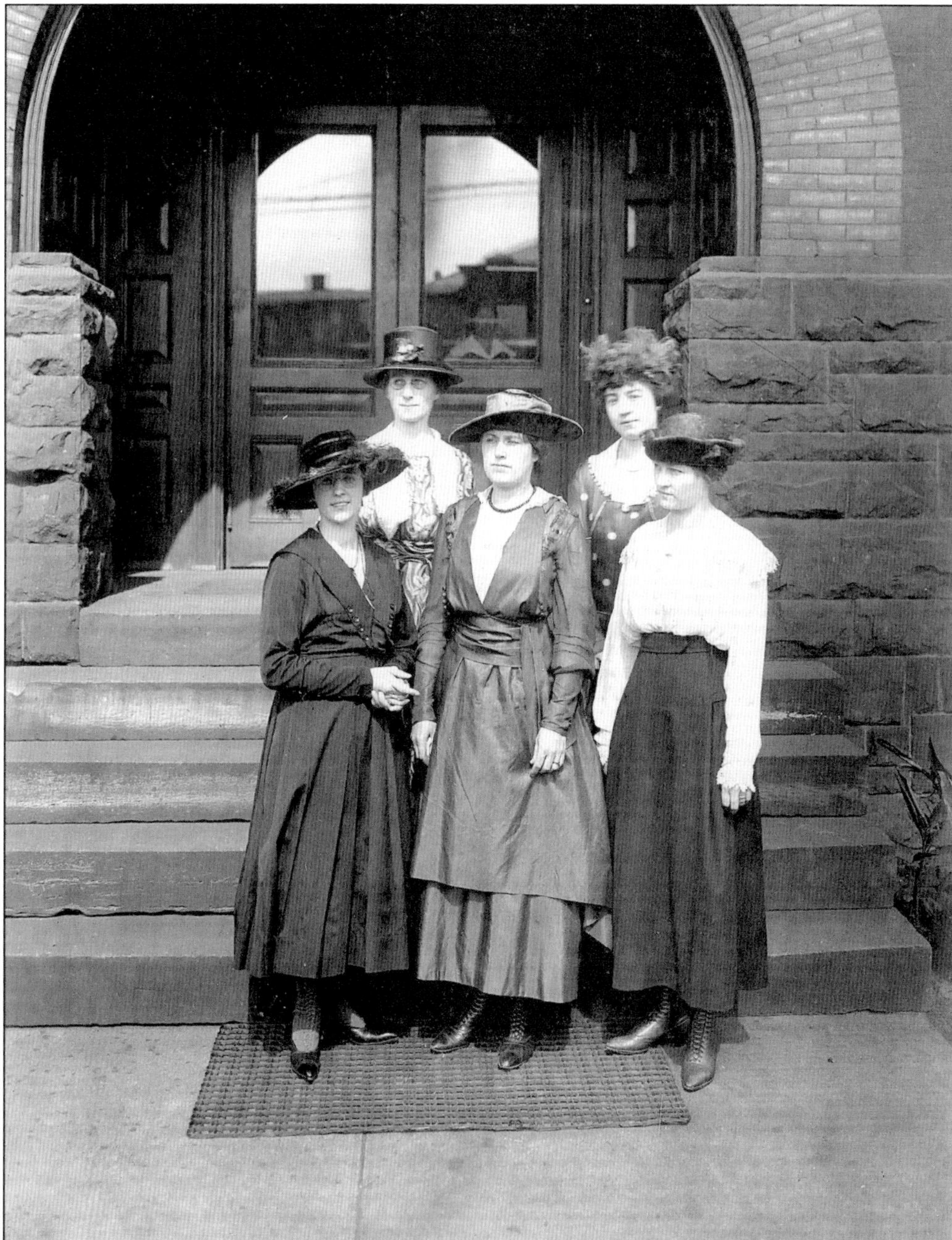

This photograph shows the War Song Singers Ladies Quartet standing at the entrance of the Westinghouse Air Brake Company's superintendent's building. The quartet raised money for Liberty Bonds during World War I. Dresses and skirts were Victorian-style, ankle length, and layered. Hats were a must; jewelry was sparse but present. Short sleeves were out of the question. These ladies appeared none too happy to be photographed, although the woman in black, on the left, seems to be smiling. The female quartet was well known throughout the area and a popular draw to any who acquired their services.

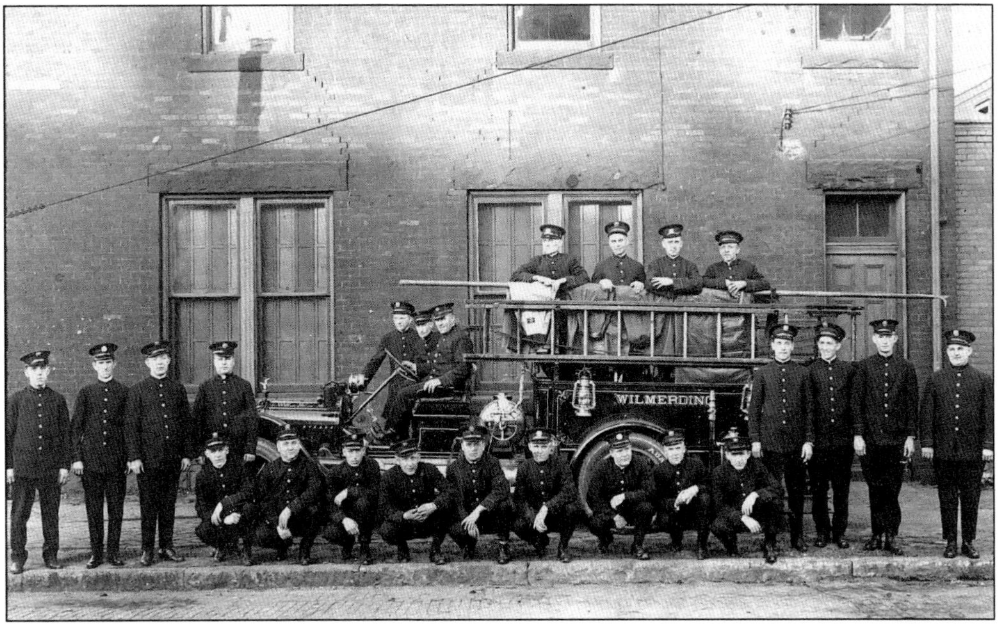

Wilmerding's first motorized fire truck, a White Chassis, was purchased in 1921. The Joseph Horne Company in Pittsburgh had previously used the White Chassis. Up until then, Wilmerding's fire equipment had been drawn by hand. However, the Westinghouse Air Brake Company offered their trucks to help fight fires in the borough.

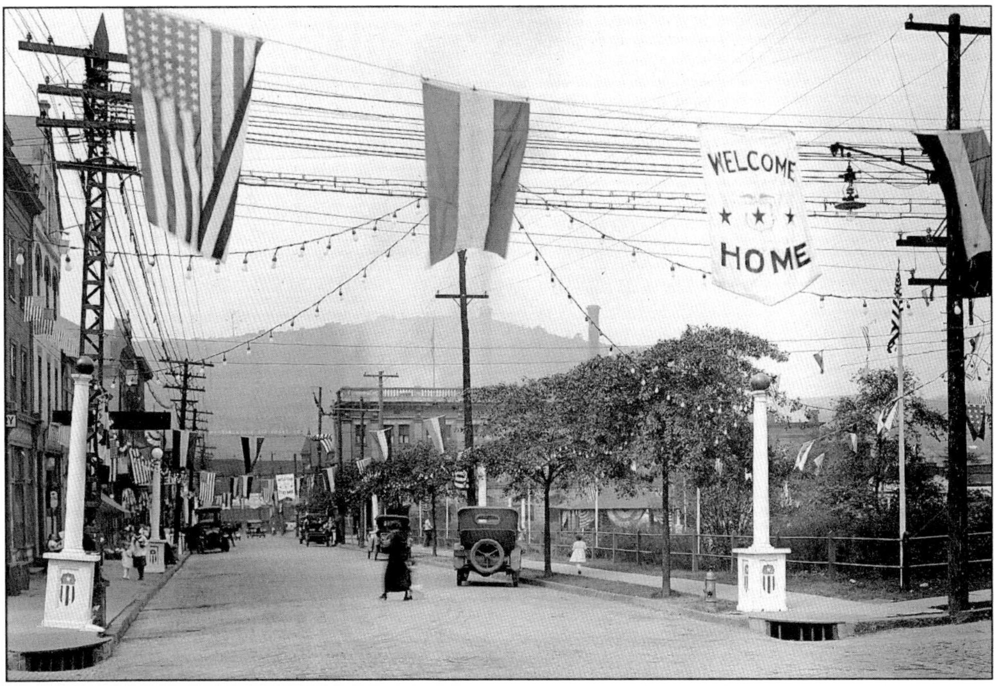

The Homecoming Celebration is shown as it appeared on Westinghouse Avenue in September 1919. The view looks north on Westinghouse Avenue toward the Westinghouse Air Brake Company plant. Lights, flags, banners, and signs were gaily hung over the streets. The park is on the right; the fence around it has since been removed.

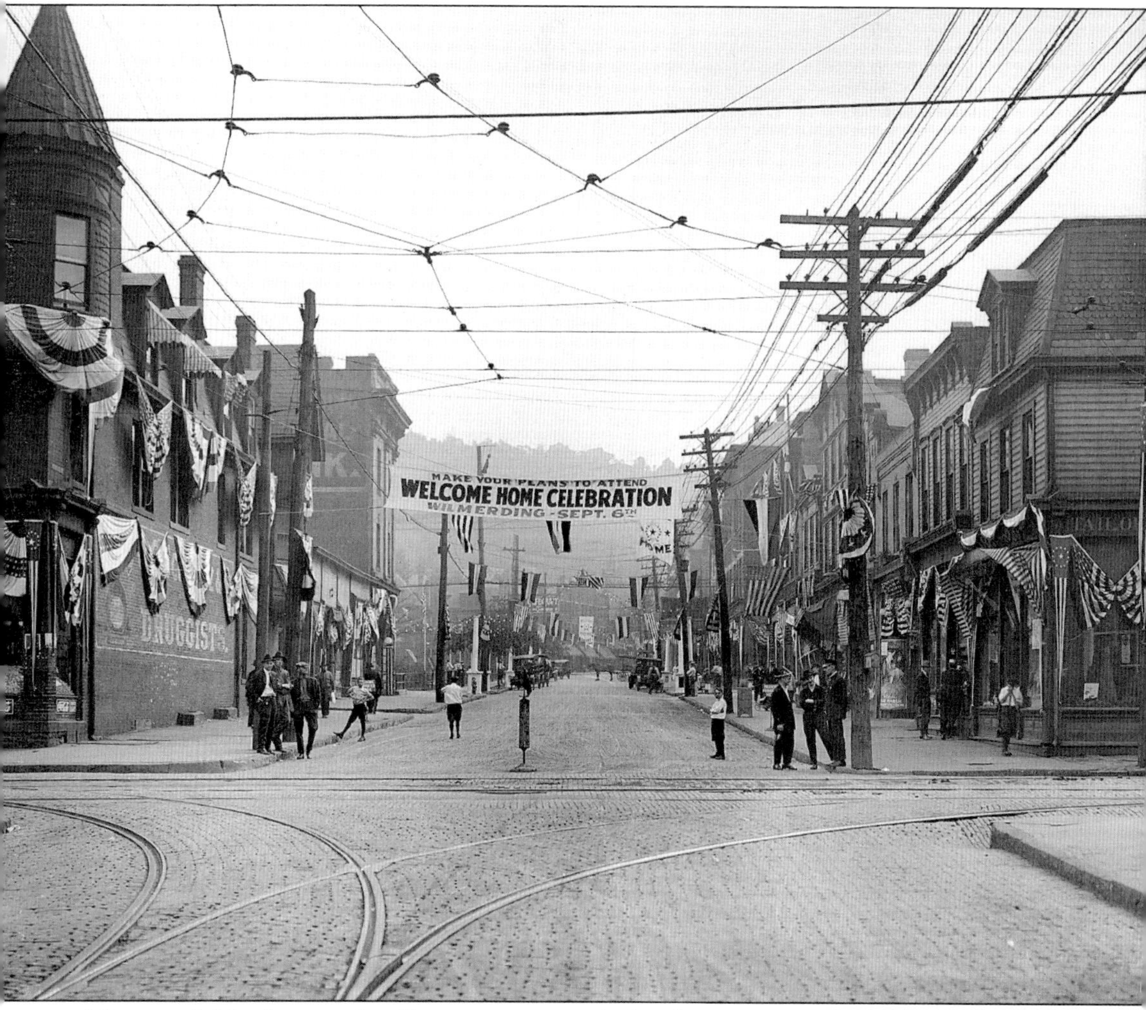

Viewers of this photograph will get a pretty good idea the extent to which Wilmerding went to get ready for its Homecoming Celebration on September 6, 1919. The view looks south on Westinghouse Avenue from the corner of Station Street. The celebration marked the return of the men and women engaged in World War I, remembered as the war to end all wars. The war ended with the signing of the armistice on November 11, 1918. Streetcar passengers board at the point this picture was taken. Notice that the tracks run to the right and to the left. Streetcars going right travel to Pittsburgh and all points in-between. Passengers who travel left end up in McKeesport. Do you see the stop sign in the middle of the street?

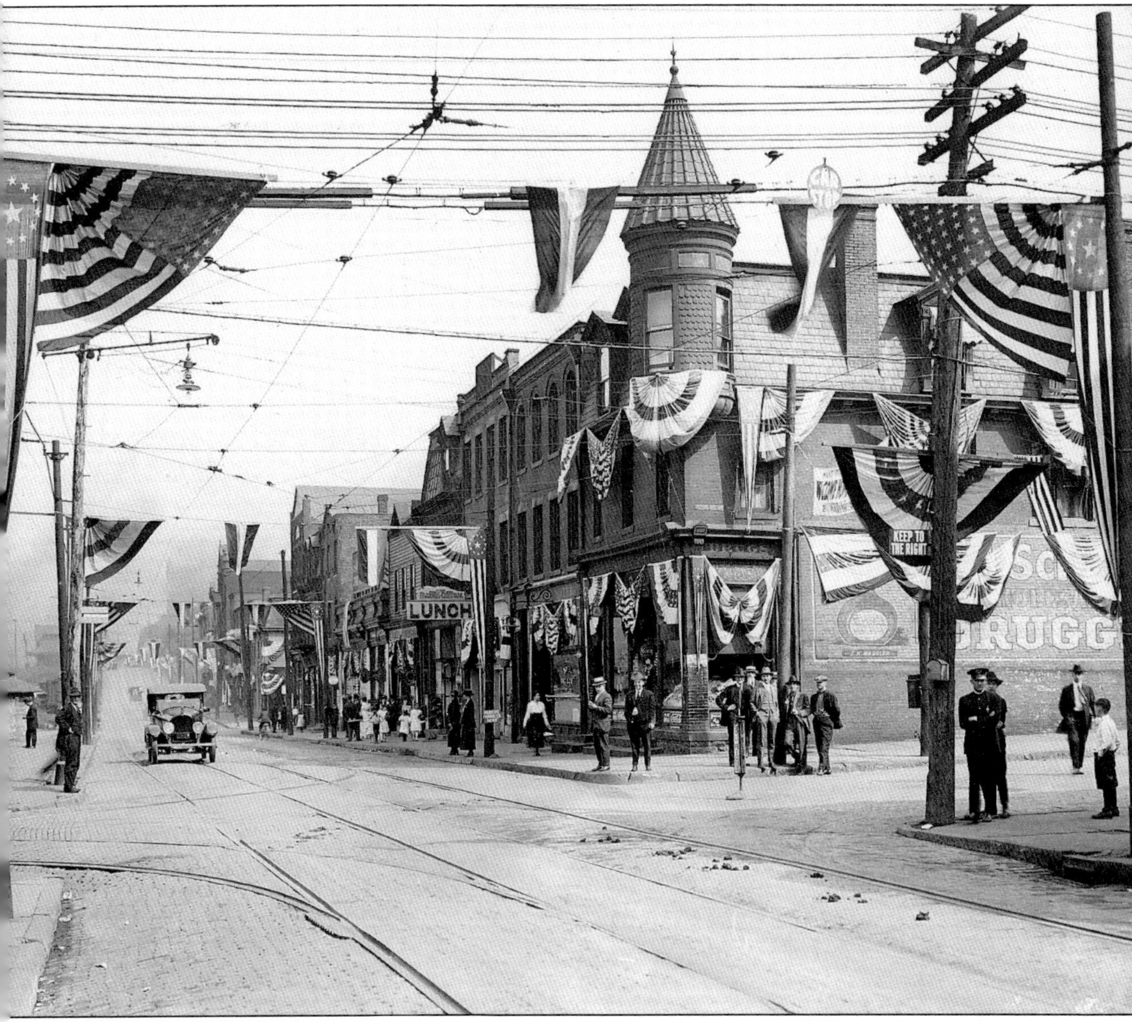

This photograph, looking east down Station Street from the corner of Westinghouse Avenue, shows another view of Wilmerding's Homecoming Celebration in September 1919. If you check the street in the foreground, the horses have just left. To the right, a policeman looks on with his arms folded. Beside the policeman stands a young boy dressed in knickers. From the stares of the men standing on the opposite side of the street, it appears they are all aware of the camera. Notice the massive string of trolley wires above the street. Not shown in this photograph, but located to the left, are the Westinghouse Air Brake Company and railroad station.

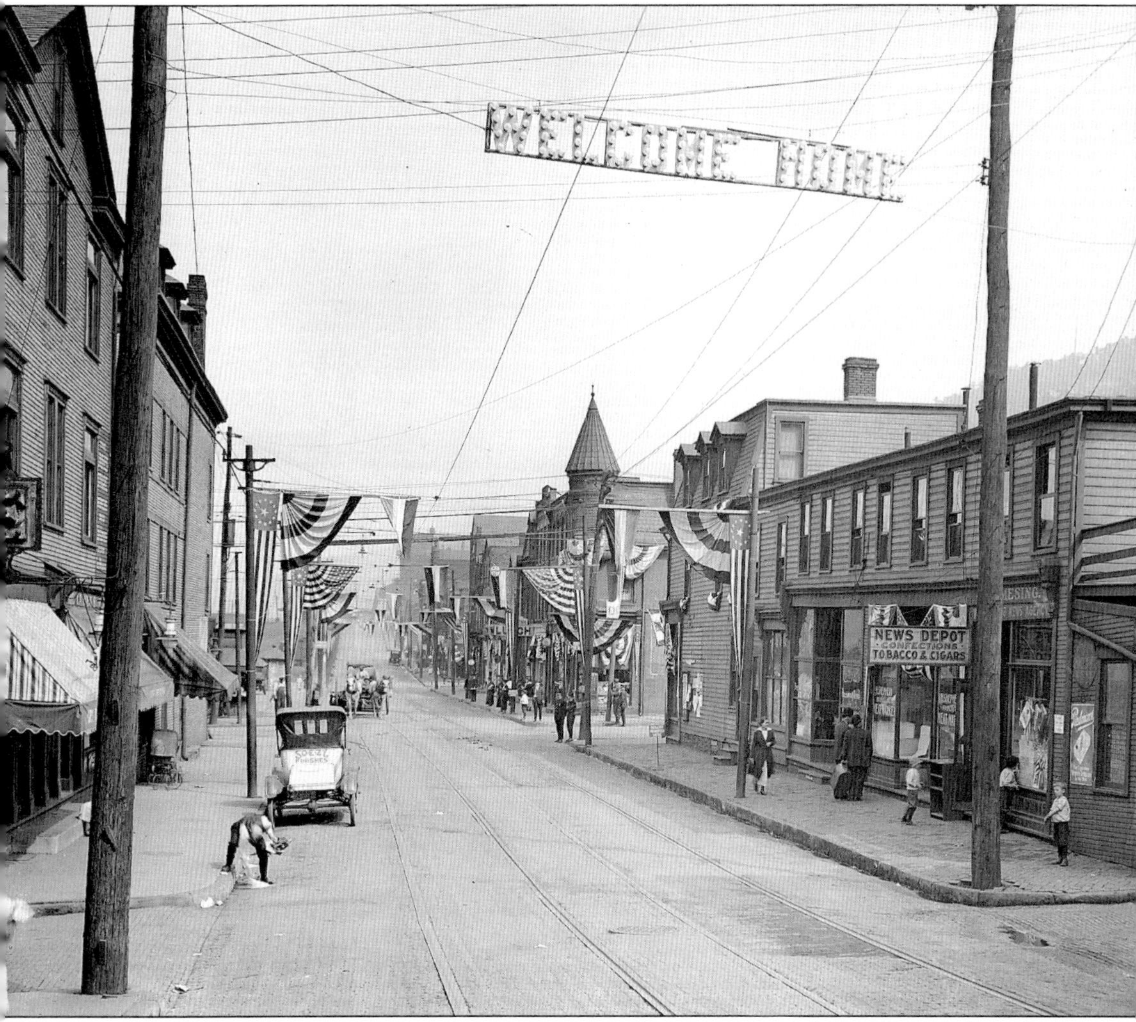

A lighted Welcome Home sign greets visitors as they return to take part in Wilmerding's Homecoming Celebration in September 1919. This photograph was taken looking east on Station Street from the alley below Caldwell Avenue. Notice the horse-drawn vendor's cart coming up the street. Since the fire department often used merchants' horses to help pull fire equipment, maybe this pair has been to a fire or two. In contrast to the horse-drawn cart, a new car is parked near the curb. "So-e-zy Finishes" is painted on the back of the car. In front, a merchant bends over to pick up trash in the gutter. Across the street, three small boys look on; two wear brimmed hats.

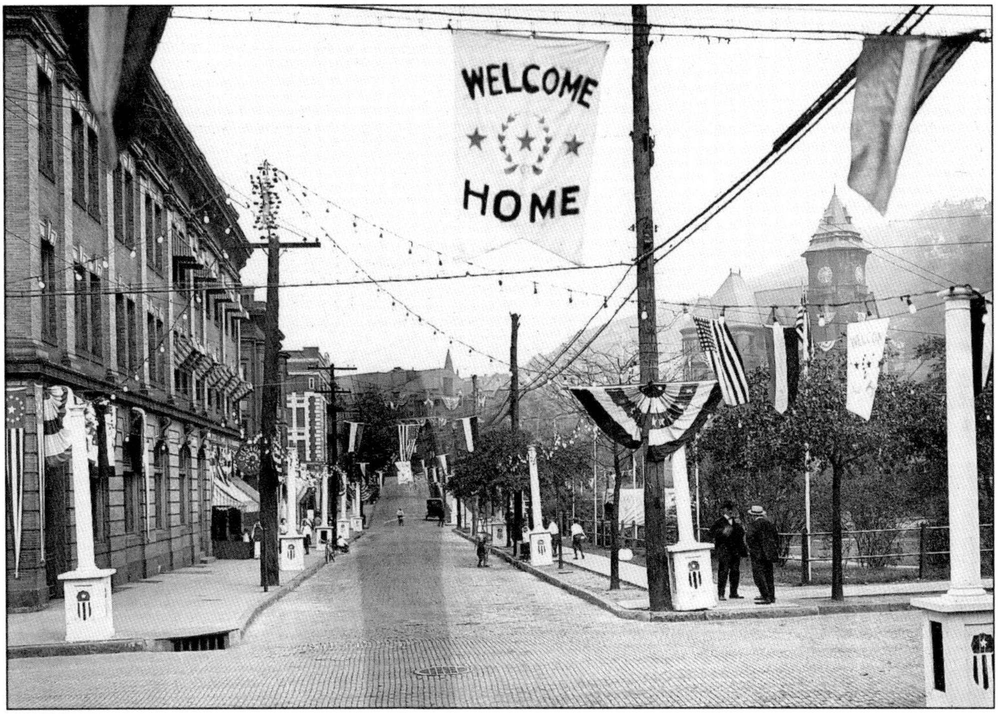

This photograph, looking east on Commerce Street from Westinghouse Avenue, gives another look at the Homecoming Celebration held in Wilmerding in September 1919. The park is on the right, and the Westinghouse Air Brake Company's general office building is seen above the park. The company's annex is on the left.

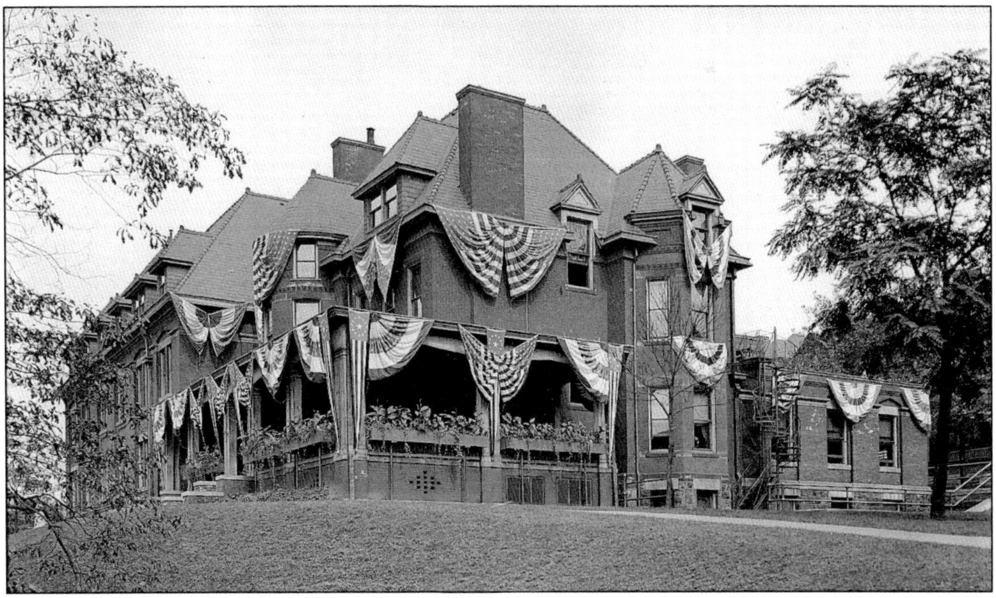

The Wilmerding YMCA celebrates Homecoming in September 1919. Flower boxes, brimming with greenery, line the porch. Colorful flags adorn the building, and the grass has been freshly mowed. The stately mansion is ready to celebrate. To the right are steps used to access Marguerite Avenue.

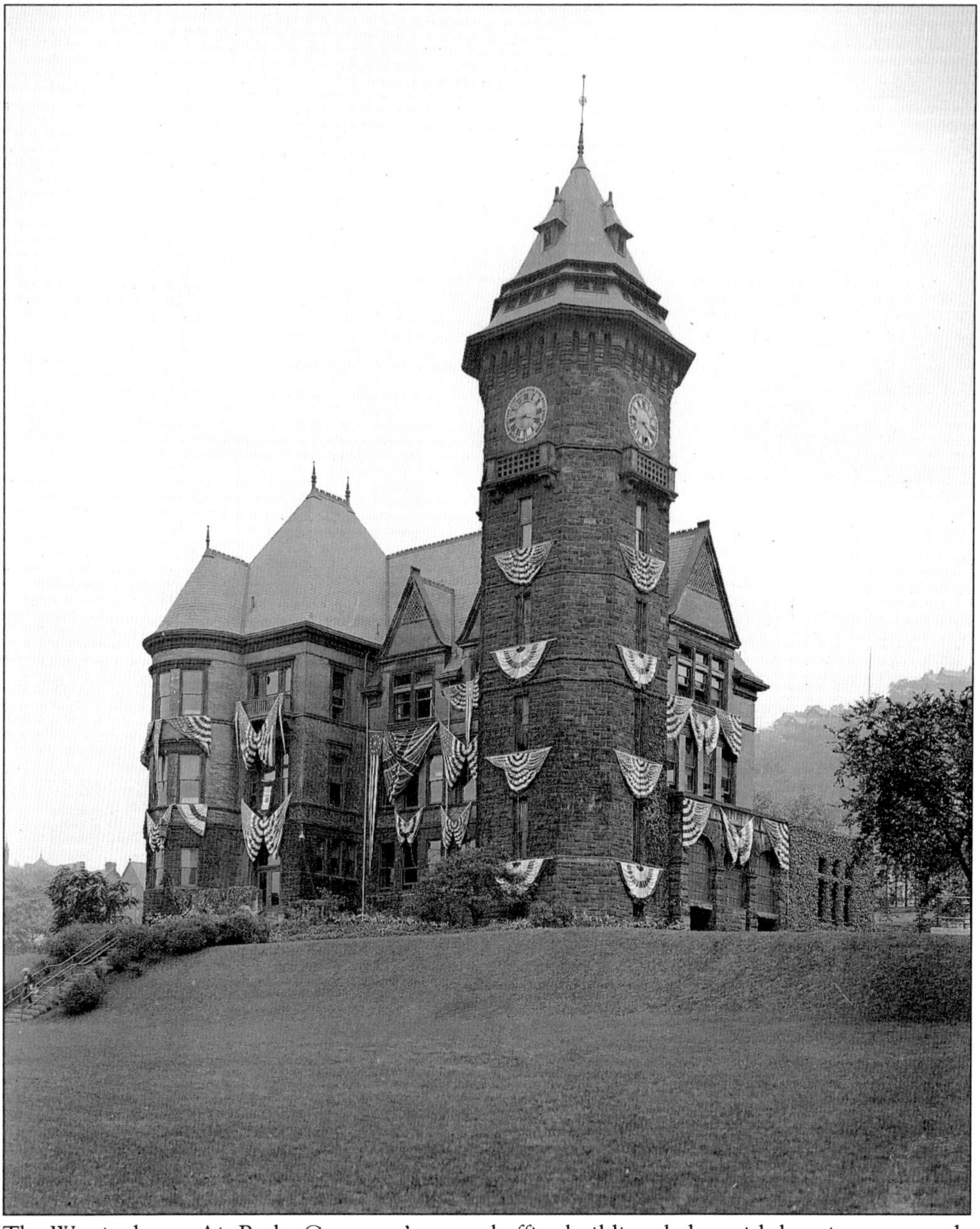

The Westinghouse Air Brake Company's general office building, laden with bunting, gets ready to celebrate Homecoming on September 6, 1919. Only 54 months earlier, air brake inventor George Westinghouse Jr. succumbed to heart disease at age 67. Never again would he hear the melodious sounds coming from that wonderful four-faced clock tower while working in his second-floor office. Originally purchased from the E. Howard Watch & Clock Company of Boston (maker of tower clocks for 10 years) and as much a part of Wilmerding as George, the corner clock struck dependably every hour and half-hour. All of Wilmerding has marked time by that old clock. Today, the clock still chimes every hour and half-hour. Some residents cannot go to sleep without first hearing the striking of the old Castle clock.

A lighted display placed against the flagpole in the park in Wilmerding during Homecoming in September 1919 pays tribute to the many fallen heroes of World War I. Two children sit on the grass to the left of the flagpole. A ladder still leans against the pole in the rear.

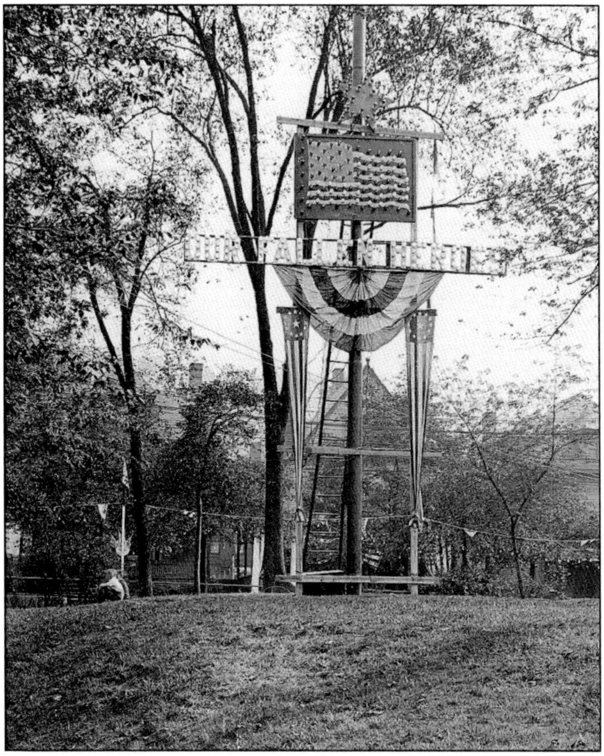

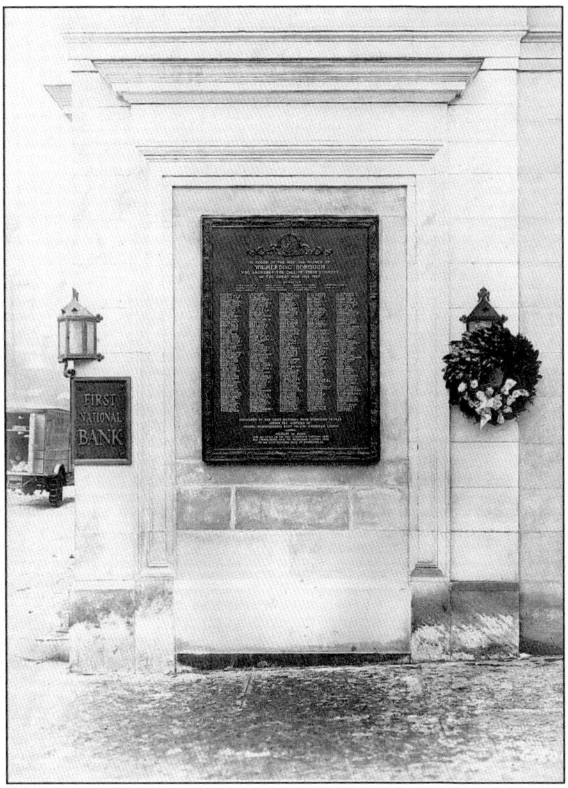

A plaque was erected on the First National Bank at the corner of Commerce Street and Westinghouse Avenue in honor of the men and women of the borough of Wilmerding who answered the call by their country to enter the Great War of 1914–1918. An open wagon stands to the left of the bank building.

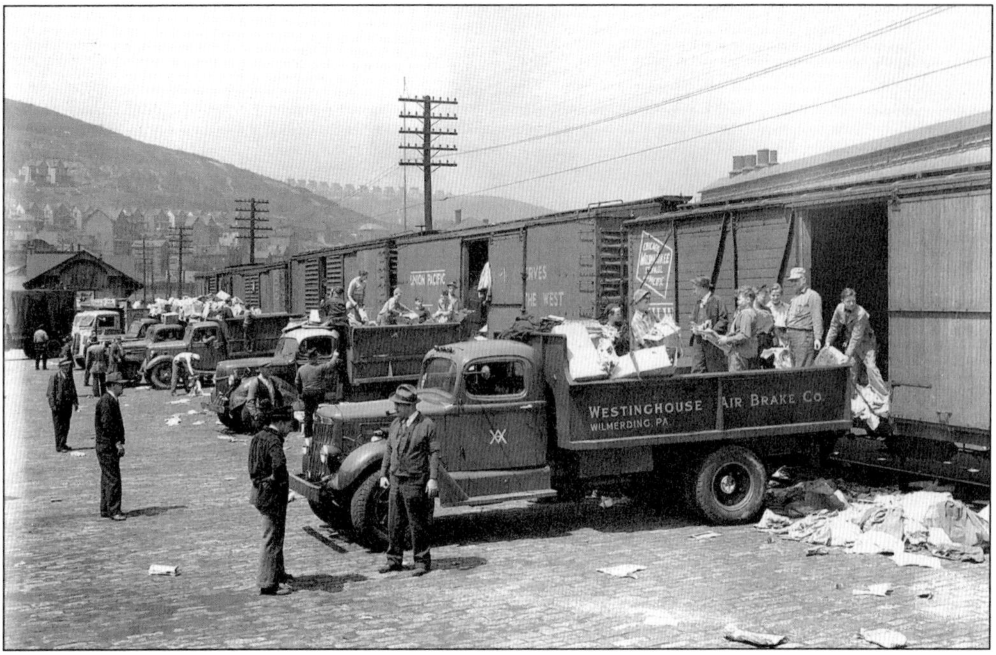

Many participated in the September 1945 wastepaper drive. Young boys and girls contributed greatly to this worthwhile project, eager to help with the defense of their country. Railroad freight cars are seen here accepting loads of paper at the freight station in downtown Wilmerding.

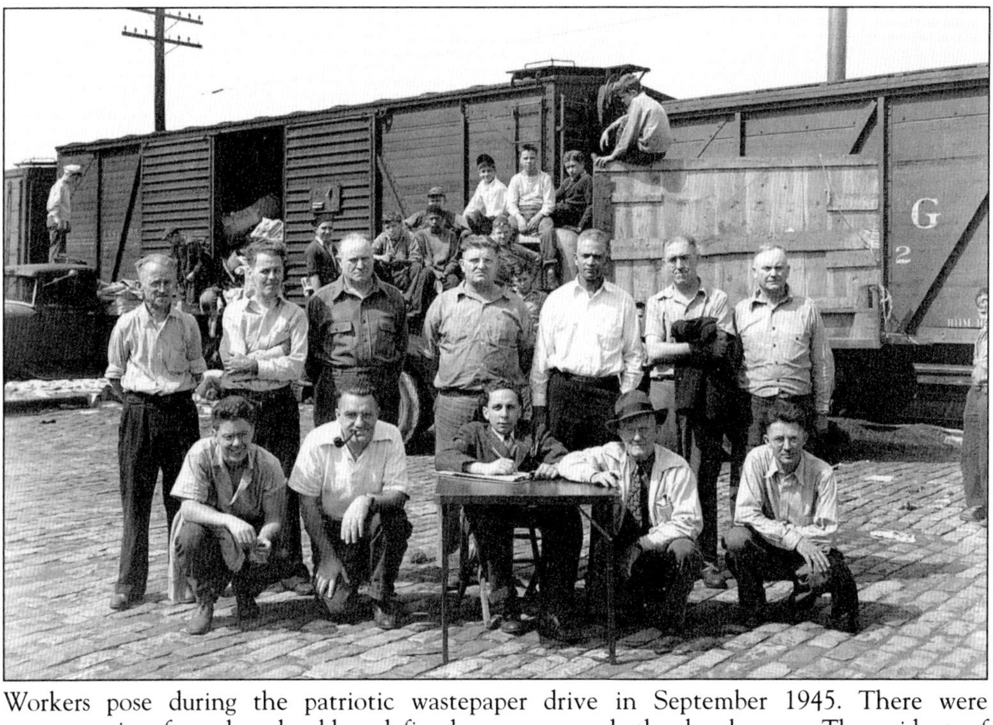

Workers pose during the patriotic wastepaper drive in September 1945. There were representatives from the school board, fire department, and other local groups. The residents of Wilmerding helped make the wastepaper and scrap tin drives successful through hard work and determination. In the background are freight cars taking on loads of paper.

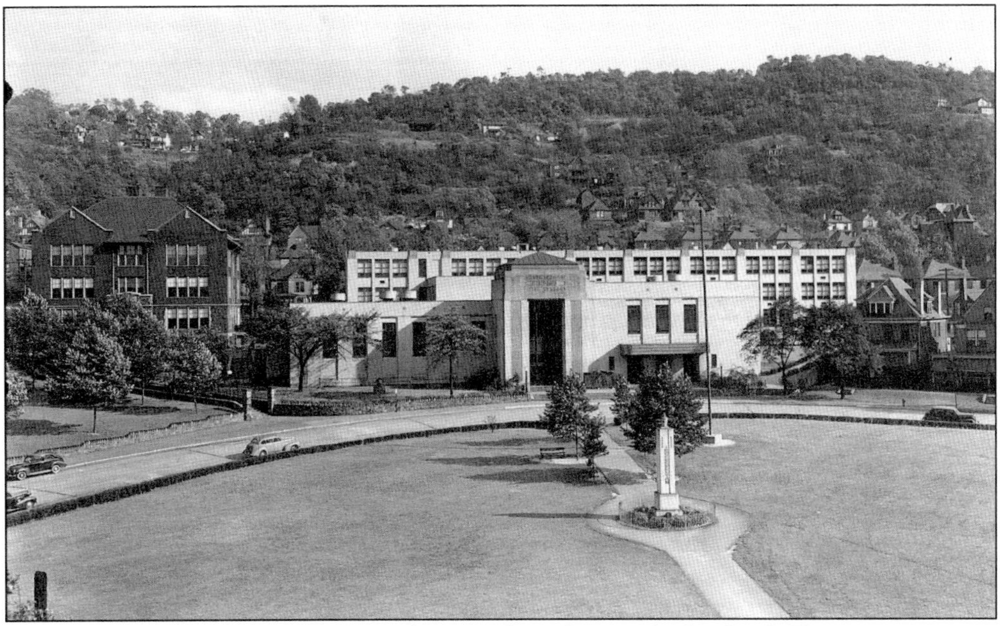

A monument was also built in the park across from the new high school. The monument was erected by a grateful community in honor of its sons and daughters who served their country during World War I. Behind the stone structure, notice the new school. To the left of the high school is the elementary school.

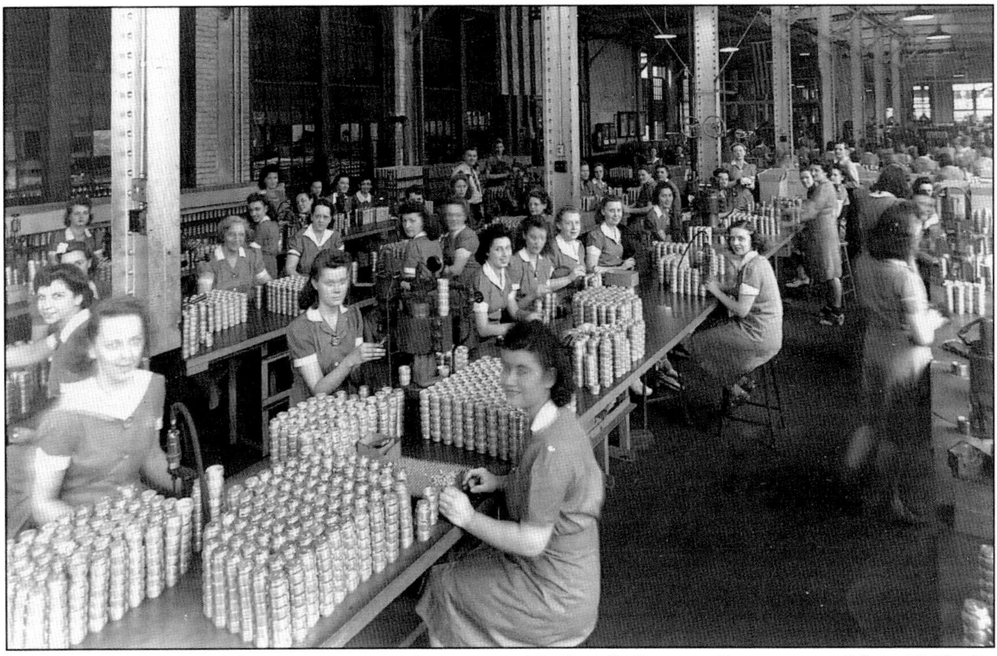

Westinghouse Air Brake Company workers assemble bomb fuses in Department U in 1942. As was the norm throughout the country during World War II, young girls and women performed jobs previously held by men who were away serving their country. This department was located on the third floor of Building 24. The Westinghouse Air Brake engineering department now occupies this location.

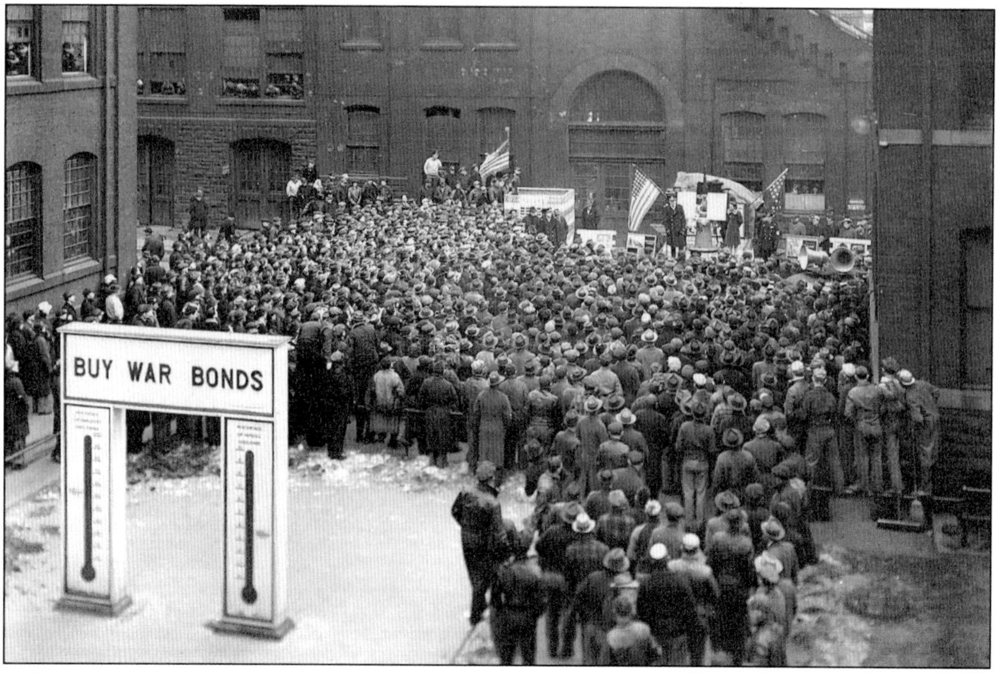

A "Buy War Bonds" display was mounted in the Westinghouse Air Brake Company yard in front of the foundry building. Patriotism ran deep throughout the United States after the Japanese bombed Pearl Harbor, plunging America into World War II. Along with the rest of the country, Wilmerding citizens and the Westinghouse Air Brake Company were anxious to serve.

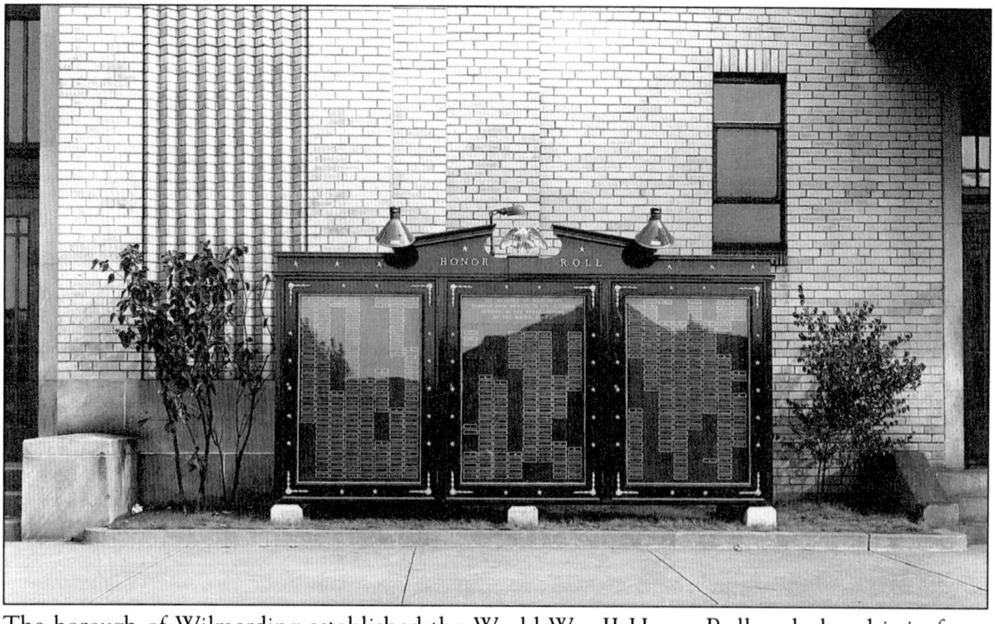

The borough of Wilmerding established the World War II Honor Roll and placed it in front of the Westinghouse Memorial High School during the 1940s. Anyone who was interested in looking up the names of friends or loved ones who fought in World War II could search the names listed on the plaque.